RULERS OF THE HOROSCOPE

Alan Oken

THE CROSSING PRESS
FREEDOM, CALIFORNIA

For information on bulk purchases or group discounts for this and other Crossing Press titles, please contact our Special Sales Manager at 800-777-1048.

Visit our Website on the Internet at: www.crossingpress.com

If you would like to contact Alan Oken, you can write to him at P.O. Box 5574, Santa Fe, NM 87502 or visit his website at www.thewisdomschool.org

Library of Congress Cataloging-in-Publication Data

Oken, Alan.
    Rulers of the horoscope / by Alan Oken.
        p. cm.
    Includes bibliographical references and index.
    ISBN 0-89594-998-9 (pbk.)
    1. Dispositors. 2. Essential dignities (Astrology) I. Title.

  BF1717.23.O54 2000
   133.5'4--dc21   99-057491

Dedication

To Marion March, a most beloved and respected teacher, friend, and contributor to the establishment of modern astrology. Thank you, Marion—your work and total dedication to our field and its practitioners has helped to create astrology as a living science for so many people around the world.

Table of Contents

List of Example Horoscopes

Acknowledgments

One of the most wonderful things about writing a book, especially after one has reached a certain age, is the ability to write what you please, but writing what pleases you doesn't necessarily mean that it will be published. In August of 1998, I visited with Elaine Gill, the publisher of The Crossing Press in Freedom, California. Elaine sat me down in her office and said, "Alan, I want you to create a series of astrological books for the intermediate and advanced astrology student. Write on any topic you like and we will publish it." Thank you, Elaine Gill, for your confidence in my work. I look forward to writing several more books in this series, which I hope will serve the astrological community and add to the tremendous efforts of so many of my other distinguished colleagues in the field.

I also want to thank a number of my contemporaries, professional astrologers all, whose friendship and support over the years have done so very much to keep me inspired, active, and involved in the progress and development of astrology in our times. A special word of gratitude is due to my respected colleague, Ray Merriman, who took the time out of his intensely busy work and travel schedule to read the manuscript and write the forward to this book. My love and deepest appreciation go out to my remarkable editor and dear friend, Erin Sullivan. Her fine and dedicated work in the preparation of this volume is sincerely appreciated. My gratitude and love to Jean Redman of "The Mystic Bear" in Albuquerque—you are the steady light in my heart. I would also like to acknowledge the organizing team and the faculty spirit of the United Astrology Congress, who have collectively contributed so very much to modern astrology. One final word of appreciation is in order to my many students and friends in the USA, Britain, Europe, and Australia, too numerous to mention but not too numerous to keep ever conscious in my heart. To all of you, dankeschön, obrigado, tusind tak, merci, grácias, grazie, dank U, good on ya mate, and many, many thanks.

Foreword

When one begins the journey of becoming an astrologer, there is inevitably the bridge to be crossed between being a student and evolving into a practitioner. In fact, it may be more accurate to say that there is inevitably a bridge to be constructed before it is crossed. How long it takes to build that bridge, and how sturdy it becomes in order to sustain one's future astrological practice depends upon each individual who chooses to make this journey. In most cases, the journey ends after one realizes that building such a structure is no simple task. There are no shortcuts available to "get to the other side."

So it is with astrology and astrologers. At first the study of astrology appears to be very much like the start of an exciting voyage to someplace new. One enters upon this adventure with a great deal of intrigue and anticipation. Sun signs, Moon signs, Rising signs…all pointing to some fascinating discovery about oneself and one's life. The study of astrology's basic alphabet of signs, planets, and even the houses is simple and exciting enough, and there are plenty of maps and tools to guide one along this initial phase of the astrologer's path.

But then comes that "great divide," that chasm which separates two worlds: the world of the student on the one side who looks over to the other side to see the world of the professional practitioner. This point of tension is similar to that of the traveler who reaches a certain point along his or her journey, but cannot figure out how to complete the trek. There are no set road maps from here to there, and a large ocean separates the two.

At what point, therefore, does the study of astrology become one's dominant language? At what point does one "cross the bridge" whereby one's view of life's reality is interpreted through the symbolism of astrology and is no longer framed within the constructs, images, and belief systems that have been shaped by one's earlier life lessons? Most importantly, what happens in those instances when the bridge one crossed was not built sturdily enough, so that the reality one now enters is out of step with the common view of life of the majority of people in one's environment? Indeed, what happens when one crosses the astrological bridge, considers oneself to be an astrologer, but never has really learned the art of chart synthesis correctly?

This is precisely what occurs in much of today's world of astrology. We have a profession in which many of its practitioners do not know the difference between a wedding reception and mutual reception! They do not know where or how to begin a consultation, perhaps spending the entire time only explaining the positions of the Sun, Moon, and Ascendant. Worse yet, there are those who call themselves astrologers and even toss in a couple of technical astrological terms, but in actuality practice something quite different, such as numerology or psychism. There are hundreds of students of our ancient science who understand all of the meanings and relationships between the planets, signs, houses, and aspects, but are at a total loss as to how to conduct a basic chart interpretation.

This begs the question: How does one go about synthesizing the various factors of a natal horoscope in order to produce a useful and successful delineation? The answer, of course, is what separates the student or hobbyist from the true and serious practitioner of the art of astrology. Just building the bridge to which I earlier referred, takes a good deal of time and the proper application of all of one's instruction, studies, and materials. The road to becoming a proficient astrologer takes many years of work and the learning of the proper rules, procedures, and techniques of this craft. One has to learn the basics, and then discover how to apply these fundamentals in their many layers so that they "fit correctly." The more one practices, the better one becomes. Not only that, but the sturdier becomes one's foundation. In time, this structure of knowledge and understanding will hold not only the astrologer's professional practice in place, but will also act as a firm underpinning by which he or she may bring others to their eventual destination either as clients or as students.

In the book you are about to read, Alan Oken assumes that you have been given the basic tools of astrology. This information is easily available in a multitude of books on beginning astrology. But what Oken provides herein is an excellent set of instructions on how to apply these factors in their correct placement and relationship to one another. In *Rulers of the Horoscope*, the reader will clearly see that the proper synthesis of astrology is not just a matter of interpreting all the planets in all the houses or signs with equal weight. The strength of a planet is tempered by the particular sign in which it is placed, or the particular house in which it resides. The relative degree of a planet's influence in the horoscope is also determined by the various relationships it forms to other planets through dispositorship by mutual sign or house reception.

This is not the easiest part of astrology to master, though with the horoscopes of many well-known persons used as illustrations, Alan Oken makes this process enjoyable. Like traveling itself, the start of a journey may appear to be easy. Yet you come to a point when additional planning and insight into the journey's purpose needs to be determined in order to continue the sojourn properly. This takes work, concentration, and practice. And you must have the right instructional guide to go with the material you have already acquired. So it is with chart synthesis, the subject of this book. This is, therefore, not a book you should read once or twice. It is a book that should be read and referred to several times on one's astrological journey, particularly if you are in the process of building the bridge towards becoming a true astrologer. *Rulers of the Horoscope* is, in essence, that link which will help to transform the student to the professional. For that person in particular, who is beyond the initial stages in his or her studies, but not yet comfortable with calling oneself a full-fledged astrologer, this is a book that you should keep close at hand. It is a book whose instructions you should read over and over again, whose directions should be followed on all the charts you read and study, just to make sure you have the methods of natal delineation properly understood. In this way, the bridge that you are building into becoming an astrologer will serve you and others for the duration of your life.

Ray Merriman, President,
The International Society of Astrological Research

Introduction

As twentieth and now twenty-first century students of the ancient art and science of astrology, we are indeed very fortunate. In addition to the hundreds of very fine astrological texts published in the last fifty years, we also have a wide range of Internet websites and other computer-based assets at our fingertips. This makes the pursuit and exchange of information about our highly specialized field of study not only extremely available, but also "user-friendly" and very enjoyable.

My own work in astrology began in 1967. Although I have become particularly interested in what is called esoteric or soul-centered astrology, the basis for my studies and practice is still very much grounded in the methods of interpretation found in the traditional, humanistic astrological systems of approach to the natal chart. You cannot safely and accurately reach for the heavens without having your feet firmly planted on Earth. In the course of these past thirty-three years, I have spoken with thousands of astrological students, teachers, and professionals, read a myriad of astrological texts, and attended, as well as given, my fair share of workshops, lectures, and seminars all over this planet. I found that there is an absolutely essential facet of astrological delineation that has been little used at best, and in too many cases either underestimated in its importance or totally overlooked. This major factor of astrological interpretative techniques has to do with the various levels of planetary and house rulerships, also known more technically as "dispositorship values and powers."

This book is specifically oriented to sharing the meaning and nature of dispositorship, as well as general and more subtle rulership associations found in the natal chart. Its purpose is to guide the reader toward a clear understanding of how to integrate this knowledge into the wider interpretation of the horoscope. These factors are very important to a comprehensive delineation of a given nativity. Once these factors are fully uncovered, the reader will then have a sense of immediate contact with the skeletal structure of any and all horoscopes. It is the skeleton of the chart upon which the body of the reading is constructed. The present work is geared to any student of astrology who has progressed beyond the initial stages of astrological investigation. The intermediate student will find the material well suited to his or her continued educational journey. Some individuals at this level may wish to review their comprehension of the nature of the houses through consulting the author's book, *The Houses of the Horoscope* (The Crossing Press, 1999). The more advanced student or professional practitioner will discover in the current text an additional means to unlock the meaning of the complexities of human behavior, thus being of greater service in his or her astrological practice to both students and clients.

It is very important to see the horoscope as an energetic map of interwoven forces waiting to be uncovered, explained, and interpreted. Once the astrological student has established a solidified comprehension of the meanings of the letters in the cosmic alphabet (the planets, signs, houses, and geometric aspects), he or she must then move on to the more complex job of synthesis. It is this task of putting all the letters into words and the words into sentences and the sentences communicated with the intent of healing, that is the greatest challenge to all astrologers.

I have noticed that there are three basic kinds of astrologers: the intellectual, the intuitive, and the integrated. Intellectual astrologers are very mercurial in their approach. They are persons who have sincerely labored and studied the meanings of all the 1,872 basic planetary positions in the natal chart until they know them all perfectly and individually.[1] They can comment at length about the difference of meaning between Venus in Aries in the Second House and Venus in Taurus in the Tenth, for example. They know why Virgo always relates to the Sixth House and why the Eleventh is connected to Uranus. It has taken them at least three and perhaps as many as seven years, to accumulate such knowledge. The highly gifted intellectual astrologer knows how to accumulate, codify, and structure data. They are wonderful researchers and their findings aid enormously in the goal of revealing the relationships that exist between heaven and earth. But the predominantly mercurial, intellectual astrologers do not know the *meaning* of the nativity, cannot see (as Dane Rudhyar would have said) "the person in the horoscope," and certainly are not prepared to bring wholism and healing into the consulting session.

Intuitive astrologers are quite Uranian in their vision of the horoscope. They are attuned to the symbology and archetypal significance of the many planet-sign-house combinations and may even be expert in the complex issues involved in understanding the indications of multiple aspect patterns. They are more energy- than mind-oriented; more focused on essence than on form. They can pick up a chart, look it over for 30 seconds or so, and get totally in touch with the man or woman living through that horoscope. The problem of primarily intuitive astrologers is that they cannot communicate their attunement to the person to whom it matters most—the client. They therefore often say to themselves, "I know this chart, but I just cannot explain it." And they are right. Once again the opportunity for creative healing is not present. Even the highly gifted, spiritually oriented, soul-centered astrologer may fail in his or her purpose when the intuitive gifts are not matched *and* blended with the hard-earned knowledge of astrological science.

The integrated astrologer is a man or woman who has developed the art of astrological synthesis. This is a person who is both an intellectual and an intuitive, one whose intent is spiritual. This person has the ability to guide the client into the next cycle of the unfoldment of life. The integration of which I speak is the natural result of the fusion of mind and heart in the expression of human consciousness. When intellect is coupled with intuition (which is itself a product of love), the potential for healing emerges. I am, of course, speaking here of the astrologer who works primarily with others as a counselor, guide, and teacher. I am not speaking of the many fine and highly gifted astrologers who are sincerely dedicated in their approach to financial astrology, mundane astrology, or any other of the many branches of the cosmic science. But as I function primarily as a teacher and consultant, I am most familiar with a humanist orientation to astrology and shall confine my comments to this area of our work. I can say, however, that an application of the present treatise on the implications of the powers of dispositor-ship is of definite value to all the many specialized fields of astrological interest, from the most materialistically mundane to the most ethereally esoteric.

No astrology text or author can give a person spiritual illumination. This must come from the evolution of one's heart. At best the writer can but stimulate and support the focus of a person's development. But the writer can present and enlarge upon those techniques of delineation and interpretation that fuse the intellectual with the intuitive and thus produce a synthesized approach to a more subtle and comprehensive rendering of the horoscope. This is my intent in this work.

Alan Oken

Santa Fe, NM

---

1. This number is derived from the 12 signs multiplied by the 12 houses multi-plied by the 10 primary planets plus Chiron and the North and South Nodes of the Moon (12 x 12 x 13 = 1,872).

Peeling the Onion

It is vitally important that the student come to experience the planets, signs, houses, and aspects of the horoscope as *fields of energy*. The entire scope of astrological literature is devoted to giving verbal definitions to the energy of life and its myriad interconnections and possibilities of manifestation. The present work is no exception. Any astrological author strives to define such factors with exactitude, precision, and perception. In this respect let us elaborate a bit upon the seven major modes of expression through which the astrological energies unfold their meanings in the natal chart. Once these primary factors are reviewed, summarized, and explored, we shall devote the rest of this book to an eighth factor, the primary subject of this work, the dispositors and hidden rulers of the chart. The reader will see from this discussion that the powers and values of dispositorship are like a needle whose thread weaves the entire chart into one integrated and comprehensive entity.

The Planets

The planets reveal the *"whats"* of the horoscope—what energy is at work? All the planets reflect the light of the Sun, the principle of vitality in the natal chart. The Sun is to the horoscope what the King is to a game of chess. The Sun has little movement of its own (it is, after all, a fixed star), but without its presence, there is no energy at all, no chess game to be played, no horoscope to be lived. Thus, in traditional, personality-centered exoteric astrology, the Sun is the center around which the entirety of the chart unfolds.[1] A weakened Sun, a solar force that is debilitated by other planetary powers (especially Saturn, Pluto, or Neptune), cannot energize in any consistent and positive way the condition of the other planets whose "light" is, after all, reflected solar light.

The planets however, are the most important features in the natal horoscope. They represent the primary differentiation of the radiation of the solar life force and therefore are the expressions of the prismatic effect of the Sun's rays manifesting through the solar system, giving color, form, conditions, and shades of meaning to the purpose of the nativity. Although the planets have their own natures and their particular effects upon one's life, they are held in place by the play of solar gravity upon their own orbital speeds. This physical phenomenon has a metaphysical counterpart. It reveals that the Sun, as symbol of the Creator, dominates its creations but is ever interacting with them and affected by them. The planets do have a life of their own, and express their own energy fields and destinies, but all of this is totally reliant upon the ability of the Sun to emanate the central point of life-giving light-substance. It is true that if there is a Mars/Sun aspect in the natal chart, for example, both bodies will affect each other. In this case, the Sun definitely further energizes Mars for good or ill according to the nature of that aspect (square, trine, sextile, etc.). Mars, however, returns the favor by adding a quality of assertiveness and aggression to the principle of solar vitality, which then radiates out and integrates with all of the other planets in the chart. In essence, all the members of the planetary family in the solar system will be touched by the energy of Mars through its direct contact with the Sun.

The Signs

The signs reveal the "*hows*" of the horoscope—how are the energies of the planets manifesting? The signs definitely have their own energy, but it is an energy of form rather than of essence. It is an energy which shapes and molds rather than creates and projects. The planets impregnate the signs with the essence of their vitality and express their nature through the form-giving dynamics of the signs in which they are placed. Venus, for example, is always seeking partnership and complementation. In the sign Taurus, she will bring into one's life relationship issues that involve money, substance, and tests of true human values, i.e., the forms of Taurean expression. But when placed in the sign of Aquarius, for example, Venus' urge to merge tends to be much more idealistic and impersonal in her approach to others, and far less materialistic and personal than when in the sign of the Bull.

The Sun's sign always has to be considered when attempting to integrate the other planets and their respective zodiacal functions. If the Sun is in Pisces, the unfolding of one's creative vitality and the expression of one's destiny is focused through an energy field that seeks universality, lack of confinement, and sensual expression. The solar force situated in Capricorn, on the other hand, indicates an individual who yearns to create predictability, solidity, stature, and structure. If Jupiter were in Sagittarius in a Pisces or a Capricorn chart, its outgoing and expansive nature would remain the same, but its expression would work out quite differently. It is true that in the example just given, Jupiter in its own sign will remain constant in its urge for higher knowledge and an understanding of the underlying laws and principles of life. But the Sun in Pisces person would tend to use the energy of Jupiter in Sagittarius to further his own solar urges for spiritual, sensual, or ideological freedom, while the Sun in Capricorn individual would tend to utilize this planet/sign combination to widen her influence in the world and use her knowledge to anchor a more expanded base for her social position.

The Houses

The astrological houses show the "*where's*" of the chart—where are the energies of the planet/sign combinations manifesting with their greatest strengths or weaknesses? The houses are the most physical indicators in the chart. They reveal "place." No matter which of the many house systems the astrologer chooses to construct the chart, all secondary house techniques are based on two primary axes: the Midheaven/Nadir (or IC) and the Ascendant/Descendant. The former reveals the relationship of the individual when standing up and the latter when he or she is lying down. Thus, the Midheaven is connected to the point in the heavens (i.e., the degree of the zodiac) that is the highest point along the zodiac at the time of birth; while the Ascendant shows the degree of the zodiac that is on the eastern horizon at the place of birth. From those angles, the rest of the houses define the individual relative to his or her world not only in a more subjective, personal sense (through the affairs and psychological conditions described by the houses below the horizon), but also in a more objective, collective sense (through the circumstances and social encounters delineated by the houses above the horizon).

The nature and function of dispositorship and the hidden rulers of the chart make it essential that the astrologer keep the "natural" chart in mind when examining the natal chart. The natural horoscope *always* has Aries on the Ascendant and all the other signs are in the order of the "natural houses," that is, Taurus on the Second, Gemini on the Third, and so on through Pisces on the Twelfth House. There is always an interplay between the natural and the natal planetary rulers of the signs on the house cusps of the horoscope, and this interplay is a major factor in a more comprehensive understanding of the implications of the chart.

This point is more fully elaborated in Chapter 3. However, as an example, let us say that Capricorn is the sign on the cusp of the Fourth House in the natal chart at birth. This is the natural house of Cancer and its ruler, the Moon. Both of these symbols, Moon and Cancer, will always affect the nature of this house and the outcome of its effects on one's life. When examining the natal Fourth House, the astrologer has to take Saturn into consideration, as he is the ruler of Capricorn. But it is also equally important to study the position of the Moon (by sign, house, and aspect) and the relationship between Saturn (natal ruler) and the Moon (natural ruler) in order to obtain a deeper perception into the effects of the Fourth house in the natus. *Planets will always be stronger (for good or ill) when they are in their natural and/or natal house or when the natural/natal planetary rulers are in major aspect with one another.* Thus, in the example cited above, it is especially favorable if Capricorn is on the cusp of the Fourth House and the Moon is trine Saturn. But should Saturn square the Moon, look for a definite increase in the challenges associated with the Fourth House in terms of the nature, events, and people associated with this house.

The Aspects

The planetary aspects reveal the "*ways*" of the chart. They show the energetic pathways of the interconnecting links between the planets. The aspects themselves are energy fields, defined by their geometric nature. Thus, what are called the "easy aspects" (30°, 60°, 72°, and 120°), generally but not always, facilitate the combination of planetary forces. The so-called "hard aspects" (45°, 90°, 135°, 150°, and 180°) often put stumbling blocks along the path. The most intense aspect of all, the conjunction (+/- 0° to 8° between planets) is quite complex in nature. Called a "variable" aspect, it requires an intimate knowledge of planetary powers (and their various mutations through the signs) in order to determine if a particular conjunction will be "easy" or "hard." The effects of primary and secondary dispositorship upon the aspects is fundamental to their total understanding. As Chapters 3, 4, and 5 reveal, it is really impossible to perceive the full effects of these geometric relationships without an examination of the factors of planetary rulership.

The Qualities—Cardinal, Fixed, and Mutable

The three qualities define and express the *motion, rhythm, and movement* of the energy fields of the signs. The effect of a planet upon the natal chart is strongly conditioned by the quality of its placement. You cannot say that a planet is cardinal, fixed, or mutable, but some planets are able to express their true nature more easily in one of these fields than in the others (see the Summary at the end of this chapter). Other planets are comfortable in two of these modalities, and others in all three of the qualities. Jupiter is expansive and excessive by nature. He is much more "at home" in the mutable signs of exploration and movement than he is in a fixed sign wherein the natural perimeters of fixity serve to restrict and limit Jupiter's need for a life without boundaries.

It might be helpful to use the wheel as a metaphor for the essential meaning of the three qualities of sign energies.

The rim of the wheel represents the cardinal signs (Aries, Cancer, Libra, and Capricorn), as it is the outer ring which pushes a cart forward on the road of life.

The hub of the wheel represents the fixed signs (Taurus, Leo, Scorpio, and Aquarius), as it holds the entire structure of the wheel together, giving it a central point of power.

The spokes of the wheel are represented by the mutable signs (Gemini, Virgo, Sagittarius, and Pisces), as they endow the wheel with space, radiation, and dimensionality of expression.

The Elements—Fire, Earth, Air, and Water

The elements define and reveal four additional major principles of manifestation. They speak about *texture, focus, and the primary expression* contained within the essential nature of the signs. In essence, fire will add vitality and creative impulse, earth will give stability and the urge for physical manifestation, air will endow communication and intelligence, while water contributes sensitivity and resourcefulness. Each of the elements conditions and modifies the natural energetic dynamics of the planets. The results can heighten a planet's potency or debilitate its effectiveness. The hidden ruler or dispositor of any planet in any element, however, may weaken an otherwise seemingly powerful influence or restore the planet's energy to a more harmonious level.

Let us say that the Sun is in Pisces and the Moon is in Taurus in a natal chart; and we shall place Venus and Mercury in Pisces as well and give this individual a sweet Cancer Ascendant. But what is this looming force coming up red and vibrant? It is Mars in Aries, all bright and glorious, having one helluva great time for himself! Mars loves his fiery cardinality, but what may be happy for a planet may not be happy for you. And what of our gentle Pisces/Taurus/Cancer friend? Mars in this case would tend to be a very disruptive force in that otherwise kindly, nurturing, and receptive individual. Yes, I know that many astrology students would think that a naturally passive Pisces/Taurus/Cancer person needs Mars in Aries to give him a little spark and spunk. Although this may indeed be true, to that otherwise docile individual, Mars in Aries may be having a very pugnacious party at the expense of the rest of the chart. The element (fire, earth, air, and water) of planetary placement needs to be fully considered in order to determine the degree of a planet's strength or weakness by sign.

Gender—Male or Female

The gender of a sign reveals its polarity. The male are the fire and air signs (Aries, Gemini, Leo, Libra, Sagittarius, and Aquarius). When planets are placed in any of these six designations, the tendency is for them to be outgoing, assertive, and electrical in nature. When they are placed in the six earth and water female signs (Taurus, Cancer, Virgo, Scorpio, Capricorn, and Pisces), the planets tend to be receptive and magnetic in their expression. The Sun, for example, is most "at home" in the male signs, except in Aquarius, when its rays may become too diffused. Yet when an Aquarian learns how to direct his or her personal, individualized, creative will within a larger social context, the Sun will thrive in the Waterman's domain. The Moon can generally provide more of her nurturing, supportive qualities when in the female signs, except for Scorpio, which indicates the need to release and transform certain patterns of emotional self-expression that inhibit caring and the right use of personal resources. But once the more selfish and possessive dynamics of Scorpio have been truly transmuted, the Moon in this position becomes quite a potent vehicle for healing and restored abundance.

Summary of Planetary Strengths and Weaknesses

Sun: The nature of the Sun is strongest in the cardinal and fixed fire signs (Aries and Leo), weakest when in the water and the mutable signs. It is stronger in Capricorn than either Taurus or Virgo, stronger in Sagittarius than in Gemini. It is also not particularly potent in either Libra or Aquarius. The Sun shines brightest in the First, Fifth, Ninth, Tenth, and Eleventh houses, and dimmest in the Third, Fourth, Sixth, Seventh, Eighth, and Twelfth houses. The Second House placement of the Sun is rather neutral, tending to be more positive than otherwise.

Moon: The Moon is strongest in the earth, female, fixed sign of Taurus and the water, female, cardinal sign of Cancer. She is also very potent in Pisces. She is weakest in all the male signs, especially in Aries, Gemini, Leo, Sagittarius, and Aquarius. She does not do well in Capricorn, and is really tested in Scorpio. The Moon can also be quite happy in Virgo and Libra, but only if the work area provides economic security and emotional satisfaction in the case of the former and when relationship dynamics are fulfilling in the case of the latter. The Moon is at her most potent when in the Second and Fourth houses, weakest in the First and Tenth, neutral to strong when placed in the Fifth, Seventh, Ninth, and Eleventh, and neutral to weak in the Third and Sixth.

Mercury: Mercury is strongest in his own signs, Gemini and Virgo, but does very well in Aquarius, Capricorn, and Aries. He is very adaptable, but tends to work better in the mutable and cardinal signs rather than in the fixed. He likes all the elements except for water. Mercury tends to be weakest in Pisces, Sagittarius, Taurus, Cancer, Scorpio, Libra, and Leo. Mercury likes being in the First, Third, Fifth, Sixth, Tenth, and Eleventh houses. He is least potent in the Twelfth, Fourth, Seventh, and Eighth (in that order), but can do quite well (depending on the sign) in the Second.

Venus: Venus is at her best when in Taurus and Libra and also shines brightly in Cancer and Pisces. She can be quite financially beneficial when well aspected in Capricorn, and very artistically expressive in Leo. She is out of favor in Aries, Virgo, and Scorpio, and to a somewhat lesser extent in Gemini, Aquarius, and Sagittarius. Venus is content in all of the elements except fire and seems to work well in all three of the sign qualities. Venus is very at home in the Second, Fourth, Fifth, Seventh, and Tenth houses and to a somewhat lesser extent in the Twelfth (where she loses her sense of structure and boundaries—although for those on a more spiritual path in life, this is exactly what needs to happen!). In actuality, she can do well in any of the houses, but the latter are her favorites.

Mars: Mars is strongest in Aries, Scorpio, Capricorn, and Leo, and is also very happy (but a bit unfocused) in Sagittarius. He is weakest in Taurus, Libra, Cancer, Gemini, Aquarius, and Pisces, but seems to work well in Virgo. He is most noble and active in the fire signs, and his great potency in Scorpio must be mitigated by the general moral "tone" of the chart. In general, Mars is not at his best in the water or mutable signs. He is a very powerful influence in the First, Fifth, Eighth, Ninth, and Tenth houses, but not particularly popular in the Second, Third, Fourth, Sixth, Eleventh, or Twelfth.

Jupiter: Jupiter bestows his blessings wherever he travels in the chart, but he is especially fond of the fire signs (Sagittarius, Leo, and Aries in that order) and two of the water signs (Cancer and Pisces). He can be very generous in earth, but this is not his favorite element and he is not particularly at ease in the airy signs. All the houses are happy to receive him, but he is at his best in the Second, Fourth, Fifth, Ninth, and Twelfth.

Saturn: Saturn can be a most beneficial influence when placed in Capricorn, Libra, Aquarius, and Gemini. He is not so pleasant in Cancer, Scorpio, or Pisces. He likes the element of earth and can do well in Virgo and to a lesser extent in Taurus. He does not like fire and is thus not particularly strong in Sagittarius, Leo, or Aries. He is a test (and if "obeyed" may eventually bestow a great victory in life) in any house in which he is placed. If well situated by sign and aspect, Saturn can be especially strong and positive in the Tenth, Eleventh, and Seventh houses.

Uranus: Uranus is very potent and positive in Aquarius, Gemini, and Libra, and can also be quite happy in Sagittarius and Aries. It is not particularly easy to have him in Leo, Taurus, and Cancer. He is very much at home in Scorpio and can be quite beneficial in Pisces if one is on the spiritual path. Uranus especially favors the element of air. His favorite houses are the Eleventh and the Third, and he is at his most disruptive when in the First or Fourth.

Neptune: Neptune favors Pisces and Cancer. He inspires the arts, but can wreak havoc with one's relationships when in Libra, and is least content in Virgo, Aries, Taurus, Scorpio (although from a spiritual perspective, this can be a very positive position), and Capricorn. The Father of the Oceans is most at home, of course, in the element of water, and least content in fire, earth, and air, in that order. He is very comfortable in the Fourth, Ninth, and Twelfth houses, and not at his best when in the First, Second, Seventh, Eighth, and Tenth.

Pluto: Pluto moves so slowly that his influence in all the signs in terms of modern astrology has yet to be fully tested. He is naturally at his strongest in Scorpio and Aries and would appear to be quite favorable also in Gemini and Sagittarius. Personally, I liked his influence in Libra because it broke down many old patterns of relationship, allowing a great deal of social experimentation to take place. Virgo seems to be a good sign for this planet, as it promotes refinement and healing, and I assume that Aquarius will be a welcoming sign, as Uranus, its ruler, is in exaltation when in Pluto's primary sign of Scorpio. Pluto is not particularly potent in Taurus, Cancer, and Capricorn. He brings out some egocentric (but highly individualizing) elements in Leo, and from an esoteric perspective, is at his most spiritual in Pisces, where the road to the redemption of the lower self reaches its conclusion. He is a powerful influence in all of the houses, but is most effective in the First, Eighth, and Tenth, and seems to be very positive in the Ninth and Eleventh as well. The Second, Seventh, and Twelfth can be troublesome spots for Pluto, but as with all positions of this planet, a great deal depends on the individual's level of consciousness.

A note concerning the Moon's Nodes and Chiron: In my experience I have found that the Nodes of the Moon are neither favorable nor unfavorable, stronger or weaker in any of the signs, as they function to bring us into those experiences which generate new and positive opportunities for personal growth (North Node) or seek to repeat old habits of social interaction (South Node) according to the signs in which they are placed. The only house positions of the Nodes that I have found to be somewhat challenging are when the South Node is either conjoined to the Ascendant or Midheaven. In the case of the former, the individual is constantly having to adjust to life experiences and environments which go contrary to one's basic nature (unless this contrariness *is* one's basic nature!). The Northern Node on the Seventh House cusp should bring in positive relationships that can help to make life easier. In the case of the Southern Node on the cusp of the Midheaven, there is some difficulty in finding one's way in life in terms of career and profession. Here the Northern Node on the Fourth House cusp can be an effective tool. It asks (and supports) the individual to look more deeply inside of herself in order to find a more profound sense of inner contact both to her essential nature and to her personal resources.

In terms of Chiron, the reader would do well to read *Chiron and the Healing Journey* by Melanie Reinhart, Arkana/Penguin CAS, 1989. This is the most authoritative and detailed book on the subject yet written and has been my source for my still experimental work with this most recently included body in astrology. Look to the house and sign position of Chiron to indicate a wound in the personality that, when healed, becomes a major source of an individual's strength.

---

1. Should the reader be interested in exploring the meaning of the Sun from the perspective of esoteric astrology, please consult the author's previous work, *Soul-Centered Astrology,* The Crossing Press, 1996.

Planetary Dispositorship Defined —
The Hidden Rulers Revealed

The word itself, "dispositor," comes from the Latin verb *disponere*, meaning "to put in different places," while *dispositum* indicates "things that are arranged in order." A dispositor in astrology has come to mean a planet which has the authority to move the energy of another planet or house to a different location in the horoscope. In this capacity, the discovery of the structure of dispositorship creates a true ordering of planetary powers. Since the astrologer's main task in reading a chart is to bring clarity out of the seemingly chaotic jumble of symbols and geometric angles, finding the real potencies and weaknesses in a horoscope and then knowing how to arrange them in order of importance is our absolutely essential task.

Another term that is sometimes used for dispositor is "ruler," but this is neither complete nor quite correct. Although we know that signs are ruled by planets, the concept and application of dispositorship to the natal chart is far more extensive than simple rulership. For example, the sign Aquarius is ruled by the planet Uranus. If the Sun is in Aquarius, the astrology student would say that the individual is an Aquarian, ruled by Uranus. Many astrology students would stop at that point and focus on the Sun's position. But the place in the chart of Uranus by sign and house *disposes* the energy of the Sun. Although the Aquarius individual would express a great deal of activity through the position of the Sun, *it is the position of Uranus that takes the energy of the Sun forward and conditions its use.* Let's take a look at an Aquarian horoscope and see how the nature of dispositorship — in this case, the simple dispositorship of the Sun — affects the chart interpretation.

Example 1: The Horoscope of Angela Davis[1]

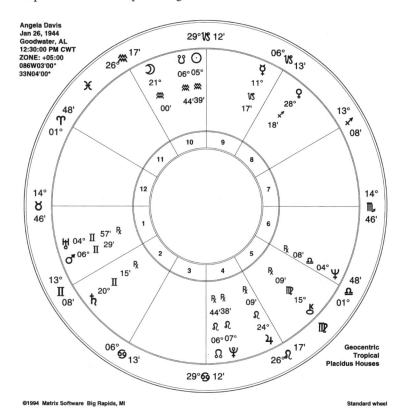

Angela Davis
Jan 26, 1944
Goodwater, AL
12:30:00 PM CWT
ZONE: +05:00
086W03'00"
33N04'00"

Geocentric
Tropical
Placidus Houses

©1994 Matrix Software Big Rapids, MI

Standard wheel

Angela Davis was a very prominent figure in the Black Liberation Movement of the 1970s. She was highly educated both in the United States and in Europe. She studied Marxism and majored in philosophy, eventually becoming an assistant professor at UCLA. Her political activities linked her with the Black Panther Party and she was arrested in connection with the murder of a judge. Davis was, for a time, on the FBI's "Ten Most Wanted" list, but after a long and highly publicized trial, she was subsequently acquitted of all charges. The Sun in Aquarius is located in the Tenth House of social standing and career. That house is most closely associated with wide-ranging acclaim and/or notoriety. The Sun is ruled by Uranus and secondarily by Saturn. Uranus is in the First House, dispositing the Sun. Thus, she fully embodies and projects through her everyday contact with the world (First House dynamics) the radicalism and revolutionary spirit of her Tenth House Aquarius Sun. These characteristics are made even stronger by the fact that Uranus trines the Sun, allowing an ease of expression between the two planets. In this case we have a positive link between the First and the Tenth houses: who she is and what she does are smoothly connected by the trine. When we add the presence of Mars (god of war) conjunct Uranus (agent of revolutions) and also trine the Sun (creative principle of vitality), we understand the violence and turbulence of her political stand and her personal life. In essence, there is no difference between the two: the personal is the political and the political is the personal. Uranus is both the natal and the natural ruler of the Eleventh House (the general public, groups, and organizations) and disposits the energy of this house in the First (projected ego contacts with the immediate environment) with Mars (natural ruler of the First). She thus easily becomes the personification of the collective group struggle, a struggle which she can clearly communicate (Mars and Uranus in Gemini) and emit through her immediate contacts with life (First House).

The philosophical background is also clearly indicated in the chart and emphasized by dispositorship. The tracing of the dispositorship pattern will show us where to place the *originating potency* of the chart. When we closely examine the movement of the planetary energies, we will see how Mercury is this underlining, stimulating planetary force. The Sun is ruled by Uranus, which disposes/deposits the solar energy into the First. Mercury, however, is the ruler of Gemini and disposes the focus of Uranus as well as the path of the energy of Mars *and* Saturn. The ruler of her Gemini planets is Mercury in Capricorn in the Ninth House, the latter being the astrological domicile of higher education, law, and philosophy. In fact, as of this writing, Davis is a professor of political science and philosophy.

There are numerous dispositorship factors in this horoscope that make its study very worthwhile and we will return to its delineation. At this point, however, let us outline and explore all of the other kinds of rulership and dispositorship factors that are inherent in a natal horoscope. These are commonly found within the structure of the natus, but are all too often either entirely overlooked or underemphasized.

Planetary Mutual Reception

Mutual reception is a facet of dispositorship that intimately links planets and/or houses. Planets are in mutual reception when they are placed in each other's signs. Mars in Aquarius and Uranus in Scorpio, Jupiter in Leo and the Sun in Sagittarius, the Moon in Virgo and Mercury in Cancer, are all examples of this kind of mutual dispositorship. When two planets are in this type of relationship, they have to be considered as a pair. These two bodies work together, enhancing or inhibiting their various functions. Yes, each of the planets has its own effect in the chart and must be understood individually. It is essential, however, that the astrologer also fully considers the effects of the combination of energies that exists when the two are brought together. It is only in this way that the full range of implications of *both* planets may be fully understood. To further complicate (but also to complete) the matter, there are two additional factors which need to be determined in order to make your analysis of the mutual reception complete. In the first place, the astrologer has to consider which of the two planets is the stronger. Secondly, are they also connected by any one of the six major aspects (conjunction, sextile, square, trine, opposition, and inconjunction)?

Determining the Relative Strengths of the Planets in Mutual Reception

The summary on the following page, although familiar to many readers, will help to make the spotting of mutual reception in a horoscope that much the easier.

A planet cannot be in mutual reception if it is in the sign of its own rulership.[2] If this is the case, it disposits its energy where it is placed. It can, however, be in its exaltation and be in mutual reception: the Sun in Aries and Mars in Leo, for example. Which is the stronger? The Sun in Aries. Although Mars is quite potent and comfortable in Leo, it is not in the sign of its exaltation, while the Sun is so placed. A planet will be weakened by placement in either detriment or fall. You will know at a glance if a planet is very strong if it is posited in its sign of exaltation, or very weak if it is in either its detriment or fall.

Summary of Planetary Powers

Planet	Honor/ Ruler	Detriment	Exaltation	Fall
Sun	Leo	Aquarius	Aries	Libra
Moon	Cancer	Capricorn	Taurus	Scorpio
Mercury	Gemini/ Virgo	Sagittarius/ Pisces	Aquarius	Leo
Venus	Taurus/ Libra	Scorpio/ Aries	Pisces	Virgo
Mars	Aries/ Scorpio	Libra/ Taurus	Capricorn	Cancer
Jupiter	Sagittarius/ Pisces	Gemini/ Virgo	Cancer	Capricorn
Saturn	Capricorn/ Aquarius	Cancer/ Leo	Libra	Aries
Uranus	Aquarius	Leo	Scorpio	Taurus
Neptune	Pisces	Virgo	Cancer	Capricorn
Pluto	Scorpio/ Aries	Taurus/ Libra	Aquarius	Leo

Venus in Leo and the Sun in Libra—which is the stronger? Venus in Leo. The Sun in Libra is in its detriment and Venus is definitely stronger, i.e., its true nature may be more easily expressed in Leo than the solar force in the sign of the Scales. Venus in Pisces and Neptune or Jupiter in Libra? Venus in Pisces, as that is where she is exalted (and air is not the strongest element for the expression of either Jupiter or Neptune).

A complication arises if both planets are in mutual reception but are also in the signs of their detriment. This occurs in "the reversed pairs" relative to the natural order of the signs: Venus in Aries—Mars in Libra; Mars in Taurus—Venus in Scorpio; Jupiter in Gemini—

Mercury in Sagittarius; Saturn in Cancer—Moon in Capricorn, etc. In this case, you need to determine which of the planets is the weaker, as it is important to discover which of the bodies will have the most deleterious influence on the chart. This requires that you know the "theme" of the horoscope.

Let us say that you are examining a chart with Leo rising. The Sun, as the ruler of the Ascendant, plays a vital role in the entire nativity (see Chapter 3). If the Sun were in Aquarius, its detriment, and Uranus in Leo (its detriment), the Sun would be the more debilitated (and debilitating). If this were a natus with the Sun in Taurus and a Libra Ascendant chart and Venus were in Scorpio and Mars in Taurus (both in their detriment), Venus would be receiving the more serious blow, as she rules and disposits both the solar and ascending potencies. This type of detrimental pairing is not helpful. I have heard it said that each of the planets in such a combination can "borrow" the strength of the other's placement by sign and thus serve to balance one another. In my experience, this doesn't work—it simply is not the case. People with Venus in Aries and Mars in Libra will confuse passion with love, affection with lust, friendship with courtship. Socially and in all forms of relationships, they will "Go!" at a red light and "Stop!" at the green (and there will be no such thing as respecting a cautionary yellow). Social, tempering yellow lights are far more respected when Venus is in Capricorn and Mars is in Virgo (or vice-versa).

Another example of relative strengths and weaknesses in mutual reception occurs when one planet is in its exaltation and the other planet is in a "neutral" sign: Jupiter in Cancer (exaltation) and the Moon in Sagittarius or Pisces. Here the Moon rules Cancer, but Jupiter is exalted in this sign *and* is the ruler of Sagittarius as well as the co-ruler of the Fish. The influence of Jupiter would clearly predominate in both of these cases of mutual receptions.

The above leaves little doubt that it is in the ability to synthesize the various elements of a horoscope that the real art of the astrologer expresses itself. Synthesis requires the development of an inner mental alchemy. This is primarily a mercurial process (Mercury in Gemini rules analysis, but in Virgo, Mercury rules synthesis), one that requires a total comprehension of the meaning of each of the elements in an "astrological unit" and then the ability to fuse these elements together. This is why it is so vital to memorize the astrological keywords and phrases that constitute so much of the work during one's initial approach to our science.[3] We can consider an astrological unit to be composed of three parts: a planet in a sign and in a house. When combining astrological influences, two and often more of these units have to be considered at any one time. The inner, synthesizing alchemy of which I speak is created through the development of true intuition. It allows one to contact the energies and subtle structural patterns of life as expressed through astrological symbology. This faculty of perception is one of the greatest gifts that astrology offers its serious practitioners. You cannot be a true astrologer without it. And once you have it, you are more than an astrologer, you are a conscious human being.

The Effects of Aspects Between Planets in Mutual Reception

Rule: When two planets are in mutual reception and also connected by one of the six principal aspects (conjunction, sextile, trine, square, inconjunction, and opposition), the effects of the mutual reception are strengthened for good or ill depending on the nature of the aspect as well as the planet/sign combination involved.

Let us take the example of Mars in Capricorn square Saturn in Aries. We can immediately determine that Mars is the stronger of the two influences because it is exalted in Capricorn, while Saturn is in fall in Aries. In this case, Mars would stimulate drive and ambition while at the same time aid the individual to create the necessary structures for success in life. Saturn, on the other hand, would tend to inhibit this undertaking by limiting the size and effectiveness of what is being created based on the individual's need to create his or her own system of rules and regulations. When Mars is in Capricorn, there is a definite ability to hold steady in reaching long-range goals. It also aids the person to cultivate and organize the material circumstances and resources in his or her personal environment relative to the needs of the personality. Saturn in Aries, however, restricts the use of such talents to an area circumscribed by the person's need to be in direct control of every operation. A square between these two planets will only emphasize the natural antipathy existing within the energies of the mutual reception. Without the square, the two planets would act somewhat more independently. This would be especially the case if each of the two were in positive aspects to other planets in the chart. A square between Mars and Saturn, for example, links them in a constant, intense battle, no matter what other mitigating and even positive astrological circumstances exist in the chart. In this case, the urge to succeed in the material facets of life (Mars in Capricorn) will constantly be up against a self-imposed ordering and sense of control (Saturn in Aries) that will limit this form of self-expression in the larger world. It is very much like driving a highly tuned car with the brakes on while all the time attempting to win the Indianapolis 500.

What would occur if Mars in Capricorn were trine Saturn in Aries? This could occur if Mars were in the first degrees of its sign and Saturn in the last degrees of its position (for example, Mars at 2° of Capricorn and Saturn at 28° of Aries—a distance of 116° and well within the orb of a 120° trine). Although the conflict between these positions would still exist (how could it not?), the individual would find that life would more easily yield solutions to the tension that the mutual reception indicates. The individual could learn how to create proper boundaries for his goals and orientation for success. He could find ways to adapt his intense urge for power within his sphere of activity to the actual boundaries of that sphere and so minimize an inherent sense of frustration that comes when Mars and Saturn afflict one another.

Some mutual receptions are very soft by nature because the natures of the planets are basically compatible. This is the case between the Sun and Venus. A semi-square between Sun in Libra and Venus in Leo would tend to produce a very artistic nature even though the Sun is in its detriment. There is the tendency in this planetary combination for the Libran individual to idealize their lovers, sometimes shaping the people and the relationships themselves into something more representative of a dream image than the reality at hand. Even the challenging nature of the aspect linking this mutual reception would not deny having partners. On the contrary, it would stimulate a very intense and passionate love life and would definitely enhance the fun of being in intimate situations. Yet the urge to create an idealized focus of relationship could lead to difficulties.

Venus in Pisces inconjunct Neptune in Libra will give a lot of complications in determining if a relationship is to be conducted on a more platonic/spiritual level or on a more personal one. There is definitely the urge to worship the partner or to be the object of that adoration—or both. Co-dependency and an "I'm a martyr for love" complex is almost certainly part of the individual's "relationship package." But this mutual reception, even with an actual inconjunction between these planets, will not deny (in fact, it will enhance) artistic sensibility, the urge to be of service to others, a generous disposition, and a very kindly nature.

Let's return to Angela Davis' chart found on page 31. Here we see that we have a very important mutual reception between Mercury and Saturn. Mercury is at 11° Capricorn in the Ninth House and Saturn is at 20° Gemini in the Second. First, we will analyze the individual astrological units; then we will synthesize these indications in order to know what they mean in terms of Davis' life.

Unit 1: Mercury in Capricorn in the Ninth

This position leads a person to the study and exploration (Ninth House) of an established philosophy of belief (Capricorn on the Ninth House cusp). The urge will be to unite one's own faculties of communication (Mercury) within the structure of this greater intellectual system (Ninth House).

Unit 2: Saturn in Gemini in the Second

The Second House is strongly emphasized in this horoscope by the fact that Taurus (the natural Second House ruler) is on the Ascendant.[4] Davis thus will be very naturally inclined to project her own system of values (Taurus) upon her contacts with her immediate environment (Ascendant). Saturn in Gemini serves to create a logical mental structure that works to establish and communicate these values (Gemini on the Second House cusp) and gives her a stance, a sense of authority in the process (the position of Saturn).

When we combine the influence of these two units by mutual reception, we see that the lessons learned at institutes of higher learning (Ninth House), especially a European philosophy learned at a foreign university (Marxism studied at the Sorbonne in Paris), are brought into her own sphere of personal values (Saturn ruler of the Ninth and dispositor of Mercury in the Second House). This information and belief system is then expanded and taught by Davis through her own position as an assistant professor of philosophy. It reaches collective proportions and brings her into the spotlight of media attention as Saturn and Uranus (both ruled by Mercury) trine her Tenth House Moon and Sun respectively. Saturn and Uranus are, of course, the rulers of her Aquarius-placed Sun and Moon.

Davis' philosophical background is clearly indicated in the chart and emphasized by dispositorship. The tracing of this dispositorship/rulership pattern will show us where to place the *originating potency* of the chart. After having examined the movement of the planetary units, we can now easily understand how Mercury (backed by Saturn) is the underlining, stimulating planetary focus of the chart. Although the Sun is ruled by Uranus, which disposes the solar energy into the First House, it is pulled back into the Ninth, as Mercury is the ruler of Gemini. Mercury thus disposits the focus of Uranus as well as the path of energy exhibited by Gemini-ruled Mars and Saturn.

Multiple Mutual Reception

It often occurs that there is a pattern of reception in a natal horoscope that yields a multiplistic ordering of dispositorship. This takes place when the path of rulership involves three or more planets that disposit one another. This obviously creates a more complicated linkage, one that will dominate many of the events and personality characteristics of that person's life. Such an example exists in several closely connected patterns in the Davis horoscope: The Sun is in Aquarius disposited by Saturn in Gemini, which in turn is disposited by Mercury in Capricorn ruled by Saturn in Gemini. The Moon is also in Aquarius and the same dispositorship factors occur (Moon to Saturn, Saturn to Mercury, Mercury back to Saturn). The Saturn factor is stronger than the dispositorship pattern we can trace using Uranus as the ruler of Aquarius:

Sun and Moon in Aquarius disposited by Uranus, Uranus disposited by Mercury, Mercury in mutual reception with Saturn. As Saturn is the ruler of the Tenth House (career, public image), its prominence is definitely underscored. This is a woman who definitely had a very public life! Once again, we come to the conclusion that the relationship between Mercury and Saturn dominates the horoscope.

As an interpretive aside, it can be stated that if Uranus is posited in either the First or the Tenth houses of the natal chart, the individual (who is usually highly individualistic) tends to embody some form of political or social principle as his own. The person, in effect, becomes a symbolic archetype of the cause, belief, or social movement of which he is a part. At the very least, he will stand forth as clearly representing himself as his own archetype. The message is: "After the gods created me, they broke the mold!"

The Final Dispositor

The astrologer is seeking to determine planetary strengths and weaknesses as well as the ordering of these relative potencies when delineating the horoscope. One of the most important factors of prominence that can be found in the chart is the location and meaning of the final dispositor. The sign and house position of this planet reveals a place of tremendous planetary influence. It is an underlining current of energy that *seeps and infiltrates* throughout the entire natal map. The final dispositor is found as the end result of tracing all rulerships back to one source. To make the final dispositor easier to find, please note the following:

1. There can be no final dispositor in a horoscope whenever there is mutual reception.
2. The final dispositor has to be in the sign of its own rulership.

Let's look at a few charts and find the final dispositor. It is obvious that in the Angela Davis chart, as there is no planet in the sign of its own rulership and that significant mutual reception exists, therefore there can be no final dispositor. The two example charts below, however, will clearly reveal the presence of such a planet.

Example 2: The Horoscope of Charlie Chaplin[5]

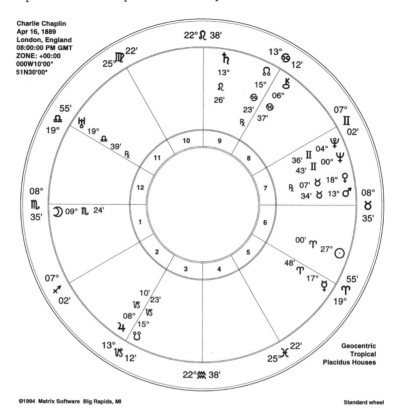

If we begin with the Sun in Aries we can trace the pattern of dispositorship as follows: first to Mars in Taurus as ruler of Aries and then Venus (ruler of Taurus) in Taurus (stop). As we will see, all the other planets will "stop" at this point (be disposited by Venus in Taurus): Neptune and Pluto in Gemini, Mercury (as ruler of Gemini) in Aries, Mars in Taurus, Venus in Taurus (stop). Saturn in Leo, Sun (ruler of Leo) in Aries, Mars in Taurus, Venus in Taurus (stop). Uranus in Libra, Venus as ruler of Libra in Taurus, Venus in Taurus (stop). Moon in Scorpio, Pluto in Gemini, Mercury in Aries, Mars in Taurus, Venus in Taurus (stop). Using the other dispositor of Moon in Scorpio: Mars in Taurus, Venus in Taurus (stop). Jupiter in Capricorn, Saturn (ruler of Capricorn) in Leo, Sun in Aries, Mars in Taurus, Venus in Taurus (stop).

Chaplin was a lover of many women (Venus conjunct the ruler of his Aries Sun, Mars) as well as a person who attracted universal appeal

— 41 —

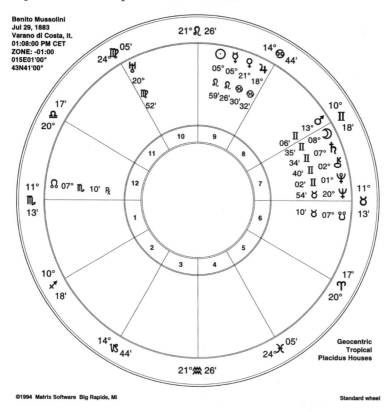

Benito Mussolini
Jul 29, 1883
Varano di Costa, It.
01:08:00 PM CET
ZONE: -01:00
015E01'00"
43N41'00"

21° ♌ 26'

24° ♍ 05'

14° ♋ 44'

☉ 05° ♌ 59' ☿ 05° ♌ 26' ♀ 21° ♋ 30' ♃ 18° ♋ 32'

♅ 20°

17' ♎ 20°

10° ♊ 18'

♂ 13° ♊ 06' ☽ 08° ♊ 35' ♄ 07° ♊ 34' ⚷ 02° ♊ 40' ⚹ 01° ♊ 02' ♆ 20° ♉ 54'

11° ♏ 13' ☊ 07° ♏ 10' ℞

11° ♉ 13'

07° ♉ 10' ☋

10° ♐ 18'

17' ♈ 20°

14° ♑ 44'

24° ♓ 05'

21° ♒ 26'

Geocentric
Tropical
Placidus Houses

Standard wheel

for his ability to partner with the hearts of millions of people all over the world. The qualities of his final dispositor also reveal that he made a great deal of money. His most popular character, the one that brought him international acclaim, was "The Little Tramp," a sad, often homeless figure with amazing compassion. Venus is the ruler of his Twelfth House, the "home of the homeless."

At the other end of the spectrum, we can examine a horoscope of someone who destroyed the lives of many people, the Italian dictator, Benito Mussolini.

Beginning with the Sun and following the natural rulership of the signs, the following dispositorship pattern emerges: Sun in Leo (stop); Mercury in Leo, Sun in Leo (stop); Venus and Jupiter in Cancer, Moon in Gemini, Mercury in Leo, Sun in Leo (stop); Mars, Moon, Saturn,

Pluto all in Gemini, Mercury in Leo, Sun in Leo (stop); Neptune in Taurus, Venus in Cancer, Moon in Gemini, Mercury in Leo, Sun in Leo (stop). The Sun in Leo is the final dispositor of the chart.

Mussolini followed in the footsteps of another Leo potentate, Louis XIV, the Sun King. His Majesty's well-known philosophy was: "*L'état, c'est moi!*" —I am the State. Uranus in the Tenth House seems to echo and support Mussolini as the archetype of the Fascism which he embodied. This doctrine played the major philosophical role in bringing him to power. Its influence can be seen in the chart, as the Sun rules the Tenth House (public standing, governments and their leaders), and is posited in the Ninth House, along with Jupiter, natural ruler of that house and the planetary significator for philosophy and belief systems. Mercury, dispositor of the huge stellium in Gemini that includes the Moon, as well as Uranus in Virgo, is also in Leo. The Sun in Leo disposits the entire horoscope just as in life Mussolini's personality and philosophy totally dominated, ruled, and ruined Italy.

Now that it is clear how to find the final dispositor, here are some rules and guidelines to interpret the meaning of this significant and often hidden ruler of the horoscope.

1. Important! If the final dispositor is also the ruler of the sign on the Ascendant, the influence of that planet will dominate the life. Give that planet high priority in terms of its overall influence in the chart. Example: Leo rising, Sun in Leo in the natal chart and also found to be the final dispositor.
2. There will be sometimes a little uncertainty in the finding of the final dispositor if the planet is placed in a sign of its own rulership, but this same sign is coruled by another planet. Examples: Scorpio, ruled by Pluto and coruled by Mars; Aquarius, ruled by Uranus and cruled by Saturn; Pisces, ruled by Neptune and coruled by Jupiter. Please examine the chart on the following page.

Along with Dane Rudhyar, Alan Leo, and Charles Carter, Marc Edmund Jones was one of the "founding fathers" of modern astrology. Profoundly intellectual, but clearly gifted intuitively as well, Jones

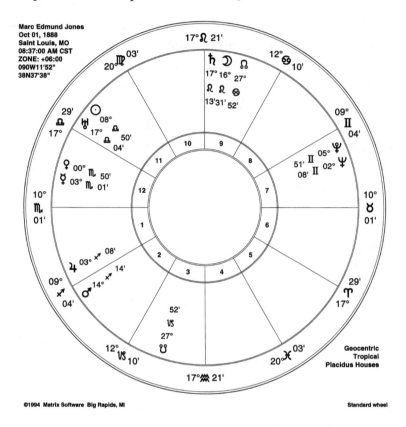

Marc Edmund Jones
Oct 01, 1888
Saint Louis, MO
08:37:00 AM CST
ZONE: +06:00
090W11'52"
38N37'38"

17° ♌ 21'

12° ♋ 10'

17° 16° 27'
♌ ♌ ♋
13'31' 52'

09°
♊
04'

05° ♆
51' ♊
08' ♊ 02' ♅

10°
♉
01'

29'
♈
17'

03'
20 ♓

17° ♒ 21'

Geocentric
Tropical
Placidus Houses

©1994 Matrix Software Big Rapids, MI

Standard wheel

contributed an enormous body of excellent work to the astrological community. He is best known for his book on the Sabian Symbols, as well as his codification of birth patterns.

Using the method outlined above, let's find the final dispositor in this chart: Sun and Uranus in Libra, Venus in Scorpio, Mars in Sagittarius, Jupiter in Sagittarius (stop). Moon and Saturn in Leo, Sun in Libra, Venus in Scorpio, Mars in Sagittarius, Jupiter in Sagittarius (stop). Venus and Mercury in Scorpio, Mars in Sagittarius, Jupiter in Sagittarius (stop). Neptune in Gemini, Mercury in Scorpio, Mars in Sagittarius, Jupiter in Sagittarius (stop).

We come to the complication I mentioned when we examine the position of Pluto. Pluto in Gemini, Mercury in Scorpio. That is a mutual reception and by definition, this eliminates the possibility of a *final*

dispositor—and it does. In fact, once we trace any of the dispositorships of the planets back to either Venus or Mercury, we are led to either
Pluto in Gemini or Mars in Sagittarius, as these two planets are the co-
rulers of Scorpio. But if we trace the line of planetary energy through
Mars instead of Pluto as the ruler of Scorpio, we do indeed come to a final (albeit not "absolutely" final) dispositor (in this case, Jupiter in
Sagittarius). The influence of this planet cannot be and should not be
underestimated. Jupiter does dominate through dispositorship a lot of
the direction of the planetary energy in Marc Edmund Jones' life. He
was a philosopher and teacher who had a huge impact on his environment (Jupiter in the First House in Sagittarius). He challenged the prevailing underlining concepts about astrology during his time and
caused a regeneration in the thinking and methods of chart interpretation among astrologers to this day. His work and words live on through
many of us who have benefited from studying his books (including,
with gratitude, the author). These last two sentences describe the effects of Jupiter in opposition to Pluto in Gemini in Jones' chart and
Pluto trine the Sun in the Eleventh House. The struggle to change the
way people think (as well as the need to dominate people's thinking
habits—a personality characteristic) is also clearly indicated in the
Pluto in Gemini/Mercury in Scorpio mutual reception. Although there
is no absolute final dispositor in the M. E. Jones chart, Jupiter in
Sagittarius has to be considered as "a" final dispositor and seen along
with Pluto and Mercury as the dominating, planetary influences.

3. To interpret the meaning of the final dispositor in terms of personality characteristics and the shaping of tendencies and events
   in a person's life, use your knowledge of what a planet means
   when placed in its own sign and in the various house positions.
   If Mars in Aries in the Tenth House is the final dispositor of the
   chart, you know that the individual, no matter what else may be
   indicated, is a fighter, a pioneer, and will assert his or her "plan
   for life" through the chosen career. There will be a very strong
   urge in this respect, to affirm personal dominance in the se-
   lected or self-created profession. The major thing to keep in
   mind is that by definition, as the *final* dispositor, Mars will be

the *only* planet in its essential dignity in this particular horoscope. No other planet will be expressing its nature as purely as the final dispositor. Use this understanding of the planets by sign and house and give the final dispositor the weight it deserves.

The following paragraphs may prove helpful in describing the nature of a planet when it is the final dispositor. Obviously the final dispositor will be in its own sign of rulership and thus be quite strong. As the meanings of the planets in the signs have been given out so frequently by so many fine astrological authors, there is no need for me to repeat the basic personality characteristics and tendencies of the various planet/sign combinations.[8] What the present work does attempt to offer is a *theme*, an underlying and *connecting thread of energy*, that the final dispositor lends to the chart. Just as important as the conditioning personality characteristics of the planet in question is the *weight* the final dispositor must be given in terms of delineating the chart. It is a major influence whose effects will be interwoven throughout all the individual's other activities, i.e., the energetic expressions of the other planets in terms of human behavior.

The Planets as Final Dispositors of the Natal Chart

Sun in Leo: The sense of self is exaggerated. In a more highly developed individual this will tend to add creativity and underscore a strong motivation to contribute to the direct welfare of one's immediate surroundings. If well aspected by the other planets, health and vitality are very strong and there is a ceaseless need to create a universe of one's own. When spiritually inclined, this individual will strive to make sure that that universe serves a positive, collective purpose. If poorly aspected (especially by Saturn or Neptune), vitality is depleted and health may suffer. The urge to be noticed and the ability to fulfill that urge in a dynamic, creative sense are not one in the same, causing frustration. In an egocentric and less spiritually developed person, life is reduced to the circumference of that ego's rulership. What cannot be immediately controlled or affected by the person's sense of self either does not exist or is discounted as being of no importance. *"If you are not me, you are nobody!"*

Moon in Cancer: The instinctual nature is very strong and powerfully conditioned by one's family inheritance, a factor I like to call the "biological karma." There is a need for personal security that extends outward to encompass all other individuals who are "adopted" into one's life. This adoption process is continual, and, in addition to people, also includes emotions, objects, and "sense-memory-units." Like the proverbial elephant, a Moon in Cancer "never forgets" (but may not consciously *know* that she is remembering!). As the final dispositor, the Moon in Cancer acts as a synthesizing memory sponge, absorbing all the life experiences through the interweaving web of planetary activity. It is vital to keep in mind that such absorption is taking place through the sieve of the psychological conditioning patterns of the early life. Thus, there is a very highly personalized filter at work throughout this entire process. The more psychologically subjective and the more unconsciously attached to the biological karma the individual is, the more egocentric is this filtering process.

Mercury in Gemini: The primary need in life is to gain experiences. This occurs through a never-ending urge to be multiplistic in activity and attitude. The individual is constantly gathering data, usually from firsthand experience and effort, but the *meaning and importance* of this information (as well as its creative application) is totally conditioned by the level of development of the individual's mind and orientation to life. Having experiences is just not the same as knowing what these experiences mean in terms of life's larger issues and principles. When well positioned in the chart by house and aspects, this constant flow of information and data is extremely beneficial both to self and others. If other indications, i.e., the sense of personal dedication, the urge and ability to contribute to humanity's collective well-being, are present, Mercury in Gemini as the final dispositor offers enormous advantages in terms of its communicative and associative functions. If poorly placed in the chart (especially if in multiple squares and/or oppositions with other planets in mutable signs), confusion can reign as too much information goes in and out without the proper discrimination and intellectual structures.

Mercury in Virgo: Many of the indications mentioned above also apply to this position of Mercury, but with some important differences. In Virgo we have a call to put ideas and information out in a practical, material way. The most basic expression for this would be: "I have got to make some money with all of this data." Mercury in Virgo still is a very personal placement. The individual has to do something personal with his own skills and abilities. Compare this with Mercury in Aquarius, when information can go over the Internet and it doesn't matter so much who programmed the information or where it came from as long as it reaches its intended audience. A person with Mercury in Virgo has to invent and promote his or her own way of doing things and the sense of accomplishment must be seen to one degree or another as manifesting in material form. As the final dispositor, life will take on a definite practical focus (no matter how spiritual the individual may be) and there will be also the tendency to accumulate many techniques, tools, methods, and processes with which to succeed (or survive) in life.

Venus in Taurus: The need for partnership characterizes the life of anyone who has Venus as the final dispositor, no matter what the Sun sign may be. Think about a person whose Sun and Ascendant is in Aries (and make sure that you think quickly!) with the Moon in Sagittarius who has Venus in Taurus as the final dispositor. This is great for Venus, but very challenging to this explosive, independent person who needs plenty of individual space in which to move and operate. The urge for sensual experiences and the need to possess (both objects and people) will be a major underlying theme of one's life. But the fiery, expansive nature of the Sun, Moon, and Ascendant tend to push the person away from what he or she seeks most to attract and *hold*. Venus in Taurus as the final dispositor brings magnetism and thus, great attractiveness into one's life. The test will be how to perceive true value in the many gifts that life presents. There is an old astrological saying: "A child of Venus never wants." But what is given is not necessarily what is needed and what one tends to hold on to does not necessarily equate with what is best to keep. The natal horoscope with Venus in Taurus will always bring up issues about refinement of desires and discrimination in terms of one's personal, sensual, and aesthetic orientation to life.

Venus in Libra: The benefits of having Venus as the final dispositor often outweigh the liabilities. Venus bestows benefits and opportunities through others, allowing one to share personal love and resources. Even if the relationships in one's life have their complications (which they usually do), Venus as the underlying major theme in the chart offers benefits of learning about balanced giving and sharing. Its placement by sign and aspect may not always bring consistent harmony, but even when she is in a less than perfect state, Venus offers many fine promises and joys. When Venus in Libra is the final dispositor, relationships will be the focus and vehicle of expression for all the other creative urges in the natal map. The subjective thread of life will primarily deal with balancing and harmonizing the other planetary influences so that the person's relationship objectives may be satisfied. Look to the house position of Venus to show where this relationship orientation will be centered.

Mars in Aries: A life dominated by Mars in Aries is a life that seeks to dominate. The area where the urge to win, achieve, and overcome all adversities to personal will is seen in the chart by the house placement of Mars when positioned in this, its own sign. No matter what else the interpretation of the map may reveal, it is the domicile of Mars in Aries that functions as the base of operations—the headquarters—of the individual's field of activity. Mars in Aries as the final dispositor in the Twelfth House, for example, indicates a person who will attempt to win life's battles by playing an unseen hand. No matter how kind, gentle, compassionate, or understanding the other indications in such a horoscope may be, when Mars in Aries is the final dispositor, the individual is constantly involved with an inner dialogue that says: "I win, you lose (unless of course, you are on my side, in which case I will fight the battle for both of us)." Of all the planet/sign combinations in astrology, Mars in Aries is the simplest to understand; its energy is the least complicated and the most direct and clearly enunciated. One just might wish to get out of the way when it is holding forth!

Jupiter in Sagittarius: The urge to know and to teach what is known predominates as an orientation of the personality. The house position that Jupiter occupies when in Sagittarius points to the area of major interest in the unfolding and expansion of such knowledge. As I pointed out in the introductory paragraph to this section, we add weight and emphasis to a planet in dignity when it is also the final dispositor. Jupiter in Sagittarius will *always* add the urge for expansive awareness through travel and higher education. But when it is also the final dispositor of a chart, this position should not be seen just as merely another important element in the horoscope—it is an astrological factor that will dominate the life. Jupiter in Sagittarius will almost always reveal a person who is centered in the search for (or if found, the expostulation of) a deep commitment to a particular religion or philosophy. This activity will be constantly challenged if Jupiter is poorly configured with Uranus (which by square or opposition will almost always be in another mutable sign). The results of this combination leads one away from any established belief system into one that is either of a "cultish" nature or to the creation of one's own (even if it is more atheistic or philosophical than theistic or spiritual). Saturn in conflict with Jupiter in this position will bring adversity and tension from existing educational and/or religious systems (especially when embodied by the father or an early environment conditioned by orthodox or fundamentalist dogma). The frequency of occurrence of this dispositorship is about once every twelve years. Jupiter was last in Sagittarius in 1995, but could not be the final dispositor in anyone's chart born during that year as Neptune was in Capricorn and Saturn in Pisces (mutual reception). Nineteen eighty-three was the last year in which Jupiter in Sagittarius could be the final dispositor in anyone's natal chart.

Saturn in Capricorn: The establishment of personal authority and control in the area of life indicated by Saturn's house position is at the heart of the horoscope. All of the other planetary energies will be coordinated towards this end. Conflicts and challenges in the flow of planetary forces (as indicated by the aspects in the chart) that inhibit or delay their "pathway and passage" back to Saturn will be experienced by the individual as limitations and restrictions to personal goals. Special strength is added to the nativity if Saturn in Capricorn as the final dispositor is trine Mars or the Sun in Virgo or in a sextile to these two planets in Scorpio. Strong debility is seen if Mars or the Sun is in Aries, Libra, and Cancer and thus in square or opposition to Saturn in Capricorn as the final dispositor. The more positive indications cited above will add as well as sustain vitality and creative impulse while the afflictions cut off the flow of vitality and strongly hamstring all creative urges. Saturn in Capricorn as the final dispositor can occur at most once in twenty-nine years for a period of some thirty months. The last time Saturn occupied this position (1988–1990), Pluto was in its own dignity, Scorpio, and thus could not function as the final dispositor of any chart. During a number of months from March 1960 to early January 1962, it was indeed possible for Saturn to be the final dispositor in the birth map.

Uranus in Aquarius: The call to create an intense focus of individual self-expression is very strong when Uranus dominates the chart in the capacity of final dispositor. Yet we have to recognize the group dynamics that will be certainly at work when a person is born with Uranus in Aquarius as his or her final dispositor. It is thus highly significant to note that people with this planet/sign combination will be very much at work at singularizing and individualizing the collective concepts and orientation of members of their own generation. Those among this group of people who are advanced human beings from the evolutionary standpoint will stand forth as examples of their generational aspirations and contributions. Please note that there is a big difference between simply being born with Uranus in Aquarius and having it as the final dispositor. The former group will be very much affected by the collective, creative, and social directions of their generation. This will express most certainly in the tendency to be ever more intimately linked by computer technology and the advancing presence of the Internet (and all of its implications upon our lives). Those people of a more advanced consciousness who have Uranus in Aquarius as the final dispositor will serve and function as innovators and archetypes of the collective consciousness of this huge number of "new people." Uranus is in Aquarius only once in every eighty-four years for a period of about seven years. Although the last time Uranus entered Aquarius was in April of 1995, it wasn't until February of 1997 that it was capable of being the final dispositor in a natal chart. Uranus remains in Aquarius until the end of 2003 and its position makes it possible for it to be the final dispositor for several periods during this time.

Neptune in Pisces: The possibility of this planet/sign combination being the final dispositor in a chart occurs only once in about one hundred and sixty-three years and for a period of about fourteen years. The next time this can happen will begin in the year 2011. Stay tuned— there will be a few incredibly gifted psychics and gurus and an enormous fleet of spaced-out astral swimmers!

Pluto in Scorpio: The frequency of this combination is once in about every two hundred and forty-nine years for a period of about twelve years. The current generation of young people born between the end of 1983 and the end of 1995 reveals a number of instances in which Pluto in Scorpio is the final dispositor of the chart. The implications are very intense! The entire generation has a powerful and destructive focus of willpower. Destruction and will are natural to life and can be most effective tools for the collective evolution of humanity. The question is: what is the *direction and intent* of these urges? When used to satisfy the lower nature of Scorpio, then, violence, sexual abuse, incorrect financial behavior, and selfishness of the basest order will be the definite results. When oriented to the beneficial goals of evolution, then the correct conservation and use of energy on all levels is bound to eventuate. Gifted and spiritually evolved people with Pluto in Scorpio as their final dispositor will transform the use of our collective resources, both financially and in terms of our natural energetic reserves. They will invent (and force) new ways toward the right circulation of our planetary wealth. Their less evolved, more egocentric, personal desire-oriented brothers and sisters will be fighting them with all the selfish willpower at their command. It is my sincere hope that the spiritually gifted and more easygoing next generation, those born in 1996 to 2002 (Uranus in Aquarius and Pluto in Sagittarius) will bring guidance, resolution, and integration to these battles. The Pluto in Scorpio generation will be strongly helped and supported by the group born in the 1970s, many of whom are gifted humanitarians and visionaries. This is a collective that has Pluto and Uranus in Libra and Neptune in Sagittarius.

1. Data source: Rodden, Lois M., *Profiles of Women,* The American Federation of Astrologers, 1979, p. 308.
2. There is one pair that is an exception to this statement and even this is conjectural: Pluto in Scorpio and Mars in Aries or Mars in Scorpio and Pluto in Aries. First we have to accept that Pluto is the co-ruler of Aries—some astrologers do and some do not. I do. The first of these incredibly potent mutual receptions occurred with some regularity between the end of 1983 when Pluto first entered Scorpio and the end of 1995 when it exited this sign. The "embodiments" of this energy are alive and well, marching (with great destructive anger in some cases and with enormous willpower in all cases) among us and will no doubt at some point in the near future come stridently into the astrologer's office for a reading of their chart! The second of these receptions (Pluto in Aries and Mars in Scorpio) would have occurred about 150 years ago and is not due to repeat until much later on in the twenty-first century.
3. See Chapter 7, p. 183.
4. See Chapter 3 for a full description of the 12 Ascendants and the position of their sign and planetary rulers.
5. Data source: Erlewine, Stephen, *The Circle Book of Charts,* Circle Books, 1972.
6. Data source: Marion March, her personal database file.
7. Data source: Erlewine, Stephen, op. cit.
8. This information is basic and fundamental to the study of astrology. Intermediate students may, however, wish to consult the appropriate section in the Recommended Reading List at the end of this book for helpful texts and reference works that discuss the effects of the planets when in their own rulerships or "dignities."

House Dispositorships and
Planetary Rulers—An Overview

When we examine the planetary dynamics of dispositorship, we are looking for the *threads of energy* that result in an understanding of relative planetary strengths and weaknesses. When we delve into the chart in terms of house contacts and linkages, we are searching for those *areas in life* in which the planets will support or undermine the structure of the nativity. The purpose of the present chapter is to present those rules of astrological delineation that point us in the direction of correct house assessment. We will also be discussing the interplay between the houses and the planets which affect them. These factors will reveal to us the pattern of the interwoven relationships that exist between these two essential facets of horoscope interpretation.

Mutual Reception by Houses

Rule: When the planetary dispositors of two different houses are in the house of each other's rulership, the houses in question are intimately linked.

Procedure: To find these relationships and examine the contacts.

Please return to Angela Davis' chart on page 31. Notice that Gemini is on the cusp of the Second House and Mercury (the house dispositor) is located in Capricorn in the Ninth. You then immediately look for the position of Saturn (ruler of that sign) and locate its position. Saturn is found to be in the Second. Saturn is thus the dispositor of Mercury and the Ninth and Mercury is the dispositor of Saturn and the Second. These contacts reveal a *double mutual reception* by planets (Mercury in Capricorn and Saturn in Gemini) and by houses (the ruler of the Ninth is in the Second and the ruler of the Second is in the Ninth). The indications are very clear.

The larger philosophical system (in this case Marxism) learned in a foreign country (her studies in Europe) are both Ninth House influences. These beliefs she will espouse, communicate, and teach as her own (Mercury) at an institute of higher learning (she was a professor of philosophy at UCLA). The nature of these beliefs would lend authority and form the structure of her own values (Saturn in the Second House). As this is a Taurus-ruled chart, the projection of personal and, especially, economic values into the context of her immediate moment-to-moment contacts with the environment (Ascendant) is an essential element of her life and horoscope. If we take this analysis just one step further, you will see that the ruler of the chart (Venus) is in Sagittarius, another indication that links the Ninth House (naturally ruled by Sagittarius) and the Second House (naturally ruled by Taurus/Venus). When we see that Venus is also in trine to *its* dispositor, Jupiter, the importance of the linkages between the Ninth and the Second houses of the horoscope emerge with amazing strength and significance. Just keep tracing the dispositorship patterns.

Linkages by Same House Rulership

Rule: When two or more houses are ruled by the same planet, they are very closely linked in their effects upon one's life.

Procedure: Locate this planet by sign and house. Find and examine *its* dispositor and note its astrological relationships. Examine the closest and strongest planetary aspect and do the same. Synthesize the results.

Let us say that Virgo is rising in the chart and Gemini is on the Tenth House cusp (MC). This means that Mercury is the ruler of both the First and the Tenth houses. Who you are (Ascendant) and what you do with your life in terms of career (MC) are linked through the position of Mercury in this horoscope. If Mercury were in Aries, for example, you could be sure that the focus for both personal (Ascendant) and professional (MC) communication (Mercury) would be very original, pioneering, and challenging to the status quo (Aries). The interplay of other planetary aspects, especially those of Mars (ruler of Aries and dispositor of Mercury), would be very instrumental in telling the astrologer about the relative strength and/or weakness in terms of that individual's communicative abilities. If Mars were trine Mercury in Aries as ruler of both the Ascendant and Midheaven, then this individual would be very forthright, focused, highly assertive, and all things considered, successful, in his method of sharing his ideas and insights with others. The house position of Mercury in this example would also be of primary significance in determining where the communicative drive (the predominant urge in the chart) would be located. A Seventh House Mercury in Aries trine Mars would definitely indicate a strong and potent orientation towards relationships. Given that in the above example, Virgo, the sign of work, is rising and Mercury is also the ruler of the Tenth House of career, work-related relationships will play a very important role in this individual's life. The trine from Mars indicates that this person tends to take on the role of leadership in such interpersonal contacts with ease and natural ability. No matter what else may be indicated in the chart, such factors of house/planet/sign relationships definitely unfold a major, if not *the* major indicator of life direction. This is astrological synthesis at work.

These points are very clearly indicated in Barbara Walter's horoscope. This is a woman who has made an incredibly successful career out of her ability to speak with famous people. She is able to prod, cajole, and extricate the most intimate details out of her interviewees. Not only are they willing to speak to Barbara Walters about their lives, they do so with the full knowledge that what is being said to her is also simultaneously being shared with hundreds of millions of people who watch and listen to these interviews internationally. Walters has a style that is probing but nonintimidating. She doesn't take "No" for an answer and manages to make the most famous of her interviewees even more open and public about their private lives and deepest feelings.

In this nativity, the Third and the Sixth houses are both ruled by Jupiter. The Third is the house of journalism, writing, and speaking, while the Sixth is the house most related to work. Jupiter is in the highly visible Tenth House of career. Thus, the affairs of the Third and Sixth combine and are expressed through the Tenth. Jupiter is in the sign of

Example 5: The Horoscope of Barbara Walters[1]

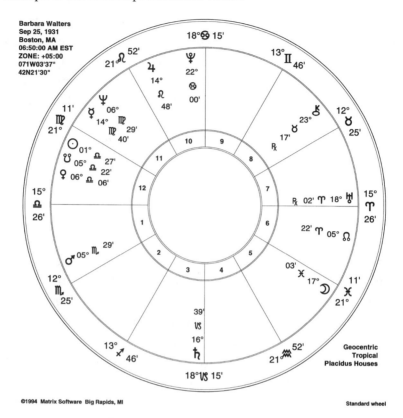

Barbara Walters
Sep 25, 1931
Boston, MA
06:50:00 AM EST
ZONE: +05:00
071W03'37"
42N21'30"

18°♋15'

21°♌52' ♃ 14° ♇ 22° ♋ 00' 13°♊46'

11' ☿ ♍ 06° ♍ 14° ♍ 29' 40' ♌ 48' ♂ 23° 17° ℞ 12° ♉ 25'

♍ 21°

☊ 01° ♎ ♎ 05° 27' ♎ 22' ♀ 06° ♎ 06'

10 9 11 8

15° ♎ 26'

12 7

℞ 02' ♈ 18° ♅ 15° ♈ 26'

♂ 05° ♏ 29'

1 2 3 4 5 6

22' ♈ 05° ☋

12° ♏ 25'

03' ♓ 17° ☽ 11' ♓ 21°

39' ♑ 16°

13° ♐ 46' ♄ 21° ♒ 52'

Geocentric
Tropical
Placidus Houses

18°♑15'

©1994 Matrix Software Big Rapids, MI   Standard wheel

show business and the arts (Leo) and its strongest aspect is a trine from a highly individualistic Uranus in Aries, ruling Leo's house, the Fifth. This is the house of one's creative self-expression. Uranus rules mass communication via the airwaves and its trine to Jupiter in Leo in the Tenth emphasizes the public demonstration of the creative potentials of the Fifth. This trine from Uranus in Aries to Jupiter in Leo also points to Walters' uniqueness in what she does.

Jupiter is disposited by the Sun conjunct to Venus in Libra in the Twelfth House (the hidden or secret relationships). Venus as ruler of the Ascendant is also the ruler of the chart.[2] This position adds an amazing degree of charm, charisma, and the natural ability to attract and connect with people. The Twelfth House position allows her to go behind the scenes and investigate the secret lives of the people who are of interest to her. It also gives her many helpful, clandestine contacts with individuals who supply her with a great deal of information relative to her creative objectives. As Venus is conjunct the Sun, this "Venusian potency" is added to the vitality of Walters' life force and is completely integrated into her persona. This factor of dispositorship (Sun disposits Jupiter and Venus disposits the Sun), plus the strong, solar Fifth House influence (Jupiter in Leo, Uranus ruling the Fifth House and trine to Jupiter in the Tenth), combine to give enormous support to the public position held by Barbara Walters in the entertainment-as-news/news-as-entertainment segment of television journalism.

Natural and Natal House Relationships

This type of house dispositor linkage falls into several categories. The principle involved is that no matter what sign is on the cusp of a house, there is always a close connection between a house and its *natural ruler*. Mars will always have some significance in terms of the First House, as its natural sign is Aries. The Tenth House will always respond to the influence of Saturn, as this planet rules Capricorn, the natural sign of this house, etc. It is important to state that even though effects of the natural ruler have an important influence, the energy of the *natal ruler* of a house (the planet ruling the sign on the actual cusp of the horoscope as derived from the birth time and place), tends to predominate.[3] In your assessment of any house of the horoscope, please note the following contacts:

1. The position in the horoscope of the natal and natural rulers and their relationship.

As an example, let us say that we are looking at a chart that has Cancer on the cusp of the Eleventh House. Cancer is ruled by the Moon and its location by sign and house would tell us how the circumstances of the Eleventh House would express themselves in the native's life. We'll hypothesize that the Moon is in Libra in the Second House. One conclusion that we could make from this set of circumstances is that the individual finds a great deal of personal comfort and security (Moon) in creating close relationships (Libra) within the context of group dynamics

(Eleventh House). Furthermore, this person is able to use her personal resources, talents, and abilities (Second House) to add to her group relationship involvements (Moon in Libra, ruling the Eleventh).

Now, let us further postulate that in this same chart, Saturn — natural co-ruler of the Eleventh — is in Gemini in the Tenth House trine to the Libra Moon in the Second House. Now we have a case in which the natural ruler of a house (Saturn) is in trine to the natal ruler of that same house (Moon). The meaning of this aspect is quite clear: the
individual has the natural tendency to assume leadership positions (Saturn in the Tenth) in regards to her involvements with her group relationships (Saturn natural co-ruler of the Eleventh). In this respect, she has a great ease in using her coordinating and organizational social talents (Moon in Libra trine Saturn in Gemini). The fact that there is a house linkage here serves to emphasize the positivity of the planetary contacts and gives added importance to the activities and circumstances of the Eleventh House in this horoscope.[4]

2. Note the presence of any natural ruler mutual house reception.

This determination is rather simple to make. All one does is examine the position of the planets in the natal horoscope and see where the corresponding natural rulers of the houses are posited. Let us say that Mars, regardless of sign, is in the Fifth House of a particular horoscope. What planet are you searching for now? The Sun, because it is the natural ruler of the Fifth. If the Sun was in the First House (naturally ruled by Mars), then the natural house rulers would be in mutual reception. Likewise, this same situation would occur if Venus were in the Twelfth House and Neptune in the Seventh; Jupiter in the Tenth House and Saturn in the Ninth; Mercury in the Eighth House and Pluto in either the Third or the Sixth, and so on. Remember, we are always looking for those hidden links in a chart that unite circumstances either harmoniously or inharmoniously in order to determine the *priority of planetary or house influence.*

In the case of natural ruler mutual house reception, the astrologer has to be very clear about the function of the planets and their "comfort zones" in terms of the houses. In the four examples used above, we can note:

- Mars in the Fifth and the Sun in the First: this is a strong and often positive contact, as these two planets are very compatible in each other's natural spheres of influence. The Sun likes to shine brightly in the First, the closer to the actual Ascendant, the better. Mars is happy to have fun and frolic in the Fifth House of amusements, romance, and children.

- Venus in the Twelfth and Neptune in the Seventh: Although this is an artistic, compassionate, and relatively "pleasant" interconnection, some difficulties may occur if the individual does not know the difference between personal and transpersonal relationships. This often results in confusion relating to emotional boundaries and degrees of intimacy. These placements also can indicate a person who is inclined to work with people who are in social distress. This is a combination frequently found in the charts of "spiritual seekers," because Neptune and Venus in these positions contribute to the "need to merge" in an ideal fashion that may be very difficult to achieve in relationships on earth.

- Jupiter in the Tenth and Saturn in the Ninth: Success in life can be attained when there is a firm basis in a philosophy or spiritual belief system that underscores one's sense of social morality. If personal ambitions override honesty and responsibility, then positive achievements will not easily be forthcoming.

- Mercury in the Eighth and Pluto in either the Third or Sixth: These positions yield a probing mind—one that is usually intensely curious and sometimes quite suspicious. Life is often geared to ferreting out secret or obscure information (Third House Pluto) or toward uncovering techniques and methodologies aiding one's ability to improve the workplace (Sixth House Pluto).

3. Determine if the dispositor of a given planet sits in the natural house of that planet.

Example: Saturn in Gemini with Mercury in the Tenth.

4. Determine if the dispositor of a house cusp is in the natural sign of that house.

The following can serve as an example illustrating both these points: (#3): Sun in Sagittarius in the Seventh House and Jupiter in Libra in the Fifth. Jupiter is the dispositor of the Sun and is in the Sun's natural house in the natal chart. Let us also say that Sagittarius is on the Seventh House cusp, making Jupiter the ruler of that house. (#4): Libra is the natural ruler of the Seventh House and Jupiter is in that sign acting as the dispositor of that house cusp.

5. Determine if either the natal or the natural ruler of a house is in that house.

Rule: A house is strengthened in importance in the natal chart whenever its natal or natural ruler is posited in that house.

The strengths or weaknesses in a horoscope are determined by the *energetic affinities* of the planets when in the houses. Mars, for example, is always a potent influence if Aries or Scorpio is on a given house cusp and Mars is in that house. It is possible that Mars could be in a different sign than the one on the cusp of the house in question. If for example, a house cusp were at 28° Aries, Mars could be in that house but in Taurus. But Mars would be more powerful if it were also posited in that house in Aries. The natal chart of Queen Elizabeth II on the following page will serve as a perfect example of this principle in action.

This chart gives us two good examples about what we are discussing. The *natal ruler* of the Seventh House is the Moon because Cancer is on its cusp; and the Moon in Leo is posited in that house. In the horoscopes of political figures or monarchs, the Moon indicates the people of that person's nation. The Moon always represents mass consciousness and our relationship to it. Thus, in any horoscope, the Moon not only represents the biological mother, but also connects us to our "tribe," to all of our biological ancestors as well as to our immediate family. The family of the

Example 6: The Horoscope of Queen Elizabeth II[5]

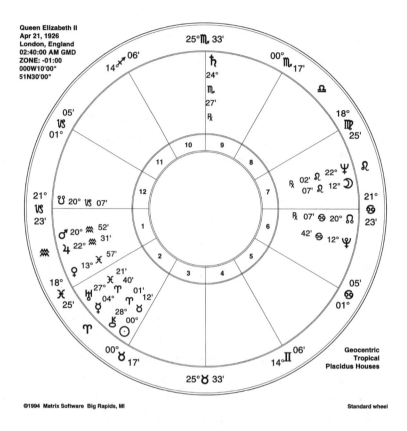

monarch is thus not only the "Royal Family," but the entire nation of which the monarch is the symbolic parental figure.

In this case, the Moon is in the royal sign of Leo. In every sense of the word, Elizabeth II is the "Mother Queen." The *Seventh House* is of course, connected to marriage and Queen Elizabeth is definitely married to the British people. In this relationship, she embodies all of the more positive qualities of her Moon sign, Leo. She is loyal, protective, faithful, regally dignified, and constant. The vast majority of the British people love her and she is proud to be their queen. In terms of her marriage to Prince Philip, it is one that embodies Leo, a fixed sign. It has endured with great dignity and without scandal for over fifty years. The Moon also represents her own mother—known as the "Queen Mother." She is another highly respected member of the royal family who coincidentally was born with the Sun in Leo!

Mars is the *natural ruler* of the First House and in Queen Elizabeth II's chart, it is located rising in Aquarius. Mars is also the *natal ruler* of the Tenth House, as the latter has Scorpio on its cusp. Thus, the energy of the Tenth is brought into the First. The meaning is quite clear: Elizabeth II embodies rulership (Tenth House) through the dynamic expression of her personality (Mars in the First House). Mars is also conjunct to the "noble" planet, Jupiter, whose color is royal purple. Mars functions also as the *natal ruler* of the Ninth House (Scorpio on the cusp), but is conjoined in the house of its *natural rulership* (First) with Jupiter, *natural ruler* of the Ninth. In addition to being the Queen of the United Kingdom, as head of the Church of England, Elizabeth II is also called the "Defender of the Faith." I am sure that most astrologers would agree that Mars conjunct Jupiter in the First, *natally and naturally* ruling the Ninth, is the perfect position for a Queen who carries such a title.

6. Note the natural house which corresponds to the rising sign.

If a chart has Leo rising, the Fifth is the natural house of this sign, and its concerns and interests will always play an important role in one's life. In a similar way, Taurus rising in a natus will always focus attention on the affairs of the Second House, Gemini rising on the Third, Cancer rising on the Fourth, and so on through the natural houses of their planetary rulers.

The Strengths and Weaknesses of the Planets When Posited in Their Houses of Honor or Dishonor

We have already seen in Queen Elizabeth II's chart how a planet's influence is greatly strengthened if it is in the house of the sign it rules *either* natally or naturally. A planet's strength in the natal horoscope also is augmented if it is in the house of the sign in which it finds its exaltation (please refer to the Summary of Planetary Powers at the end of Chapter 1, pages 25–28). Because the Sun is exalted in Aries, it is very powerful when placed in the First House. The Moon is exalted in Taurus and thus is potent when in the Second. Likewise, look for Mercury in the Eleventh, Venus in the Twelfth, Mars in the Tenth, Jupiter in the Fourth, Saturn in the Seventh, Uranus in the Eighth, Neptune in the Fourth, and Pluto in the Eleventh houses. These are all highly potent positions.

Potent is *not* the same as "positive." Saturn in the Seventh House indicates that interpersonal relationships and the need for clearly contracted partnerships, will be major factors in the individual's life. But the difficulty of other planetary contacts (let's say Saturn is square to Venus and opposing Uranus) can bring enormous conflict and difficulty into such relationships. But should Saturn in the Seventh be well aspected, then its "potency" will be quite positive indeed!

Similarly, planets are weakened by their positions in the houses that are ruled by the signs of their detriment or fall. The Sun is in detriment in Aquarius; thus, its position in the Eleventh House is not one of its strongest. The Sun is in fall in Libra, so a Seventh House Sun will not be radiating its vitality with the same vivacity as it does in the First House of Aries, its sign of exaltation. Once again, please refer to the above-mentioned table in order to ascertain the signs in question and then merely transpose this to the corresponding house positions. In this way, you will find that the Moon is weak when in the Tenth or Eighth, Mercury when in the Ninth or Twelfth, Mars when in the Second or Seventh, etc.

But what do we mean by "weak"? The Sun could be in Aries in the Seventh House and trine to Mars in Leo. This is definitely not a weak Sun, as it indicates a person with a tremendous amount of vigor and vitality. But its position in the Seventh, even when in such a powerful sign and aspect combination, compromises its *essential nature*. The Sun is not happy when it always has to shine in relationship to someone else (Seventh House). It is not at its best when it has to function *relative to* the actions and energies of another person. The Sun is most natural when others respond to its radiant fire and is most at ease when other people/planets are receptive to it and not the other way around. Thus, a person with the Sun in Aries trine to Mars in Leo in the Seventh may often experience that his or her assertive, fiery nature is somewhat limited in its scope and function, as the Sun (sense of selfhood) is very dependent on others to show it when and where to shine.

In terms of dispositorship factors, let us say that Capricorn is on the Fourth House of a given chart and we'll place Saturn in Aries in the Seventh. Capricorn is the sign of detriment for the Moon, so its position on the Moon's natural house (Fourth) is not particularly harmonious. Saturn becomes, therefore, the dispositor of this house and Saturn's detriment is found in Cancer, the natural sign ruler of the Fourth. Furthermore, Saturn is in Aries, its own detriment and posited in the Seventh, the house of its sign of exaltation, Libra. Just with these dispositorship factors alone and not modified by any other astrological influences, the astrologer could reach the following conclusions:

1. The individual finds himself in a very important but challenging relationship with the more authoritarian of his two parents.
2. This parent's psychological effects on the individual play themselves out objectively through the native's relationship dynamics.
3. These psychological patterns are expressed through issues of control in one's marriage or other forms of partnership, leading to very limiting sets of circumstances in terms of the major relationship(s) of one's life.

Other planetary aspects to Saturn (especially from Mars, ruler of Aries), the placement of the Moon and Venus in the chart (natural rulers of the Fourth and Seventh), will affect these conclusions, but these three factors are basic and have to emerge as part of the astrologer's approach to delineating Saturn's meaning in this particular example.

Aspects Between House Rulers

This is the last but certainly one of the most important and complex of the many dispositorship factors affecting the expression of the houses in the natal chart. The astrologer must always consider any of the major aspects that may exist between the dispositors of any given set of houses.

Rule: The relationships between the events, people, and circumstances as indicated by house position in the natal chart are fundamentally affected by the nature of any major aspect between the house rulers.

This is more strongly noted if these are the *natal* planetary rulers, and more subtly should they be the *natural* rulers. We must also keep in mind that if the *natal* ruler of a house is in aspect with the *natural* ruler of that house, support is either added or removed to the *natal* ruler's effectiveness relative to the nature of the aspect and the aspecting planet. Let's look at a couple of examples.

If you will reexamine the horoscope of Angela Davis (see page 31), you will see that Saturn is the natal ruler of the Ninth House and is sextile to Jupiter, the natural ruler of this domicile. It has been previously shown how important the educational and philosophical background of experience was to Davis' life. This is backed up in a most positive way, i.e., international travel for educational purposes came easily to her (as indicated by the sextile between Jupiter and Saturn and their mutual functions in terms of the Ninth House of her horoscope).

This chart also reveals a trine between the natal rulers of the Fifth and Eleventh houses (Sun and Uranus). These are the same in this case, as the natural rulers and the strength of these positions is thus increased and magnified. This planetary situation resulted in Davis' ability to integrate herself smoothly and prominently within a group ideology. Her sense of personal identity (Sun) merged with great facility into the collective identity of the group (Uranus). She gave this group a tremendous creative boost of energy (the Fifth House ruler trine the Eleventh House ruler), brought this group into the public eye (Sun in Aquarius in the Tenth), and embodied the group identity (Aquarius on the Eleventh House) in a most unique and personal way (Uranus in the First).

The *Diary of Anne Frank* is a testimony to a young girl's brief and brave passage through life. It remains as one of the most important witnesses to the greatest tragedy of the twentieth century, World War II, and the Holocaust in particular. In the natal chart of Anne Frank on the following page, the Eighth House (death) is ruled by Uranus, which is posited in the Tenth House (public acclaim) and trine to Mars in the First. Mars is the natural ruler of both the Eighth and the First and the natal ruler of the Tenth and dispositor of Uranus. A prominent Uranus in a natal chart, specifically its placement near either the MC or the Ascendant, is indicative of a person who stands forth as an example or ar-

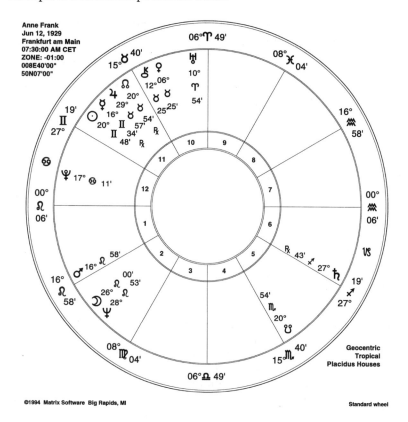

Anne Frank
Jun 12, 1929
Frankfurt am Main
07:30:00 AM CET
ZONE: -01:00
008E40'00"
50N07'00"

©1994 Matrix Software Big Rapids, MI

Geocentric
Tropical
Placidus Houses

Standard wheel

chetype of some larger issue. At the very least, this position points to a highly individualistic person.

Anne's tragic death adds strength to her testimony and the nature of the plight of all the many millions of people, Jews and non-Jews, who suffered and were killed under the tyranny of the Nazi years. The house dispositor relationship between Mars and Uranus adds enormous potency to the reality of her legacy to humanity. Uranus in Aries trine to Mars in the First House not only endows Anne with personal courage, but also makes her a symbol of her times and the experiences of a myriad of other victims of this collective and horrendous massacre. Mars in the First personalizes her experience. Pluto, however, the other natural ruler of the Eighth and co-ruler of Aries, is square Uranus from the more universal Twelfth House and is in the sign of mass consciousness, Cancer. The interconnections between the personal and the higher octave or collective planets take Anne's life out of the level of one individual incarnation and into a wider and more profound example of the collective experience of humanity. Pluto and the Eighth House, however, are not just indicators of death. They are also the doors to the path of resurrection and eternal life. Anne's contribution to the transformation and evolution of the human spirit lives on.

---

1. Data source: Rodden, Lois M., op. cit., p. 190.
2. See Chapter 5 for a full discussion relative to the significance of the chart ruler and its placement in the horoscope.
3. When Aries is rising and all of the other signs are on their own house cusps, i.e., there are no intercepted houses, this type of horoscope is known as a "natural chart." There will be no linkages of the types now being outlined, as the natal and natural rulers of the houses are the same. Such natural charts are relatively few in number and are only possible in certain latitudes relatively close to the equator. They are impossible to find in any locations in countries far north or south of the equator, such as Scandinavia, Great Britain, Australia, South Africa, Canada, etc. Some astrologers use a system of house division called "Equal House," in which case *any and all* horoscopes with Aries rising would constitute a "natural chart." Although not discounting the work of those astrologers who favor this system, the author does not use it, preferring to calculate his horoscopes using either the Placidian or Koch system of houses.
4. A suggestion: some readers may find it helpful to draw a horoscope, putting Cancer on the Eleventh House cusp and then follow the order of the signs around the wheel (Virgo will be rising). Place the planets in the positions indicated in this example and observe the results.
5. Data source: Jones, M. E., *The Sabian Symbols in Astrology*, Sabian Publishing Society, 1966.
6. Data source: Rodden, Lois M., op. cit.

The Ruler of the Horoscope
and Its Dispositor

The determination of the ruler of the natal chart and its careful and detailed delineation is an essential key element to the meaning of the birth chart. I like to say in this regard, "Wherever the ruler is in your chart, that's where you are!" The house position of this important planet and the relationship it has to *its* dispositor will tell the astrologer a great deal about the natural unfoldment of a person's life and most specifically, *where* the individual will focus much of his or her life energy. One could also correctly say that the house placement of the chart ruler will reveal where an individual will spend much of his or her time. The zodiacal sign of the ruler and its other significant interplanetary relationships reveals *how* and with *whom* that time is spent and much about the results of this expenditure of vitality. Thus, in this chapter we want to accomplish a number of things: We need to find out how to discover and interpret the importance of the ruler of the nativity. This requires a study of this planet's significance by sign, house, and major aspect contacts to any other planets in the chart. In this respect, we are especially interested in uncovering the relationship between the ruler and its planetary dispositor. Finally, we ought to clarify the difference in meaning and weight between the chart ruler and the final dispositor.

Determining the Ruler of the Natal Chart

Definition: There are only two circumstances that determine rulership of the nativity: a) The ruler of the horoscope is the planet that disposits the sign on the Ascendant; b) If a planet is within 5° of the Ascendant in the First House or 3° of the Ascendant in the Twelfth House, it takes over rulership.

Let us deal with the first of these conditions at length and then come back to the second, which has some very interesting complications connected with its proper delineation and synthesis into the whole of the horoscope. Actually, it is very simple to determine the ruler of the Ascendant. Just look at the sign on the cusp of the First House and find its ruler by house and sign. In all cases Venus rules the chart when either Taurus or Libra rises, Mercury if either Gemini or Virgo is on the cusp of the First, Jupiter rules a Sagittarius Ascendant, the Moon a Cancer one, Saturn dominates when Capricorn rises, and of course, the Sun is the ruler when the Lion is on the eastern horizon of the natus.

That leaves us with the signs of the zodiac that are ruled by two planets: Aries, Scorpio, Aquarius, and Pisces. A number of contemporary astrologers tend to consider Mars as the primary ruler of Aries and Pluto as its co-ruler, although an equal or even larger number do not give Pluto any influence over the Ram at all. The author is very inclined towards Pluto as co-ruler of this sign. Aries is birth and what is born does not come out of nothingness. Death precedes birth and birth precedes death. The two are very much locked into the cycle of life. Just try to start a successful new love affair without the correct process, recognition, and ritual of the death, funeral, and mourning of the old one. The ghosts of the past (and their living memories and presences in the form of ex-spouses and ex-lovers) have to be put to rest and reintegrated into one's life from an entirely new perspective. It is only then that the new love may hope to flourish as a life unto itself.

It is true that the interrelationship between Aries and Scorpio, as well as the First and the Eighth houses, can be understood from the fact that Mars is very definitely the ruler of the former and co-ruler of the latter. On a personal level, in terms of the direction of the will of the ego to dominate its surroundings (Aries), or in terms of the direction of the desires of the lower self to fuse others to its dominance (Scorpio), Mars has definite rulership over these two signs. Pluto tends to work from a larger, deeper, more inclusive, often unconscious, and definitely slower place in one's life than does Mars. Pluto involves collective or universal processes and events (see Anne Frank's chart). It also speaks about the evolutionary dynamics of death; by this I am referring to the "little deaths" we experience all throughout our life. It is through these often torturous experiences that we learn to detach from desires and stimulate our subjective urge for regenerative refinement. It is here that Pluto has its more profound effects; Mars is much more obvious and immediate.

In horoscopes with Scorpio rising, as a general rule consider Mars as the primary ruler. The vast majority of people on Earth function from the nature and demands of their personal desires and egocentric behavior patterns and motivations. In the lives of people who are "crossing over" and who are in the battle of transforming their personal lives into the transpersonal, the position of Pluto as co-ruler will speak about that area in life (Pluto's house position) where the energy of regeneration may be found, assisting the necessary transformation of personality reorientation. If, for example, Mars is in the Second House at birth, there will be separatist drives and conflicts relative to the use of money and personal resources. If, in this same horoscope, Pluto is in the Ninth House, the individual will have the opportunity to come in contact with the higher knowledge that may serve to resolve the issues surrounding the natal placement of Mars. Once the individual achieves the wisdom of these transformative Plutonian lessons, he may then channel such understandings back into his contact with those personal resources. The results will then prove to be much more successful. Let us keep in mind that Pluto is indeed the "higher octave" of Mars. Once a certain degree of death occurs, i.e., death to the lower urgings of the personality, Pluto can instill a "higher octane" energy into the martial engine that governs the personality (from Mars' natal house position) to such a large degree in life.

In terms of Aquarius, even though it can be said that in the current world age, Uranus is taking over an increased role as the ruler of this sign, we still have to consider Saturn as its co-ruler. Uranus essentially represents the urge for individualization. It is the planet which calls to each of us to be the incarnation of our own Being. Yet we do not live alone on this planet. There are rules, structures, and a network of subtle and not so subtle social patterns and regulations that require our attention, adherence, and acquiescence. The more individualized each of us becomes, the more important and specific become our social role and function. Every step in the expansion of consciousness demands an equal increase in our sense of responsibility for the light we carry. In the Aquarian Age, the lightning bolts of Uranian inspiration absolutely require the lightning rod of Saturnian structure to safely download our unfolding awareness into right human relationships.

As for Pisces, Neptune is very definitely the major ruler of this sign, Jupiter's rulership having ebbed considerably with the recession of the influences of the orthodox religions of the Piscean Age. The current explosion of fundamentalist fanaticism is far more Neptunian than Jupitarian (it certainly isn't "jovial"). In this author's opinion, Jupiter's current connection to Pisces is much more a question of *energetic affinity* than actual rulership. In the Piscean Age, an era in which exoteric, dogmatic Protestant theology combined with ritualized orthodox Catholicism to dominate the psychology of the Western world, Jupiter was a far greater influence over the Fish than it is now. In contemporary horoscopes with Pisces rising, look to Neptune for definitive rulership of this sign and to the position of Jupiter to reveal:

1. The urge to find a personal belief system that supports the Piscean orientation for universality.
2. A place where ideology meets and confronts reality, supporting or challenging the individual's religion, spiritual path, or educational tradition.[1]
3. Certain activities that provide expansive opportunities either to escape from the mundane and/or to enhance the ordinary with a more spiritual, or at least encompassing, vision.

The Sign on the Ascendant and the Delineation of the Ruler

In traditional, exoteric astrology, the sign on the Ascendant is one of the four most important features of a horoscope. The other three consist of the positions of the planetary ruler of the chart, and the Sun and the Moon.[2] Briefly stated, the Sun represents the future as it stands for the potential creative engine in a given life. We could say also that the Sun is our contact to the "Eternal Now," as we constantly draw upon this source for the vitality of our life in all of its many forms of expression. The Moon is the agent of the past, as it contains the history of one's biological karma and the subconscious, psychological conditioning patterns at work in one's life. The Moon, therefore, governs our automatic, instinctual response patterns, especially when emotional situations or personal security situations are aroused.

The Ascendant is our contact to the immediacy of our environment. It reveals how we interact with the surrounding circumstances and, as such, we can say that the Ascendant represents the current moment, the "immediate now." The Ascendant is also the color we add to this matrix of experience as well as the focus of expression for our character and personality. The sign on this all-important cusp describes that character, that personality, that ego-in-action. The statement the Ascendant makes is: "Here I am in the clothes that I wear to cover the nakedness of my Being (the solar force)."

The First House is much like a room covered by glass on all sides. I live inside of this room and its glass walls, ceiling, and floor are tinted with the hue and color of the sign on my Ascendant. If my glass were tinted violet, everyone looking into my room would see all of my furniture, carpets, and me through this violet tint. In the same way, as I look out of my room, the world around me also takes on the coloration of my projected personality.

The Intent and Theme of the Ascendant

This text assumes that the reader is already familiar with the various differences in character and qualities of personal expression that occur when the twelve signs rise.[3] I will therefore not go into lengthy details concerning all of these many personality-centered implications. Instead, I would like to summarize the underlining, essential *intent* of each of the signs when on the cusp of the First House. This intent will express itself throughout the *theme* of the life.

Aries: The creation and exploration of new experiences that implement and awaken self-awareness. Aries rising stimulates the consistent testing of one's personal strengths and weaknesses through an approach to life that is very confrontational in nature. The dynamic urge of the personality is to project oneself outward and forward towards the accomplishment of one's immediate goals. As a rule, little thought is given to the consequences of such actions. Boldness, courage, and a piercing drive either win or lose the day. Discrimination in the nature and manner of one's self-assertion must be cultivated. Aggressive behavior must be transmuted from an instinct urge to the conscious ability to integrate personal objectives into the larger structure of one's life. Social opposition occurs when Aries-rising individuals overstep their boundaries and move consciously or unconsciously into other people's physical or psychic territory.

Taurus: The individual has a great need to make the most out of his or her personal abilities and resources. Life is based upon what one values, and Taurus-rising people do their utmost to anchor these values in material form. If there is a lack of self-esteem, the person is likely to feel thwarted and restricted by material circumstances. This can come as a sense of "never having enough" and consequently, "never being good enough" for the situations at hand. If a healthy sense of self-worth is present, then one feels that there is "always enough." Magnetism is a potent force inherent within the fabric of the personality, manifesting as the consolidation of the emotional nature in substance. Therefore, the Taurus-rising individual must develop a sense of discrimination in his or her expression of personal desires, since what is focused upon generally manifests. There is a cyclical destruction of these forms, leading to refinement through discrimination.

Gemini: The nature of the personality is geared to a distinct orientation to the creation of variabilities and dualities in the manner of one's self-expression. The subjective purpose for such mutability is to enlarge the breadth and depth of one's life experiences. Sometimes such multifaceted activities are at cross purposes, leading to diffusion and confusion of intent and purpose. The more highly evolved Gemini-rising individual will work to create unity in diversity, harmony through polarization, integration through experimentation. The focus of life is upon the need to communicate. The more naive Gemini will only express and understand his or her personal opinions. The gifted

Twin is able to be in touch with Universal Mind, allowing the Gemini-rising person access to all people's thoughts, ideas, and concepts.

Cancer: The primary urge of the personality is to create a secure foundation both subjectively within oneself and objectively in the environment. This will serve as a magnetic anchor for the further building of individuality. If the early life was abusive and unstable, the chances are that the individual will spend many years in a frantic search to manifest his or her concept of security. Much of the life energy is spent determining the correct modes of self-nurture in order to bring this about. If a firm and positive psychological foundation is achieved, then the Cancer-ruled person will serve as a nurturer and supplier of those feelings that help others gain a greater sense of personal integration and wholeness.

Leo: The main purpose of the life is to integrate all the facets of the personality (the physical body and material environment, the emotions and the desire nature, the mind and thoughts) into a functioning unit capable of objective creativity. In essence, the individual must become a conscious co-creator of his or her life. When such integration is not established, the Lion projects the shadow of the Sun. This type of Leo-rising person is immature and this shadow can overcome the light of personal vitality, giving rise to fear and inhibitions. The other extreme produces an individual who thinks of him or herself as the center of the universe, demanding respect and attention, but giving very little in return. The primary concern is a relationship between "myself and me." The tests in life serve to bring about the eventual release from the burden of immature self-involvement.

Virgo: This is a life geared to the practical dynamics of personal interchanges with the environment. The dynamic urge of the personality is to develop a fuller range of both internal and external resources so that the individual's creative potential may be released into the physical environment in a multitude of ways. This orientation leads to the collection of a great variety of processes, methodologies, and techniques that serve to develop individual potential. In the life of the immature Virgo rising, there is a lack of discrimination and no manifestation of focused intent. This results in a highly critical nature, one that projects the lack of self-satisfaction onto the lives of others. In the life of a more developed person with Virgo rising, there is a deep sense of knowing how to synthesize the various component parts of life into a harmonious whole. Right discrimination, i.e., the ability to assess true value, and proper elimination are keys to success.

Libra: The process of awakening to one's greater life potentials and the increased ability to project the personality successfully into the environment takes place through a constant interplay with others. The Libra-rising person usually has two ways in which he or she comes into a more evolved sense of self-awareness. The first is to oppose and be opposed, so that one defines oneself and one's social role through what one "is not." The second is to identify and complement, so that this same need to participate in the world takes place through an understanding of what "one is." Thus one is either in harmony with or quite contrary to the prevailing influences in the environment. Both of these tendencies are usually present in the personality and alternate depending on the nature of the immediate life circumstances.

Scorpio: The transformation and refinement of the nature of personal desires becomes the main method of evolutionary self-development. In the lives of most Scorpio-rising individuals, the intent of life is directed by desires. Often, although not always, these are sexual in their orientation. As the general desire nature is thwarted or becomes a source of great confusion and conflict, the individual is forced to find alternative and more refined ways of self-expression. Love may eventually overcome desire, for example, so that the sexual life becomes less obsessive and more harmoniously integrated into the whole of one's existence. Releasing and letting go of compulsions on all levels allows the transmutative process to enter the life with greater ease and success. This will give rise to the cyclic unfoldment of the personality and the consequent release of more potent creative potentials. The more highly evolved Scorpio-rising person acts as a catalyst for healing in all of his or her relationships.

Sagittarius: This is the most projective sign in the zodiac. In his search for a personal identification with universal truth, the Sagittarian individual usually projects his inner concepts of reality onto the screen of the environment, making all people players in his personal drama. The urge to expand one's horizons dominates the life when this sign rises in the natal chart. As a dual sign, this expansion is likely to occur in two ways: through the mind and through the desires. The mental urge leads to the aspiration to come into contact with a sense of life that is encompassing and inclusive, i.e., the higher self. This leads one to study, learn, and travel. If the lower, animal aspect of the Centaur dominates, then the senses rule the life. Expansion here takes place around and below the waist, as sensual and sexual appetites provide the aspirational focus. Life may be said to be conditioned by one word: purpose. This can be the purpose to know the mysteries of life or the purpose to find pleasure in all and everything.

Capricorn: This is a life in which many lessons are learned, leading to the attainment of the right use of will and power. As a result, there is a need to bring about the development of those techniques that perfect one's understanding of the relationship between structure, order, and form. Until and unless this is learned, the individual will feel encumbered, limited, and restricted. The early life is often difficult, with conflicts between oneself and the authoritarian aspects of the parents' personalities. At times, the childhood is conditioned not so much by an overly strict and dominating parent, but by abuse or neglect. Material conditions and social acceptance play very important roles in life. True evolutionary progress is made when, from a pinnacle of success, the Capricorn-rising person turns his back upon his *attachment* to such goals, and begins to use the will and power thus acquired in the service of others. The achievement of true creative objectivity may be said to be the prime intent of this sign when it rises.

Aquarius: The urge to create a distinct sense of self will involve personal integration through a method, study, group, or other stimulus that aids in the process of individualization. This requires the person to be able to discriminate and prioritize his or her life within an enormous field of possibilities and great generalities. The sense of self can be so diffused that the Aquarius-rising person may see him or herself as exactly the same as everyone else. This is great for ideological egalitarianism but does little good towards the development of a creative focus of self-awareness. There is another extreme possibility—the Aquarius-rising person feels totally different from everyone else and as a result considers him or herself as a social outcast or alienated misfit. The more mature and integrated Aquarian understands that each person is a different unit within the One Organism in which we all live and breathe and have our being. This is a person who is definitely him or herself but is also at the same time just like everyone else. In essence, he or she has become a world citizen and a "universal being."

Pisces: The intent underlying the evolution of a Piscean personality is to find a universal sense of self in any given social context. This requires developing a sense of universal compassion, an empathetic response to life that allows the individual the capacity for total inclusivity. The conflict that often occurs along the way has a lot to do with maintaining a sense of personal identity while obtaining this global sensitivity. The Fish who tends to swim downstream usually is self-annihilating, often in the form of substance or relationship abuse. The upstream, higher nature of the Fish tends more to meditation over methadone, illumination over hallucination, and divinity over depravity. Pisces embodies the true meaning of the word "sacrifice." This word has two Latin roots: *sacra* (meaning "holy, sacred") and *fice*, coming from the verb meaning "to make." The highest intent of Pisces rising, therefore, is to make life sacred.

Once the rising sign has been noted, the ruling planet may then be immediately determined and located in the natal chart. It is vitally important to observe the zodiacal sign in which the ruler of the chart is posited. The influence of this sign must be blended with the sign on the Ascendant in order to come up with the correct interpretation of the effects of the ruler on the chart. This process requires a solid understanding of the basic alphabet of astrological science. But once this is accomplished during the early phases of study, the rest of this procedure will be very "astrological." The reader may wish to approach the synthesis of this information in the following order (we shall be using Princess Diana's horoscope throughout this chapter to illustrate these five points):

1. Note the Ascendant and its intent and theme.
2. Find the ruling planet and delineate its essential meaning.
3. Integrate this meaning into your understanding of the planet's sign position.

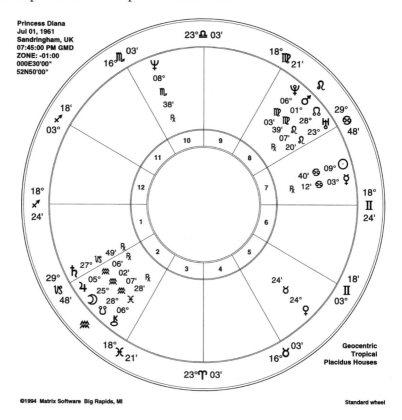

Princess Diana
Jul 01, 1961
Sandringham, UK
07:45:00 PM GMD
ZONE: -01:00
000E30'00"
52N50'00"

Geocentric
Tropical
Placidus Houses

©1994 Matrix Software Big Rapids, MI   Standard wheel

4. Do the same in terms of the planet's house position.

5. Determine the dispositor of the ruling planet and note its position by sign and house and observe if there are any major contacts between the two. This constitutes certain factors of "secondary dispositorship," about which I will speak in greater detail.

The natal chart of the late Princess of Wales not only reveals the life of a very special human being, whose creative potential for serving humanity was so abruptly and tragically ended, it also provides us with many fine and perfect examples of the points of delineation under discussion. Princess Diana has a Sagittarius Ascendant and therefore the intent and theme of her life may be stated as:

The expansion of life's experiences so that the mind may be led to an eventual contact with the underlining truths contained and hidden within the forms of daily life; the development of a universal belief system.

The Essential Meaning of the Ruling Planet and Its Effects on the Horoscope

We have determined that the ruler of the horoscope is the planet ruling the sign on the Ascendant. This ruling planet embodies the energy that is the *vehicle of expression and source of power for the Ascendant*. It is a predominating influence and its nature, sign, and house position are very important. The following is a brief description that seeks to encapsulate the meaning of the planets when in the role of the horoscope ruler:

Sun (Leo rising): A "double engine," carrying not only the source of vitality of the entire chart, but bringing out that vitality as the creative potential of the personality. The Sun's natural sign on the Ascendant carries a great deal of weight in the nativity. Life will have an extremely personal touch, because the individual often conceives of him or herself as the alpha and omega of all events. There may thus be some considerable difficulty in getting "out of the way" so that the collective life force may move through the individual and relieve some of the weight of having to carry the egocentric personality. When matured and spiritually developed, there is a sense of deep unity connecting one to the creative potential in everything and everyone. The Sun in a Leo-rising chart then illuminates with selfless vitality, especially in and from the area of life defined by the natal house position.

Moon (Cancer rising): Life is very much conditioned by early environmental circumstances, especially the nature of the relationship with one's mother. The Moon, along with its sign, house, and planetary aspects, often portrays the mother's life circumstances around the time of the birth, and during the first seven years of the individual's life. The inheritance of certain family traits, both biological and psychological, will act as the screen that patterns one's emotional responses to environmental circumstances. The need to be nourished by and nourishing to the people and situations in one's immediate surroundings is uppermost and will be conditioned by the qualities of the Moon's sign placement. If the personality is immature, one can never fully expect to "leave home." If developed, "home" is synthesized into the evolving dynamics of the personality and the process of individuation moves forward.

Mercury (Gemini rising): The personality seeks to express itself through the rational mind. The personality's opinions, the method by which it codifies, processes, and communicates data, the way it orients the events of life, all proceed from the activities of the lower mind. This can create dissipation of creative energy. It may also bring about challenges to the integration of one's feelings, and consequently inhibits the development of real intuition. When highly developed, Mercury as the ruler of a Gemini Ascendant acts as the "Messenger," bringing information and experiences from the higher mind/self to proper externalization through the dynamics of the personality. The mind may then act as a "conduit of return," processing information "back up" once again from the personality to the higher self/soul. At this point, the ego ceases to identify itself with the dualities of mind, and works instead to resolve those dualities.

Mercury (Virgo rising): Much of what is said in the previous paragraph holds true, but with several major shifts in emphasis. The process of communication seeks an expression in material form, not just in the "form of ideas," as in the Gemini Ascendant. The mind is impressed with the need to orient the events of life so that the individual has an actual physical place and fits into a larger scheme of things, and thus the part and the whole become one. The process of synthesis (bringing things together) becomes more important than analysis (taking things apart). When matured, the urge for and the ability to bring wholeness predominates the life. This will be expressed through the sign Mercury tenants and will be centered on the circumstances of its natal house position.

Venus (Taurus rising): The "urge to merge" predominates, as Venus is essentially a magnetic energy field, drawing to *herself* (when in a female sign) or drawing *herself* to (when in a male sign) the circumstances and people indicated by her sign and house position. The need to experience the sensual side of life is very strong when the Bull rises. This often manifests as the drive to create/acquire those material possessions and life partners that correspond to the individual's personal tastes and values. Venus' sign will indicate the method of approach to these factors; its natal house position will reveal where and under what circumstances these important acquisitions take place and where the resulting life lessons occur.

Venus (Libra rising): The orientation to life is geared to the dynamics of the learning experiences that come about through relationships. Harmonies and imbalances within the self will be immediately sensed (or created) by the individual, and polarized and externalized. This clarifies the life lessons to be mastered and creates their resolution. The house position of Venus reveals where the Libra-rising individual will focus most of his or her relationship contacts and the sign will show how the individual goes about interacting with others.

Mars (Aries rising): Life is geared to the assertion of self for the purpose of activating any latent responses in one's immediate surroundings. The ability to find or create an environment that allows for a continuously projecting personality is supported or thwarted depending on the position of Mars by sign. Psychological and social complications are more likely (such as a "passive-aggressive" personality) if Mars is in a female sign with the Ram on the Ascendant. Life will respond negatively if the objective of self-projection is the attainment of purely egocentric personal conquests. Conditioning factors in the form of severe opposition from others will definitely come about to modulate such immature behavior. Once developed, Mars always fights the right battle and is victorious in its greater purpose.

Mars (Scorpio rising): When immature, the satisfaction of personal desires is the underlining motive in all events, circumstances, and relationships. The forms that these desires take is conditioned and defined by the sign that Mars tenants in the natal chart. Battles are fought *through* this sign and *from* its natal house placement until death overtakes the offending dynamics of the personality, and the higher nature of the individual emerges.

Jupiter (Sagittarius rising): When functioning as the chart ruler, Jupiter expands and enlarges the entire spectrum of life experiences. Its purpose is to allow the individual to literally "widen his or her horizons." When immature, this broadens the breadth and scope of the personality, exaggerating all personal actions, needs, desires, responses, opinions, etc. When evolved, there is a *sense of one-pointed orientation* that gives direction, purpose, and meaning. Expansion then becomes the road to universality and the gift is the ability to see the macrocosm within the microcosm. The path to this unfoldment (or to the dissolution of the lower self) is effectuated through the house and sign position of this planet.

Jupiter (Pisces rising): The message is the same, but the emphasis shifts from a mental, fiery one to an emotional, watery one. Growth thus takes place through the feeling nature. One is then an ever-expanding focus of compassion or a never-ceasing searcher of sensual stimulation.

Saturn (Capricorn rising): Structure, order, process, form, perimeters, and boundaries are the keywords when Saturn rules. Life is expressed and personal restrictions overcome through an intense awareness of the interconnected patterning that links all things in life. When there is either a lack of intelligence or consciousness (or both) and such structures and patterns remain unseen and unrealized, a deep sense of limitation and restriction dominate the life. In a figurative sense, Saturn rules blindness. Once vision is attained, this sense of personal restriction is transformed into a focused sense of purpose in terms of serving others. The weight of personal responsibility is lifted from an inner depression into an outer creative potential that becomes most effective. The house position tells where this sense of obligation to oneself and others is most prominent. The sign shows how it is to be fulfilled.

Saturn (Aquarius rising): The above-mentioned characteristics are applied much more to the world of ideas, ideals, and the social dynamics of relationship, than to the more earthy, often financial or professional, Capricornian modes of expression.

Uranus (Aquarius rising): The need to individualize the nature either through some highly focused form of self-expression or within the context of a specialized group is a major life concern. Originality, that aspect of life that sets us apart from others or gives the illusion of such separateness, is designated and defined by the house and sign position. Uranus as the ruling planet will always function to focus life first on personal uniqueness and then, after the development of the personality, to a more mature state, to interpersonal interconnectedness.

Neptune (Pisces rising): The life urge is to uncover the transpersonal within the personal. Neptune's rulership thus gives rise to an orientation that dissolves any set of rigid limitations and does away with the lines defining any given set of circumstances. When highly developed, this can be the gift of seeing into the potential of another person, looking beyond the restrictions of the projected personality. It can also endow the ability to tune into the hidden resources and potentials of an interpersonal business situation and uncover latent treasure. It may also be the talent to identify and bring forth the spiritual truth from the most common of life's circumstances. Yet the reverse may also be true: the individual with Neptune as the chart ruler may be unable to assess the practical realities of any situation, placing there instead an illusionary, glamorous projection of false hopes and unfulfilled aspirations.

Pluto (Scorpio rising): Life evolves and unfolds through a series of slowly emerging crises. These situations require the absolute transformation and reorientation of the underlining circumstances involved. It is incumbent upon the individual to be able to identify these obscure but incredibly potent life themes and take on the necessary work of transformation. If this work is sincerely undertaken, the house position of Pluto will act as a great source of strength and riches. If the required transmutation does not take place, the individual then becomes attached to a constant repetition of his or her non-regenerative activities, thus losing a great deal of vital energy. The position of Mars will point to the nature of the desires of the lower self and define their expression within the context of this larger transformative process.

The Ruling Planet by Sign

A planet is said to rule the horoscope when it is either the ruler of the sign on the Ascendant or a planet closely conjunct this point. The sign position of the ruler reveals *how* the nature of the planetary ruler expresses itself. This is quite simple to understand, as the reader has already studied the various planet/sign combinations in his or her earlier astrological studies. The important thing here is one of *weight*, and in this respect, it is essential that the astrologer give proper importance to the sign rulership of the chart ruler. It will then be necessary to blend the two, i.e., the sign on the Ascendant and the sign in which the ruler is posited. Let us say for example, that an individual has Taurus rising with Venus in Scorpio. Scorpio is not one of Venus' favorite signs, in fact it is the sign of her detriment or dishonor. Why? As we have seen, the life theme of Taurus rising requires: "The need to create and integrate with the physical forms of self-expression that evolve directly from one's *personal values and resources*." When Venus is in Scorpio, the urge is to attract and use *other people's resources*. This thwarts the essential and natural orientation of Taurus and brings the individual with Taurus rising into many interpersonal conflicts. Such conflicts are based on the need of the Taurus-rising/Venus-in-Scorpio person to transform the other person's values into a reflection of one's own. This Taurus/Scorpio conflict will be a very important theme throughout this individual's life.

To keep our thoughts constant with the theme of the text, I will list the twelve signs and their keyword thematic definitions. Each of these passages contain two interpretations. The first is applied (a) when the ruler is well situated in the chart and the second (b) when the ruler's position is challenged by aspect or placement in the chart, or is operating through a lower form of its possibilities. Again, the important thing to hold in mind is that these characteristics are to be *emphasized as the energetic field* through which the ruler is operating. The nature of the planetary ruler is emphasized when in:

Aries: (a) as an urge to evoke new experiences in the environment and to stimulate increased creative potentials for oneself and others; (b) to stimulate a direct response from the environment that serves to support a very highly personal form of self-expression and to dominate the field of circumstances in which the individual finds himself.

Taurus: (a) as an urge to impregnate physical forms and circumstances with greater creative potential and thereby nourish the environment through the right use of personal talents and resources; (b) as a need to reduce the circumstances of life to their physical and/or sensual levels of expression in order to satisfy the personal desire nature.

Gemini: (a) as an urge to increase communicative possibilities through the diversity of personal knowledge and experience and resolve all dualities into greater harmonies; (b) as a tendency to dissipate vital energy through the continuous creation of unresolved interpersonal conflicts of communication.

Cancer: (a) as an urge to bring the circumstances of life into a more integrated and solidified foundation for self-expression and the proper cultivation of methods of nurturing both oneself and others; (b) as a tendency to express the nature of the ruling planet in Cancer from an unconscious urge for the preservation of non-regenerative instinctual patterns and psychological characteristics.

Leo: (a) as the ability to use the energy of the ruling planet in Leo to project a powerful focus for the sustained release of positive, creative potential; (b) as a need to dominate and control the environmental circumstances using the energy of the ruling planet as a vehicle for personal recognition.

Virgo: (a) as an urge to utilize all variable and possible personal talents and environmental resources in order to bring forth an increase in individual usefulness; (b) as a sense of incompletion, frustration, or dissatisfaction with the field of expression signified by the ruling planet.

Libra: (a) according to the nature of the ruling planet, the personality is endowed with charisma and magnetism that allows unification with others in relationship dynamics that enhance mutually beneficial creative possibilities; (b) as an orientation to create oppositional and conflicting circumstances that prevent such unity from taking place.

Scorpio: (a) as an urge to transform and refine the energy of the planet, thus liberating it to be more creatively potent; (b) as a series of crises that point to the perpetuation of selfish or egocentric life patterns. Such activities are based on the needs of the lower desire nature and serve to devitalize and diminish creative potentials.

Sagittarius: (a) as an urge to expand upon the qualities and creative dynamics inherent within the ruling planet, thus bringing it to a focus of greater creative possibilities; (b) as an exaggerated expression of its true nature with results that bring waste and imbalance.

Capricorn: (a) as the tendency to utilize the most developed qualities of the ruling planet for the purpose of personal and social achievement; (b) as a tool for domination, control, and the improper use of the personal will, or as a vehicle to restrict or restrain the creative potential of the others through the nature of the ruling planet.

Aquarius: (a) as an ability to use the energy of the ruling planet as a connecting link between people for collective benefits, or to develop something very unique and original from the placement of the planet in the chart; (b) as a force which dissipates, diffuses, confuses, or annihilates the creative potential inherent in the planet's position.

Pisces: (a) as an urge to bring a deeper sense of meaning into the circumstances signified by the ruling planet in such a way that healing and wholism is engendered; (b) as a negation of the practical consequences of the activities of the planet in question, resulting in a loss of balance, proportion, and structure.

The Ruling Planet by House

The house position of the ruler is of extreme importance, as it shows *where* in one's life the major focus of the externalization of the personality will take place. The house position of the Sun tells you a lot about the place of the source of *vitality*. It speaks to you, as it concerns a sense of primary strength that filters throughout the chart. But the house position of the ruler of the Ascendant tells you what the individual does with this vitality in terms of projecting him or herself in the *activity of self-formation*, in terms of the ego-in-action. The solar house may be the bank vault where the energy of life is stored, but the house position of the ruler tells you where it is primarily spent.

In Princess Diana's chart, you have the Sun in Cancer in the Seventh House of marriage. There is no doubt that much of her life centered on the fact she was *married* to the Prince of Wales. Her social position was created through this marriage (Libra on the Tenth House) and she could draw upon her vitality, create an identity, and radiate to the public (Sun in the Seventh) because of this position. She also gained tremendous prestige and power from the fact that she was the mother of the heir apparent to the throne. Ultimately this would lead her to become the next Queen Mother of Great Britain (Sun in Cancer).

But what of Lady Diana Spencer herself? What about her own activities as she strove to express and integrate her own sense of personal identity that transcends (and thus includes), her marriage, social position, and parental status? For this we have to return to the Ascendant and the position of its ruler, Jupiter. When we go back and reread what was said earlier in this chapter about Jupiter as the ruler of the chart when Sagittarius rises, we see that:

1. Jupiter expands and enlarges the entire spectrum of life experiences. Diana certainly became a larger-than-life figure. Indeed, at the time of her death, she was the Princess of Planet Earth.
2. When immature, Jupiter as ruler broadens the breath and berth of the personality, exaggerating all personal actions, needs, desires, etc. Diana had good reason to feel hurt, abandoned, and betrayed. But she also threw herself down a flight of stairs when she was pregnant, and created an enormous series of highly self-dramatizing episodes for the general public and especially for the British Royal Family.
3. When evolved, there is a sense of one-pointed orientation that gives direction, purpose, and meaning. Over time, Diana's awareness of the world's sorry political and social situation stimulated her own innate humanitarianism.
4. Jupitarian expansion becomes the individual's path to universality of consciousness. I believe that at the time of her death, Diana was entering a place in her life that was evolving toward a true spiritual direction regarding her attitude to world service. Had she lived, she would have made a remarkable Queen Mother (Sun in Cancer) to the world.

Let us recall what was stated when the ruling planet (in this case, Jupiter) is found in Aquarius. There is "…an ability to use the energy of the ruling planetary as a connecting link between people for collective benefits, or to develop something very unique and original from the placement of the planet in the chart…." Anyone with any familiarity with the events in Princess Diana's life will be able to see these dynamics of rulership at work in her life. The situation gets even more interesting and specific when we examine the house position of the ruler and its other factors of dispositorship.

Ruling Planets in the Houses

The energy of the ruling planet tends to express itself in the:

First House—as a strong embodiment of the planet in question. A person who has Gemini rising with Mercury in that sign in the First House, for example, will be much more vibrantly communicative than a person who has Mercury in Gemini in any other position in the horoscope. The individual will *be* Mercury in Gemini: constantly thinking, speaking, and moving. He or she will often *look and act* like Mercury in Gemini: slender, restless, nervous, actively intelligent, hands always waving about in the air. This position describes a man or woman who *acts the part* of Mercury in Gemini: taking the role of messenger in all social situations, and functioning most comfortably as a go-between or liaison. A man who has Libra rising and Venus in that sign in the First House will not just be charming, he will be the personification of charm. A woman with Capricorn rising and Saturn in that sign in the First House will not just be authoritative and masterful, she will be the embodiment of the urge to master her environment, and a symbol of authority unto herself (unless Saturn is strongly afflicted—especially by Neptune or the Moon—in which case she may feel dominated and overwhelmed by the environment and seek to withdraw). On the other hand, a person with Leo rising and the Sun in Leo in the First, definitely considers him or herself as the center of the universe. When interpreting the position of the ruler in the First House, the astrologer should use his or her knowledge of the meanings of the planets when in their own signs and give this interpretation very strong emphasis. You may wish to use the information in this chapter relative to the thematics of the signs and planets as a helpful and succinct guide to support your conclusions. In any event, always note the rule which states: wherever and however the ruler is placed, that is where and how *you* are.

Second House—as a natural urge to use one's own talents and resources in life. It is very important to recognize that the Second is not just the house of money and personal financial assets. It speaks to us of a much larger set of issues: our own self-worth and sense of personal values. The Second is the treasury house of our talents and abilities, as well as the storehouse of our wealth (or lack thereof) on all levels. It is definitely true that if the ruler of the chart is located in the Second, and in an earthy sign, personal material considerations will be of extreme concern and interest. But what if the ruler of the chart were in this house in an airy sign—say Virgo rising and Mercury in the Second in Libra? In this case, the emphasis would be more in terms of the wealth of personal ideas and how these ideas could be communicated with others for mutual creative possibilities and benefits. When the ruler of the horoscope is found in the Second House, life will always be asking the individual to make the most out of what he has, for he will be the source of his own supply. The more that this individual identifies his individual source with the source of *all* abundance, the richer he will be. Learning how to do this may be an important lesson in this lifetime.

Third House—as a need to communicate, integrate, and establish a strong sense of oneself *through* the energies of the specific planetary ruler. Please notice my point of emphasis. The ruling planet is taking the individual on a voyage. It is a voyage not just of self-discovery, but of self-making. The purpose of being in any incarnation is to expand the creative potential of the Being who is incarnating—that's you! Each horoscope is the map of the next phase of this giant undertaking and the house position of the ruler is where the primary life voyage takes place. There may be many side trips—especially if the ruler and the rest of the horoscope strongly emphasizes the mutable signs and/or the cadent houses (such as the Third)—but the "major trip" is located by the ruler's house position.

I am speaking here in a traveling metaphor because in the Third, we have come to the astrological house governing short journeys. When the ruler of the horoscope is located here, it will become apparent during the course of the chart reading that the individual has a strong inclination to explore many different highways and byways. If Venus is the ruling planet and located in the Third, it will be through relationships (and possibly finances) that travels through life will be made. If Jupiter is the ruler and located in the Third (especially in Aries, Gemini, Sagittarius, and Pisces), then the individual will open many books during the course of his life.

Should Mars be in the Third and the ruler of the chart, we can safely assume that the individual will have to fight many battles to defend her opinions and ideas. We would discover that the temporary losses that always accompany the influence of Mars open the doors to greater insights and gains as her wounds are healed and her lessons learned. The placement of the ruler in the Third will also often describe an important relationship with a sibling or other close relative (except for the parents and grandparents, who belong in other parts of the horoscope[5]). A well-placed Venus as ruler in a female sign in the Third points to the importance of a lovely and loving sister (or sisterly best friend); an afflicted ruling Saturn in the Third can easily indicate an older brother who has been a dominating and very problematic influence upon one's life, etc.

Fourth House — as a life lesson that is very concerned with the creation of a home base, a foundation, and a point of personal, psychological security. The Fourth deals with one's "biological karma," the dynamics of interchange with one's parents in a definite physical sense, but also with one's entire psychological inheritance. It speaks of one's "internal message" and consequent subconscious motivational patterning. Tsar Nicholas II had Saturn in Sagittarius in the Fourth House in his natal chart. Saturn was in opposition to his Sun and ruling planet, Mercury in the Tenth. Thus, his entire public image, as well as his total self-image of "Supreme Autocrat" (one of his actual titles) was not only inherited by virtue of his position as Tsar, but also firmly anchored by his biological and subsequent psychological structure.

This ancient philosophy (Sagittarius) of the monarch as absolute authority inhibited any individualized attempt at rulership (Saturn's opposition to the Sun) and was further complicated by the fixity of the Sun as well as the ruling planet (Sun and Mercury in Taurus).

The placement of the ruler of the chart in the Fourth House has a profound meaning. In most instances, it is not the easiest of positions, as it is antithetical to the primary significance of the First House — the

Example 9: The Horoscope of Tsar Nicholas II[6]

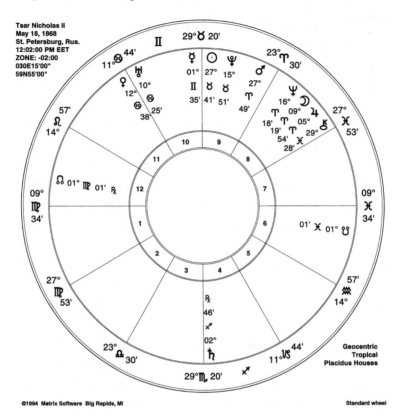

Tsar Nicholas II
May 18, 1868
St. Petersburg, Rus.
12:02:00 PM EET
ZONE: -02:00
030E15'00"
59N55'00"

Geocentric
Tropical
Placidus Houses

Standard wheel

urge to create new experiences for the evolving ego. The Fourth is the house most concerned with the past, not with the present, and certainly not with the future. Yet a well-positioned ruler (by sign and aspect) in this house can do a lot to anchor and secure a person so well within the boundaries of his own psychological domain, that it makes the addition of greater supportive structures that much easier to achieve.

If, for example, Libra rises and Venus is well situated in Capricorn in the Fourth, the individual may have a strong financial footing upon which to build and grow. At the very least, Venus in this position will reveal a legacy of traditional and established codes of family values and social behavior that can only be of help to this individual as she makes her way up the social ladder.

I use this example of climbing the "social ladder," as almost anyone with Libra rising and a well-placed Venus in Capricorn in the Fourth as his or her ruler, will seek a good marriage and a secure and socially advantageous position. It is, after all, a major part of their inherited motivational pattern for achievement in life.

Fifth House—as a stimulation to advance one's creative talents and potentials. This is usually a very positive position for the ruling planet, as it tends to enhance and support the possibilities of the ruler by adding the natural vitality of all Fifth House placements. The Fifth tends to embrace the ruler and add creative possibilities. I am speaking, of course, about a well-placed ruler in this position. If the ruler is in a sign that is not amenable to the natural fiery expression of this house, such as Cancer rising with the Moon in Scorpio in the Fifth, the potentials of the ruler may be diminished.

The Fifth has a great deal to do with the joys of life: children, romance, games, and those creative endeavors which bring pleasure and satisfaction, increase and smiles. Naturally, an afflicted ruler in the Fifth can bring difficulties with children, troubles in romance, turn the urge to play games into serious gambling losses, etc.

In the example given above, the Moon in Scorpio as the ruling planet in the Fifth when afflicted (say by a square from Saturn in Leo) can easily bring disappointment with one's offspring or even deny children altogether. The statement that the ruling planet wants to make in this house is: "I am me and here is the proof of what I can do. Here are some of the fruits of my tree all ripe and ready. Now let me make a wonderful compote out of them! I'll even give you some so that you can enjoy what I have created, too." A person with a strong ruler in the Fifth, such as Leo rising and the Sun in Sagittarius in the Fifth, is much less concerned with public reactions to his actions than to his own creative plans and projects. Such an individual is far more concerned with his own ability to produce examples of his own skills and talents and is less involved with their wider social ramifications.

Sixth House—as the inclination to find the tools, techniques, methods, and skills that refine and improve oneself and one's abilities. In essence, when the ruler of the horoscope is placed in the first five houses, the concerns of life tend to be quite personal, or at least, revolve around the dynamics of the ego as they unfold relative to one's own sense of being (First), resources (Second), ideas and methods of communication (Third), psychological roots (Fourth), and the ability to activate all of these factors into a powerful statement of the creating ego (Fifth). Conditions begin to change once the ruler is found in the Sixth House — here, the tendency is to be dissatisfied with the status quo and to search for additional tools of self-expression.

There is a reaching out into life that speaks less of the personal immediacy of self-projection (Ascendant) and much more of the urge to find a place in a larger scheme of things, a place in which there is an active and often practical interchange with life. The urge for self-improvement can express itself through a concern about health, one's own or others, through one of the healing arts. A well-placed Saturn as the ruling planet in the Sixth may incline one towards more traditional methods of healing, while Uranus as ruler in this domicile may indicate that this orientation is geared more towards alternative healing systems and techniques.

The Moon is the "collector" of the solar system. When she is well placed in the Sixth, she will be very busy gathering in those processes and skills that can be safely stored away in the individual's "cupboard" and taken out and used when the need arises. On the other hand, the Moon afflicted in the Sixth when Cancer rises is often an indication that nothing is ever right, safe, or secure, and that one's health is often in jeopardy (just like mama's used to be). Very often, the need to find one's place in life is connected with one's job or field of service. A strong and clear example of rulerships at work here would be a chart that has Aries rising and Mars in Virgo in the Sixth. The basic statement is: "Nothing is ever 100 percent right with me. I am in conflict with my job surroundings and if I am the boss, I have arguments with the people I need to help me." If Mars is afflicted in this position, this statement is even more intense in its expression. Digestive problems, like peptic ulcers, could result if the individual doesn't find a way to get a grip! If Mars is otherwise well placed (for example with a trine to Saturn in Capricorn), this statement could be modified as follows: "Although I usually find some fault or lack of perfection in my work environment, I almost always can find ways to remedy the situation and make things stronger and better than they were before." In this case, help may come from an older and more experienced worker or executive (Saturn).

Seventh House — as a very strong need to join with another or to polarize oneself against another in order to establish a stronger sense of self. The need for constant interchange and reflection (especially if the ruler is placed in this house in an airy sign) may have some definite debilities. If "I" always rely on "You" to let me know who I am or am not, then I am setting myself up for some pretty intense relationship situations. I leave myself open for co-dependency to occur (especially if my ruler is either Venus or Neptune in the Seventh) and a lot of psychological vulnerability (especially if my ruler is the Moon or in the sign of Cancer or afflicted by the Moon or a planet in Cancer). If, on the other hand (and when things concern Libra or the Seventh House, there is always "another hand"), I have a strong ruler well placed in the Seventh, I can always be sure of a partner who will strengthen and support my actions and sense of well-being. I will also be able to find those "significant others" that allow me to have a positive effect on their lives and thus validate my own self-worth and creative possibilities.

In effect, when the ruler of the Ascendant is in the Descendant, the affairs of the First House, the essential "I-amness" of life, are shifted into the realm of "otherness." The Seventh House is both the house of marriage as well as the house of open enemies. It is certainly the place where we seek (and sometimes find) the complement to ourselves, but it is also the place where the "shadow self" lives and breathes and has its being too. You know that there are going to be problems in establishing a cohesive and integrated sense of self should Aries rise and Mars be in Libra in the Seventh. Yet it just may be that out of the often chaotic circumstances in relationships that is engendered by such a rulership position, that the individual may come to resolve his battles for personal integrity. He may eventually learn how not to polarize himself through his relationships and will end his chaos. If the objective of one's life is to bring people together for harmonious mutual or collective purposes, then a well-placed ruler in the Seventh may just be what is required to fulfill this goal.

Eighth House — as the need to transform the nature of the personality so that it is better equipped for more refined and powerful creative possibilities. An Eighth House ruler is quite the test! It tells the astrologer that the individual has to undergo many crises of transformation in order to give birth to his or her greater good. This definitely involves the transmutation of the part of the nature that is signified by the planetary ruler.

If it is an afflicted Moon in this position, then unhealthy attachments to one's biological karma (and most specifically, one's mother), have got to go. If it is Venus, then our relationship with money or the motivations we have in creating relationship (especially if Venus is in a cardinal sign) have to be profoundly altered, etc. If the ruler is well placed and free of affliction in the Eighth House, the job may have already been accomplished and the individual has an incredibly powerful tool to help others do the same. Certainly one's sexuality will play a very important role in life. Sexuality is important in all lives, but in this case the focus on the nature of one's sexual expression and the social dynamics that come as a result of fulfilling one's sexual needs will be a dominant life theme.

Leo rising with the Sun in Pisces in the Eighth, for example, is an immediate indication of a person with enormous passion. The release of such passions purely for the sake of personal pleasure and relationship dominance (a very Eighth House theme) may easily lead to that individual's self-undoing. Yet if the compassionate and healing nature of the Fish is developed, the transformative magnetism of an Eighth House Sun as ruler can endow this same individual with a very loving and embracing nature. Such qualities may even be expressed sexually, but the orientation within that sexuality will not be selfish, but instead will bestow vitality and upliftment to both oneself and one's partner. The key to the right use of energy when the ruler of the chart is in the Eighth House also includes the transformation of other people's resources. For instance, a strong Jupiter in the Eighth as the ruler may be an excellent indication of a person who can, through a keen eye for investments, make money for other people. Jupiter here can also reorient a person's philosophical or religious leanings, bringing universality where prejudice, or at the very least, where narrow-mindedness, once reigned.

Ninth House—as a way of expanding one's horizons through foreign travel, higher studies, religious orientation, or any other means that takes us beyond the limits of the personality. If the ruler of the chart is weak by position in this house, there is a reluctance to travel. Travel in this sense not only indicates getting on an airplane and going to a distant land, it also means moving beyond the established boundaries of our personal, inherited value system.

It can be a very frightening journey to be pulled up from one's roots and taken away to a place where the language, customs, and food are different from what we know at home. Just think about your voyage to the land of astrology and metaphysics! Think about how much resistance there was from some old part of yourself (and from the more familiar faces around you) when you left behind your family's values, your religion of birth, and your mama's cooking when you became a vegetarian.

If you examine the natural chart, you will see that Sagittarius and the Ninth House are 150° away from both Taurus and the Second and Cancer and the Fourth. The 150° angle, or the inconjunct, is an aspect that forces adjustments under situations that are not the easiest to handle. So the Ninth House ruler, although opening many doors and dimensions, also challenges the status quo of our natal/birth values (the Second) and the whole of our biological karma (the Fourth). When well placed in the Ninth, this set of challenges and the resulting expansive transition that we make are easy to achieve, natural in fact. A strong Ninth House ruler is of great benefit to one's life and the ruling planet placed therein will reveal from whence these blessings flow.

Here are three examples: If Venus is the ruler and in the Ninth, relationships will open the way to a wider and more expanded view of life. If it is Neptune, inner inspiration will tear away the veil of the personality and reveal a path of inspiration. If Pluto is the well-aspected ruler of the horoscope and located in the Ninth, look for major transformative experiences to come out of one's spiritual and planetary voyages.

Tenth House—as a tremendous need to establish oneself in the world and to bring a sense of fruition to all efforts of personal self-expression. When the ruler of the First is located in the Tenth, the need for personal accomplishment is strong. Not only does it need to be personal, but it must be public as well. The closer the ruler is to the actual cusp of the Midheaven, the stronger is this urge. Life tends to be governed by the impulse to achieve prominence relative to the planet concerned, as self-identity is very much linked to recognition of oneself as *that planetary force.* Thus Sagittarius rising and Jupiter in the Tenth points to a person who wants to be seen (and who often sees himself) as a great scholar, adventurer, athlete, or spiritual teacher. Capricorn rising with Saturn in the Tenth indicates a man or woman who has to be the CEO of some company, a political leader, or at the very least, a figure of authority in his or her chosen field. (With Saturn in this position, it may take some time to get there.)

Mars in the Tenth with Aries rising shows the need to be the first or the best at what one does, while Mars in this position with Scorpio rising says to the world, "I got here after enormous struggles and I mean to stay!" (especially if Mars is in a fixed sign). Afflicted rulers in the Tenth House are not a pretty sight! Frustration follows frustration as one seeks to achieve a place of prominence only to be met by blockages or successes that are less than what one had envisioned.

As the natural ruler of the Tenth House, hard aspects from Saturn to the ruler in this position are especially difficult. Strong and positively placed rulers in the Tenth (especially if backed up by a good aspects from Saturn and/or the Sun, or at the very least, one or both of these bodies in a strong and complementary position in the chart), are very influential in bringing about the worldly success that such a person covets and is naturally inclined to achieve.

Eleventh House—as the need to extend oneself into the larger world through activities that involve groups, organizations, or forms of mass communications. The Internet is a good metaphor for the Eleventh House because it links the individual into a network of interconnecting sources and contacts. When the ruler of the horoscope is in this domicile, the individual tends to want to take his personal "theater" and bring it to the attention of many people. There is, however, a difference here between a Fifth House person who likes to play "show and tell" and the Eleventh House person whose version of this game is quite different. In the former case, the Fifth House person is the star and the other people are the audience ready to appreciate what he or she has done. In the case of the Eleventh House person, the situation is a bit more complex. The Eleventh House person may be the originator of what she creates, but she is also an active participant, one among the many, a unit seeking integration into the collective. When the ruler of the horoscope is in the Eleventh House, the scope of one's activities and the nature of one's aspirations involve the active participation and response of many individuals, or groups of individuals. There is often the urge to utilize one's talents and abilities for humanitarian purposes or at the very least, to reach out and involve many others. This sense of connecting with (as opposed to the Fifth House need to project outwards to) people is very strong and especially so if the ruling planet is in an airy sign.

Mercury in this position as ruler, for example, would tend to indicate an individual who has an enormous need to communicate ideas, ideals, and opinions with many others. Virgo rising with Mercury as the ruler in Cancer might point to a person who collects and stores data, information that can be distributed via computer or other communicative channels. Libra rising with Venus as the ruler in Leo in the Eleventh, for example, may indicate a person who is open and friendly to everyone she meets (and she would tend to meet a lot of people), creating the immediacy of a personal bond under even the most impersonal of communicative circumstances. Such an individual could work in telemarketing, greeting each invisible and unknown customer as if he or she were a very close friend. Venus in this context could also indicate an artistically gifted individual, one whose work reaches a large number of people through such means as television or computer advertising—especially if Venus in this position were trine or sextile to Uranus.

Twelfth House—as a distinct tendency to work or function from behind the scenes. No matter what the other indications of a horoscope may be, if the ruler of the chart is in the Twelfth, the individual has an incredibly private facet to his or her personality. Often such people find themselves alone, sometimes unwillingly, but more often by choice. There may be a natural gift for research, laboratory investigations, or occult or metaphysical studies. There is also a clear orientation toward associating oneself with individuals who either are in obscure positions in life or who are in various forms of distress. This would especially be the case if Venus or the Moon is the ruler of the horoscope and either of these planets is found in the Twelfth. Depending on the overall nature of one's life, such hidden relationships could range from the propensity for clandestine lovers through working with inmates in a prison to healing patients in a hospital. For a very busy Twelfth House man or woman—all three! In essence, a Twelfth House ruler indicates someone whose sense of personal perimeters are not anchored, fixed, or secure.

From a positive perspective, this gives a person unlimited access to others and vice versa, because there are no boundaries to stop or prevent such communication. People who tend to be gifted intuitives, psychological counselors, and healers often have strong Twelfth House positions, including that of the ruler. Yet, there is a great drawback to this position should the individual's sense of personal integrity be weak or challenged by life. One then is too easily penetrated by other people's projections, making it very difficult to hold one's own ground. Such a person can be swept away by the "slings and arrows of outrageous egos," or even normal and healthy ones.

The Twelfth is also known as the "house of hidden treasure" and some planets, such as Jupiter and Venus, do quite well in this domicile, although they need to be well aspected by planets that are above the horizon of the chart, thus bringing such subjective treasure out into objective light. Planets in the Twelfth afflicted by Neptune are especially debilitated, as the tendency for the dissipation and dissolution of that planet's energy is increased. This particularly is the case when the afflicted body is the ruling planet, because the energy involved embodies the individual's sense of himself. A strong sense of self can be obscured when in the Twelfth. Or the person is identified with a more lofty spiritual or humanitarian principle. A square, opposition, or a conjunction from Neptune to the ruler in the Twelfth House can make matters worse. If, however, the ruler in the Twelfth is strong and healthy by sign and aspects, the individual tends to be incredibly resourceful both spiritually (especially when in fire or air) and materially (especially when in earth or water).

Secondary Dispositorship

Our analysis of the planetary ruler is not complete unless we examine the position of its own dispositor. This investigation will reveal many more details concerning the way the intent and theme of the life unfolds. The astrologer should note the sign and house placement of the secondary dispositor as well as any major aspects that this planet makes to the ruler of the chart. For an excellent example, let's continue with our delineation of Diana's horoscope (page 79).

We have determined that the position of the ruler of this horoscope is Jupiter in Aquarius in the Second House. One of the most profound urges in Diana's life was to use her own talents and resources to anchor her sense of self-worth (and by extension, her personal values) in a way that reached large numbers of people. This was a source of great conflict for her as well as being the impulse which stimulated her personal growth and development.

Jupiter is disposited both by Uranus in Leo in the Eighth and Saturn in Capricorn in the First. Uranus' position in Leo tells us that Diana's personal set of values and her particular talents and resources have to be expressed in a personal, highly individualistic and dramatic fashion. Indeed, her very clothing and style of dress made an incredible statement of who she was and her spending of her husband's and public tax money to support her wardrobe led to much criticism and controversy. This type of excessive spending can be easily seen in the chart by dispositorship factors.

Jupiter is in Aquarius, the sign of public resources. Uranus, its ruler, is in the Eighth, the house of one's partner's money as well as the house of taxation. Uranus is square to Venus in Taurus (the sign of personal finances). Thus, she used her husband's and the public's money as if it were her own. The square between the two indicates the difficulties that came from such activities. Yet the humanitarian and idealistic dynamics of the combination of the above astrological influences also points to the outcome of this spending. One of the most publicized (the combined influences of Aquarius and Sagittarius are involved in the area of public relations) and most praised of Diana's activities was the eventual sale of her wardrobe. This gesture on her part raised a small fortune for charity and fetched far more money than the original cost of the clothes themselves. Her dresses became even more valuable after her untimely passing (Uranus is in the Eighth House of death).

The transformation of personal wealth so that it may be used for the benefit of other people is an Eighth House process. All the fixed signs and their respective, succedent houses are concerned with value. Taurus and the Second House are indicative of personal value, resources, and wealth. Leo and the Fifth House marks these Second House potentials with an irrefutable statement: "These objects are very definitely mine and no one else's!" This sign and house allow the individual to personify what they value and possess through the dynamic projections of personal self-expression. Scorpio and the Eighth House represent the path of conflict and point of fusion between what is personal (Taurus) and what belongs to society and the collective in which we live (Aquarius). It is through the portals of Scorpio and the Eighth House that the individual either anchors more fully the desires and needs of the personality, increasing egocentricity accordingly, or releases these urges for greater spiritual and social awareness. If this transformational process is correctly established, then the door to the collective consciousness of humanity opens wide. This, of course, is Uranus and the Eleventh House, where the collective resources of humanity are gathered and where we reap the rewards for how we formulate our lives in terms of the social contribution that we make (Tenth House).

Uranus in the Eighth House is a potent position.[7] Uranus is exalted in Scorpio and thus has an especial affinity with its natural house. We should also note that Scorpio is on the cusp of the Eleventh in Diana's chart. This is a form of mutual reception, i.e., the natural planetary ruler of the Eleventh House is in the natural house of Scorpio, while Scorpio is on the Eleventh House cusp. The astrology student has to be aware of these affinities and keep them in mind as they will reveal the subtle interconnections found throughout a given natal map. These positions contribute to the fact that Diana's death would come suddenly by accident, and be very public. Literally, moments after the automobile crash that took her life, the scene was being photographed and sent around the world. I should add here, that the presence of Mars and Pluto in their own natural house — the Eighth — are dispositors of the Eleventh (the public, publicity, public relations). All three planets (Uranus, Mars, and Pluto) conjunct the North Node in the Eighth, heightening the publicity surrounding Diana's sad end.

The conjunction of the North Node in Leo to Uranus only enhances Diana's ability to reach a huge number of people and stamp her individual mark in the collective consciousness. In mundane astrology, the Moon represents the masses and the subconscious links that bind people together into biological and social units. We should also bear in mind that the Moon represents one's family and by extension, one's tribe, race, or national grouping. In the horoscope of rulers, monarchs, and political leaders, the Moon stands for the people that one governs and affects as a result of one's social position. Saturn, Capricorn, and the Tenth House (the responsibilities that come from one's social position) always stand opposite the Moon, Cancer, and the Fourth.

Please note: The North and South Nodes that are most often used in astrology are those of the moon and they have great significance in the delineation of any horoscope. Their positions are calculated based upon the place in the sky where the orbit of the Moon intersects with the Earth's orbit around the Sun. This means that it is through the placement of the Nodes in the chart that the individual connects with the mass consciousness of the human race. The more advanced and highly developed our own consciousness, the more we come to know ourselves as members of the human family. Thus, people with lower levels of consciousness are prejudiced and separate by nature. Racial hatred, religious fundamentalism, human and animal persecution are instigated through people so traumatized and fixated by the umbilicus of their biology that they never emerge from the murky waters of their unnurturing womb.

In essence, the position of the North Node gives us the opportunity to expand our consciousness. It is from the position of the North Node that we acquire those new experiences in a given lifetime that open our hearts and minds to one another. In the horoscope of a person whose destiny brings them into contact with large numbers of people, the North Node is even more significant. Diana's ruler is Jupiter in Aquarius, its dispositor is Uranus conjunct the Northern Node. Is it any wonder, then, that her life would be celebrated and her death mourned by billions?

The position of the South Node pulls us back into the collective unconscious womb. It is a place from which we do not advance. It functions to inhibit personal growth and, at its most harmful, insists upon focusing on those portions of our past (both individual and collective) that serve no cohesive purpose for our growth. Diana's Moon is conjunct the South Node. The Moon is the dispositor of her Cancer Sun and Mercury and the latter is both the natal and the natural ruler of her Sixth House of health. Is it no wonder, then, that Diana's illnesses involved food disorders? The more she insisted upon being accepted by a family that could not embrace her, the more she rejected her own self-nourishment, her own self-worth, and ultimately, herself (Moon in the Second House). Note that the Moon disposits the Seventh House Sun and Mercury. In this case the ruler of the Seventh, indicating her husband Prince Charles, is in the Seventh in Cancer. The ruler of a house positioned in that house adds to the importance of that planet. The fact that the significator of marriage is in Cancer tells the astrologer that the husband's family (Cancer) was a very important influence in her life. When we see that Mercury is inconjunct Jupiter, it is no wonder that there was so much conflict between Diana (Jupiter) and her original modes of self-expression (Aquarius) and Charles (Mercury) and his family (Cancer).

Saturn as co-ruler of Aquarius also has a very important role to play as the secondary dispositor. We should note that the sign on the Second House cusp is Capricorn, thus emphasizing Saturn's importance because it is also the dispositor of the house wherein the ruler is placed. Saturn is in its own sign, indicating the traditional background (and its particular set of strictures and restrictions) from which Diana came.[8] Saturn is also retrograde in Capricorn, revealing how deeply entrenched such social rules and regulations were in terms of her way of life. Her need to rebel against these social dynamics is marked by Jupiter as the ruler of expansive Sagittarius in the revolutionary sign of Aquarius. Jupiter is also retrograde in this sign, indicating that the need to expand and overthrow established rules of conduct is also profoundly marked in her character.

It can be safely stated that after Diana Spencer, the British Monarchy (certainly ruled by Saturn in Capricorn) will never be the same again.

1. This is relative to the house position of Jupiter. Please remember that the houses refer to those areas *on earth* through which the planetary forces express themselves. Earth always brings forth the "gravity of reality," which is not always the favorite field of expression for either Jupiter, Neptune, or Pisces.

2 In esoteric astrology, the Ascendant is *the* most important point. Please refer to the author's book, *Soul-Centered Astrology*, for more details.

3. Intermediate students may wish to consult the Recommended Reading List at the end of this book for suggested works that will expand this understanding.

4. Data source: The author's personal contacts in Great Britain.

5. The reader may wish to consult the author's earlier book, *Houses of the Horoscope*, The Crossing Press, 1999, to see "who belongs where" in the chart.

6. Data source: Jones, Marc E., *The Sabian Symbols*, p. 392.

7. In this chart, a tendency to public death is seen astrologically as follows: public = Eleventh House, death = Eight House. Scorpio, the sign of death, is on the Eleventh House cusp. The *natural and the natal rulers* of the Eleventh are in the Eighth and Mars and Pluto are the natural rulers of this house, strengthening their influence. I point out that Diana tried to commit suicide on several occasions. The natal ruler of the Eighth House is the Moon in the sign of the public, Aquarius. In addition, the dispositor of the Eighth House ruler (Uranus) is in opposition to the ruler of the Eighth (Moon). There is yet one other, slightly more subtle factor of dispositorship pointing to this tragedy. The dispositor of Uranus is the Sun. The Sun (the vital life principle in any chart) is disposited by the Moon, and the Moon is in opposition to Uranus in the Eighth ruling the Eleventh. I realize that this is a highly complex analysis, but if the reader goes through the above astro-logic carefully, the natures of these positions clearly reveal themselves.

8. The First House equals a person's early environment, especially prior to the first Saturn return at age 29.

The Ruler of the Horoscope
and Its Aspects

When the Ruler of the Horoscope Is a Planet Conjunct the Ascendant

We have up to this point only spoken about the ruler of the horoscope when it is the ruler of the Ascendant. As I earlier indicated, there is another case for planetary rulership, which occurs when there is a planet within 5° from the Ascendant that is posited in the First House or located within 3° from the Ascendant in the Twelfth House. Such a planet and its condition by sign and aspect would tend to dominate the chart as its ruler, but the planetary dispositor of the Ascendant would still play an enormous role in the life.

Let us say that 12° of Virgo rises in a chart and Uranus is at 14° of that sign. Uranus in Virgo would tend to rule the nativity, but the position of Mercury would also be vital to expressing the full implications of the Ascendant. The astrologer should note if there are any aspects between the two, for example, Mercury at 10° Capricorn trine Uranus. In this example, we have a person who is very original in his or her self-expression. There is a tremendous need not to be like everyone else and to develop a personality that is unmistakably unique and singular. These characteristics have to be expressed through the nature and interests of the sign, Virgo. Thus, it would be common to find such a person revealing the focus of their individuality through the particular sphere of their work. With Mercury in Capricorn trine to Uranus and the Ascendant in Virgo, such an individual would have an easy time developing individualistic ways and means to bring efficiency into the workplace, and finding unique ways of creating practical improvements in their environment.

A planet conjoined the Ascendant will also mark a person's appearance and character strongly and with great vibrancy. Keep in mind when delineating the chart that the individual will totally embody the nature of the planet on the Ascendant *through* the coloration of the sign. *Please note:* Study the condition of the natal and natural houses which the planet in question rules. Thus, if Mercury conjoins the Ascendant, look at the Third and Sixth houses as well as the houses with Gemini and Virgo on their cusps. If the planet on the Ascendant is Saturn, for example, then the Tenth House should call your attention, as well as the Capricorn and Aquarius cusp houses. If it is the Moon on the Ascendant, then the Fourth and the Cancer cusp houses are to be carefully examined, etc. An understanding of the affinities between the rising planet and its natal and natural house rulerships will tell you a great deal about where and how the individual works out a great deal of his or her life interests and natural orientations.

The following is a brief list of some of the more important features and behavioral characteristics when each of the planets rise and conjoin the Ascendant:

Sun: A "sunny" disposition. The urge to dominate the environment with one's personality is strong. The individual has a hard time seeing the difference between the environment and oneself. The immediate environment *is* the self and everything and everyone revolves around that sense of personal identity. This person can have a generous, warm, and energizing persona (especially when the Sun is in the fiery and airy signs) but a highly egocentric nature. The individual has to learn how to *see* other people and appreciate that each person is also a Sun. Personal appearance and clothing will be very important and the hair will be a marked physical feature.

Moon: As one would expect, home and family are very important. The individual has been highly affected by the inherited emotional patterns of the birth family and early environment. There is a tremendous need to create a protective womb around him or herself, one that only permits the entrance of people deemed safe and secure. You do not have to be well known to the person with the Moon conjunct the Ascendant to be accepted, but you do have to feel like family, otherwise the individual tends to be very standoffish to whom he or she considers "psychic strangers." The face is often roundish; the skin and musculature can tend to be soft. Food will be an important facet of the person's life.

Mercury: The disposition is nervous and the individual is restless and eager to be on the move. Even in the more sedentary signs of Taurus and Cancer, Mercury on the Ascendant will still impact the nature and create the urge for an intense exploration of the immediate environment. The rational mind dominates the life, leading one to communicate through the written and/or spoken word. The physical body tends to be slender with an abundant use of hands and arms when speaking. In the earthy signs, the hands will be especially important to one's line of work. In the watery signs, there will be a marked tendency to rationalize one's feelings through one's actions. In the airy signs, communication and interpersonal relationships are definitely the focus of self-expression. In the fiery signs, there is the need to inspire others with one's creative urges and thoughts.

Venus: A well-formed body and a lot of personal charm and magnetism characterize this position. Even if the individual is not classically beautiful, there is that "special something" about this man or woman that attracts other people. Relationships will play an important role in one's life because the individual is oriented to sharing. Here we have the personification of the "urge to merge." One drawback is a tendency to create each relationship in one's own image, ideal, or concept of what a complementary partner should be like. There is a need to create harmony and balance in the immediate environment. This trait can manifest as the need to *be* beautiful and harmonious at all times, thus avoiding personal conflict at any cost.

Mars: Assertive and dominant in character and demeanor, when Mars is conjoined the Ascendant, the individual is not open to any form of compromise. Competition is strong and there is an attitude of "me versus them" which plays itself out in every interpersonal encounter. The personality is combative and challenging. This is an individual who becomes bored when there are no battles to fight. Therefore, there is a tendency to create confrontations when none exist. The individual is direct and often indiscreet; as subtlety is definitely not the way of his or her self-expression. These characteristics are most obvious when Mars is in the male signs. A propensity to passive-aggression and strategic moves are more the predominant theme when Mars is in the female signs. Sexual orientation and activity will play an important role in one's motivations and be a strong factor throughout life. Look for a prominent nose and piercing eyes.

Jupiter: A large body and an imposing demeanor characterize the life when this planet conjoins the Ascendant. This is an individual who is ever searching to widen his or her horizons. There may be a great deal of travel during one's lifetime, as well as a never-ceasing need for education (especially if this trait is supported by a strong Ninth House influence). This can be modified if Jupiter is in Cancer or a fixed sign and/or afflicted by Saturn or the Moon. Then the tendency to travel is often frustrated and limited by family or other circumstances close to home. There is the tendency to exaggerate self-importance (especially if Jupiter is in Leo or in strong aspect to the Sun from this position). It is difficult for a person with Jupiter on the Ascendant to accept life as it is. There is a great need to enlarge upon existing circumstances. If in Virgo, look for the individual to make a lot of fuss over very small, highly personal matters. If in Cancer, great kindness is offered but there is a tendency to overemphasize one's personal feelings in all things. If Capricorn is Jupiter's sign, the pursuit of personal ambitions will dominate the life. In this, as in all other instances, use your knowledge of the signs to modify the nature of the planet.

Saturn: The personality tends to be serious and the demeanor can be somber or even maudlin when Saturn rises. The sense of personal responsibility over the affairs of life is highly noted. If Saturn is well placed by sign and aspect on the Ascendant, there is a sense that if one just works long and hard enough, any goal may be accomplished. If Saturn is debilitated (especially to the ruler of the Tenth House), the life attitude is that no matter how arduously or assiduously one may toil, the goal seems ever to be beyond achievement. This is a person who has to learn how to cocreate his or her own boundaries rather than to allow oneself to be circumscribed by the limitations in the environment. Personal security and one's material conditions may be overly emphasized, especially if in the watery and earthy signs. A dark beauty, a depth of earthly knowledge, a sense of having "been here" before, are all characteristics of this planet when it is on the Ascendant.

Uranus: An unusual and unique person who is often quite unpredictable in his or her ways of self-expression. There often is a need to be different in appearance (especially the case with Uranus in Leo or Aquarius). There is a sense that one does not belong or does not quite fit in with the prevailing social environment (especially true when Uranus is in Virgo or Capricorn). One is a rebel, an outcast, different from all the rest, even different from other people who also have Uranus on the Ascendant. There is an attraction to unusual people and a need *to be* an unusual person. Usually this is not difficult to achieve. If in the mutable signs, life is the most unpredictable. If in the fixed signs, there is the frustration that life is not unpredictable enough. If in the cardinal signs, one makes one's own life as unpredictable as possible.

Neptune: There is a distinct tendency to be enigmatic, both in oneself and to others. There is a definite psychic sensitivity that, although it may not make one psychic, certainly sensitizes every environmental and social set of circumstances. One is usually not particularly comfortable in public. The individual ego structure may not be strong enough to handle other people's vibrations. Too many people in one's environment is experienced as too much psychic energy that has to be absorbed and processed. Saturn or the Moon on the Ascendant may give a person the ability to block others off and shut down. This is not the case with Neptune. Neptune on the Ascendant can indicate a person with the urge to tune out and disappear even when they are with you, but such individuals can never fully block out other people's energy. They may try to create artificial boundaries such as alcohol, cigarettes, or other drugs. They may even attempt to find a sense of personal centeredness and protection through a sincere dedication to meditation and other spiritual practices. What is true is that these individuals are incredibly sensitive and definitely need time by themselves on a regular basis. When positive, Neptune in this position gives a disposition to a spiritual life of service. When in difficult aspects (especially with Mars, Saturn, or the Moon), there is a tendency to depression, weak morals, and self-destructive habits and practices.

Pluto: There is a marked tendency to undergo consistent cycles of transformational crises in self-discovery. An internal tension is always present, much like a slow moving and highly pressurized lava flow waiting for the time to rise to the surface and erupt. This inner magma is magnetic, giving the individual a sense of personal power. Depending on the aspects between Pluto and the other planets, this power may be well regulated and correctly used (Pluto trine Saturn), abused (Pluto square the Sun), or diffused (Pluto inconjunct Mercury in an airy sign). The person with Pluto on the Ascendant has a great effect on his or her environment and may effectuate strong changes in the status quo. This is essentially a loner, a person who is constantly being pulled or motivated by something very intensely magnetic and enigmatic existing deep within him or herself.

The above descriptions were given with an emphasis on First House placements. Should the planet be located slightly into the Twelfth House, the same characteristics are to be noted as being in effect, yet the awareness of the *conscious projection* of these traits may be somewhat diminished. Thus, a person with the Sun on the Twelfth House side of the Ascendant may definitely have a "sunny disposition" but be less aware of the nature of his or her "sunlight" than is the person with the Sun just slightly inside the First House. This particular difference is very subtle, the appreciation for which can only be gained through the experience of reading lots and lots of charts. The ability to differentiate the colorations and hues of energy come with the territory, so to speak. It is a gift, a faculty of intuition, one that is obtained as a return on the investment of years of dedicated study to the incredibly beautiful art and science of astrology.

A good example of a chart in which the ruling planet of the horoscope is conjunct the Ascendant but 2° into the Twelfth House is the horoscope of Chris Sizemore. Sizemore was the person about whom a best-selling book was written and a subsequent successful movie was made. This was *The Three Faces of Eve*, the true story of a woman who suffered from a type of schizophrenia known as multiple personality disorder. There were more than just "three faces" of Sizemore. In time she developed over a dozen distinct personalities. Eventually, and with personal determination and proper psychiatric support, she managed to restore her mental health.

Example 10: The Horoscope of Chris Sizemore[1]

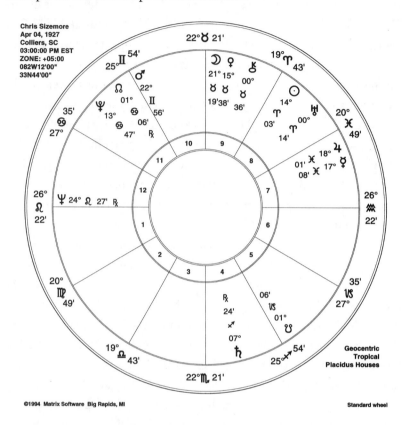

Chris Sizemore
Apr 04, 1927
Colliers, SC
03:00:00 PM EST
ZONE: +05:00
082W12'00"
33N44'00"

Geocentric
Tropical
Placidus Houses

©1994 Matrix Software Big Rapids, MI

Standard wheel

The horoscope shows that Neptune in Leo is on the Ascendant. It is disposited by the Sun in Aries in the Eighth, which is exactly square Pluto in Cancer. Pluto is disposited by the Moon, which is square Neptune. The challenge to integration of personal identity is shown clearly through this pattern of planetary force fields. Sizemore's psychic sensitivity and vulnerability is evident by the placement of Neptune. Its angular square to the Moon reveals a person who has a difficult time creating a firm emotional structure. A more positive interplay between the Moon and Neptune endows a person with the ability to be aware of other people's feelings. Any affliction between these two bodies makes it very difficult to stabilize such sensitivity. Simply stated, Sizemore had no emotional boundaries and was open to a constant invasion of emotional forces that worked to disintegrate a sense of personal wholeness. Esoteric astrology would state this condition as follows: There is a "leak" in the auric force field preventing the energies of the lower astral plane to enter freely into the consciousness.[2]

Her afflicted Neptune on the Ascendant in the Twelfth reveals a tendency to mask and unmask, to veil and unveil oneself without the necessary objective ability to control the process. A good actress, for example, is very aware of her shape-shifting. There is a firm sense of self at the center of her *dramatis personae*. Sizemore was indeed a very good actress, but Neptune's position in the chart and its dispositorship pattern shows that no such firm sense of self existed. Leo rising dramatizes self-projection and adds to the tendency for Sizemore to personify her various personae with costumes and full characterizations. Thus, her "faces" included such various women as a gentle blind lady, a sexy harlot, a virgin who would refuse to be intimate even with her husband, and several other "characters." In addition, the Sun is the dispositor of the Ascendant and Neptune is square Pluto. This aspect adds intensity to every form of self-projection, but it also gives a highly self-destructive urge and destabilizes the sense of personal identity so essential to a person's mental health.

When the Planet Conjunct the Ascendant Is the Ruler of the Sign on the Ascendant

As I have mentioned previously, one of the major keys to the correct delineation of the horoscope is the ability to judge the weight of planetary emphasis. We have just seen how important the ruler of the horoscope is to the interpretation of a nativity. This potency should be given additional attention when the ruler of the Ascendant is on the Ascendant and in its own sign.

This situation occurs if Mars is in Aries conjunct an Aries Ascendant; Venus in Libra conjunct a Libra Ascendant; Saturn in Capricorn conjunct a Capricorn Ascendant, etc. The astrologer should follow the guidelines of interpretation outlined above, paying attention to the fact that the planet will be expressing its nature through its most potent modality. *This planet/sign combination will definitely dominate*

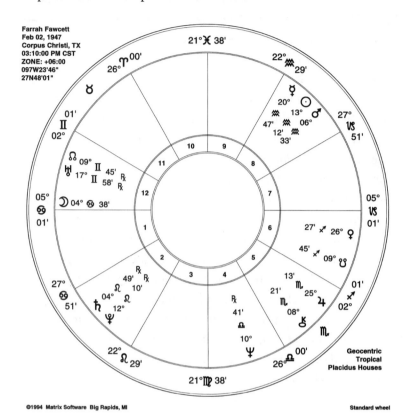

Farrah Fawcett
Feb 02, 1947
Corpus Christi, TX
03:10:00 PM CST
ZONE: +06:00
097W23'46"
27N48'01"

Geocentric
Tropical
Placidus Houses

©1994 Matrix Software Big Rapids, MI   Standard wheel

the life. There is *no* dispositor of this planet, so the energy remains totally a matter of First House expression—it travels to no other house! The individual is the total personification of the nature of the ruling planet. Even more emphasis has to be given if the ruling planet in its own sign is conjunct the Ascendant and is also the *final dispositor* of the chart. Here the "secret ruler" will definitely not make a secret out of itself, of that you may be sure!

The above horoscope chart is of an actress who first came to the public's attention as a model and spokeswoman for beauty and cosmetic products, especially hair care products. She rose to stardom in the television series *Charlie's Angels.* Later in her career, Fawcett surprised many people with her fine performance as a battered woman in the film *The Burning Bed.*

The chart has Cancer rising with an exact conjunction of the Moon in Cancer on the Ascendant. Fawcett's Sun is in Aquarius with the Sun conjunct Mercury and trine Uranus in Gemini. Mercury and Uranus are in a very powerful and positive mutual reception. These three planets make a grand trine with Neptune in Libra. The airy emphasis of the chart shows that Fawcett would have no trouble reaching large numbers of people. The rulers of the Ninth (publishing) and Eleventh (advertising, communications to the general public) houses are Uranus and Mars respectively. Mars is in the Eighth House of residuals and royalties (Fawcett has made a fortune from her commercials and advertisements).

People who are strongly under the influence of Uranus tend to be so individualistic that they often stand out as symbols and examples for large numbers of people. That is the very special duality associated with Uranians. They are so much themselves that they function as representatives for others. Uranus is very well aspected in the Twelfth House, as it is trine both the natal (Mercury) and the natural (Neptune) rulers of this domicile. This position allows her to reach huge numbers of people and makes her very much a universal archetype of beauty. At one time, hundreds of millions of women wanted to look like Farrah Fawcett. She even married the perfect male archetype, Lee Majors, known more popularly as *The Six Million Dollar Man*. Neptune, ruler of cosmetics, hair, film, and glamour in general, is the ruler of her Tenth House of career and trine to both the Sun in Aquarius and its dispositor, Uranus, in Neptune's own house. This is a very potent combination of planetary energies and patterns, greatly strengthening the indications in the chart for stardom.

The Moon conjunct the Ascendant in Cancer allows Fawcett to be the embodiment of the glamorous woman with her creamy complexion and incredible hair (all Neptune/Moon indicators). The fact that the illusion of glamour would be embodied by her through her career is seen by the rulership of Neptune in Libra (giving an added "touch" of Venus) over her Tenth House. What is very interesting to the astrologer is the fact that Fawcett gained most respect for her talents and abilities (the Moon also rules the Second House) not as some hyper-commercialized, breathy Barbie Doll, but as the *least* glamorous of all female archetypes—the battered woman. In this role, she appeared without any makeup except for that which depicted her as swollen, broken, black and blue. In this respect, we can see how her Cancer Moon square Neptune and inconjunct Mars allows her to portray a woman at her most victimized and least beautiful. It was in this role that Fawcett's natural Uranian aptitude for embodying an archetype served in a most Aquarian and humanitarian way to bring the plight of such women out of the closet (Uranus in the Twelfth). Thus, Fawcett was able to take two of the most extreme facets of femaleness (the glamorous goddess and the battered victim) and project them both through the incredible potency of her personality (Moon in Cancer conjunct the Ascendant). It is very interesting, sad, and ironic to note that in 1998, Fawcett had her sometime-lover arrested for assault and battery. She had become her other, darker projected image.

The Final Dispositor and the Planetary Ruler

Let us at this point attempt to clarify the difference in weight between the final dispositor and the planetary ruler of the horoscope, if they are not one and the same. The planetary ruler and its position by sign and house will be the planetary energy that the individual tends to embody, project, and personify. A Venus-ruled person will always be the *embodiment* of Venus, ever seeking to balance his or her actions with those people who are the *object* of their self-projections. And in the case of the Venus-born, there will always be an object. A Jupiter-ruled person will always be the *personification* of Jupiter and will thus strive to enlarge upon the scope of his or her actions. A Saturn-ruled person as the embodiment and personification of this planet will continuously attempt to break free of boundaries or to project their personal limitations upon their environment, actions, and activities. In essence, issues of control will always dominate the life. Once the astrologer has determined the planetary ruler, it is then a simple matter of applying the keyword concepts of that planet to the activities and characteristics of the individual concerned.

The final dispositor is a planetary energy that *permeates* the horoscope. It is an energy that, like a thread in a loom, weaves its way up and down, in and out, of all actions and activities. Thus, if Mercury in

Gemini is the final dispositor, the need to communicate one's ideas will be the common thread found in every and all activities. The individual may not be the personification of Mercury. The individual may not be necessarily nervous, wiry, and exceptionally restless, as one would tend to be if Mercury were the ruler and conjoined the Ascendant (especially in an airy sign). This may be a person who is ruled by Jupiter and will thus seek to enhance, enlarge, and exaggerate his or her activities and personality traits, but *underneath* this more obvious and objective urge will be the mercurial theme of communication.

Assessing the Affinities Between the Ruler of the Horoscope and Its Dispositor

One of the most important factors involved in the correct and total delineation of the ruler of the horoscope is the nature of any geometric aspects between that planet and any other body. Of these considerations, the primary one is the presence of any aspect *between the ruler and its dispositor*. Thus, if Aries is rising (and there is no other planet conjunct the Ascendant), the ruler of the horoscope would be, of course, Mars. Let us say that in a given chart, Mars is in Gemini; then any aspect between Mars and Mercury would count as one of the first three considerations in judging the quality and effects of Mars upon the nativity.[4] In this case, you know that the intent and theme of the life of a chart with Aries rising is: the creation and exploration of new experiences that implement self-awareness, and the consequent testing of personal strengths and weaknesses that are essential to this process of self-development.

As Mars in this example is in Gemini, the mode of expression of the intent and theme would be through direct (Mars) and highly personal (Aries rising) ways of communication (Gemini). The individual would be very prone to express her opinions and ideas in such a manner that her thoughts would always "carry the day." Personal assertion, the urge to "make space" for the presence of the ego, would come through her efforts and particular means of communicating. Should Mercury be square Mars in Gemini, for example, these tendencies would be overly intensified. The individual would often find herself in the role of mediator and go-between, but her intentions would not be to link people for mutual benefit and creative compromise. This would be much more the case if Venus were in Gemini. This Mercury square Mars as ruler person is not primarily a diplomat (although she might effectuate such a role if Mercury were in Libra trine Mars and Venus were also positive and prominent in the chart). She travels between people and activates communication and interchange in order to convince others of *her* ideas, opinions, and concepts. We are dealing here, after all, with an Aries Ascendant!

Assessing the Effects of Other Aspecting Planets to the Ruler of the Horoscope

In assessing the effects of aspecting planets to the ruler of the horoscope, it is very important to pay attention to several factors:

1. Are the two planets compatible? Even though essentially antithetical planets can be modified into a compatible expression when linked by trine or sextile, some planets are much more at ease when they are combined with certain others. Even a trine between Venus and Saturn, for example, will not give relationships that are purely Venusian, i.e., romantic and free-flowing. Venus/Saturn combinations *always* bring responsibility, but the trine will make these responsibilities easier to handle or will result in some financial or social benefit. The Moon and Venus will always produce some form of kindly results in one's life and even a square between the two cannot prevent this from happening. Moon/Venus will bring sensual pleasure and romantic idealism, but the square can make such pleasure and idealism an impediment to assessing the true nature of the relationship at hand. The Moon square Venus does not like to be sensible, just sensuous![5]

2. What is the sign of the ruler's dispositor? Example: Capricorn rising, Saturn in Gemini (ruler), Mercury in Virgo (dispositor of the ruler).

3. Is the resulting combination of planets and signs essentially harmonious or inharmonious?

4. What is the nature of the aspect, if any, between the ruling planet and its dispositor: trine, sextile, square, etc.?

5. Should the dispositor of the ruler be in the ruler's sign, the significance of the dispositor is heightened and should be given more weight in the analysis of the horoscope. This factor will always produce a planetary mutual reception between the ruler of the horoscope and its dispositor. The nature of this mutual contact will be one of, if not *the*, dominating factors in the horoscope. Any aspect occurring between these two planets is of extreme importance. Examples: Libra rising with Venus in Cancer sextile the Moon in Taurus; Aquarius rising with Uranus in Libra trine Venus in Aquarius; Scorpio rising with Pluto in Sagittarius trine Jupiter in Aries; Capricorn rising with Saturn in Gemini inconjunct Mercury in Capricorn, etc.

6. If the dispositor of the ruler is in its own sign, the nature of that planet/sign combination will be a very potent force in life. Examples: Cancer rising, Moon in Gemini with Mercury in Virgo; Aries rising with Mars in Cancer and the Moon in Cancer; Libra rising with Venus in Scorpio and Mars in Aries.

7. If the dispositor of the ruler is conjunct this planet *in the same sign of the dispositor's rulership*, then the power of the ruler is diminished and the strength of the dispositor is increased. Returning to our earlier example of a chart with Aries rising, let us say that Mars in Gemini is found to be conjoined Mercury in that sign. Mercury's influence would definitely overpower Mars. The tendency of an Aries-rising individual is to move forward in a direct line until the object of personal projection or desire is won over and the goal is achieved. The focused and sequential one-pointedness of Mars is diminished in Gemini. The tendency here would be to move in at least two directions simultaneously. The nature would be very restless, the disposition nervous, with a tendency to jump to quick and impulsive conclusions based almost exclusively upon one's own data and information. Although fast reflexes and a lightning mind are some of the benefits of this conjunction, a narrowness of opinion and a tongue

Example 12: The Horoscope of Bill Clinton[6]

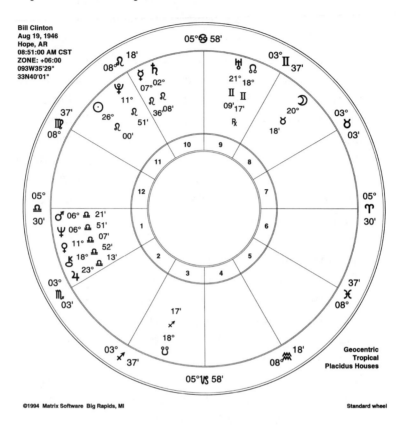

Bill Clinton
Aug 19, 1946
Hope, AR
08:51:00 AM CST
ZONE: +06:00
093W35'29"
33N40'01"

Geocentric
Tropical
Placidus Houses

©1994 Matrix Software Big Rapids, MI   Standard wheel

which can often be too sharp for its own good are some of the drawbacks.

The horoscope of President William Jefferson Clinton is filled with many examples of dispositorship and rulership factors that can serve to illustrate a number of previously mentioned points of delineation. As we seek out the potencies and powers in this chart, several factors immediately come into view.

The chart is dominated by two planets: Venus and the Sun. Venus is the ruler of the horoscope, as Libra rises and Venus is in that sign in the First House. Venus is also the dispositor of the huge First House stellium as well as the Moon in Taurus, the Midheaven, the Descendant, and the Southern Node. The Sun disposits all of the other planets and major points in the chart.

• Ascendant, Mars, Neptune, Venus, Chiron, Jupiter in Libra disposited by Venus in Libra; Moon in Taurus disposited by Venus in Libra; Descendant in Aries ruled by Mars, Mars in Libra disposited by Venus in Libra; Midheaven in Cancer ruled by the Moon in Taurus disposited by Venus in Libra; South Node in Sagittarius ruled by Jupiter in Libra disposited by Venus in Libra. Venus is in her own sign.

• Sun, Mercury, Saturn, and Pluto in Leo ruled by the Sun in Leo; Nadir in Capricorn ruled by Saturn disposited by the Sun in Leo; Uranus and the North Node in Gemini ruled by Mercury in Leo disposited by the Sun in Leo. The Sun is in his own sign.

Venus in Libra in the First House gives personal charisma and charm. The Sun in Leo in the Eleventh House gives the ability to connect with huge numbers of people and the placement of Pluto as well in that sign and house adds will and power in connection with political groups of powerful people (plutocrats!).[7] The combination of Venus and Leo as the two dominating forces of the chart enhances personal magnetism and makes it easy for Clinton to bring large numbers of people into his personal sphere of influence.

Mars and Neptune are conjoined the Ascendant. The combination of these two planets is often indicative of sexual complexities and difficulties in a person's life, as it does not allow for a sense of clear boundaries in terms of the use of personal sexual energy. As Libra (partnership) is the predominant sign (along with Leo, the sign of romance, lovers, and pleasure), it is no wonder that Clinton has suffered from various forms of relationship and sexual addictions. As if the placement of Mars, Neptune, and Venus were not enough to bring about such challenges, we should also take a look at the placement of the Moon.

The Moon is in Taurus in the Eighth and the only aspects to the Moon are a square to the Sun and Pluto in Leo and an inconjunction to Jupiter in Libra. In addition to relationship factors, Venus is also one of the major significators of money in a horoscope. The Moon in Taurus (personal resources) is in the Eighth House (other people's money) and is disposited by Venus in Libra. Scorpio is on the cusp of the Second

House of money and its rulers, Mars and Pluto, are afflicting both of these financial significators. Mars does this through its placement in the sign of its detriment, Libra, and by its conjunction with Neptune and Venus. This is not a "tidy" conjunction. It does not allow for clarity in any area of major concern to Venus (the dispositor of the conjunction): romance, money, and here especially, Clinton's self-worth. It is easy to see how Clinton's self-worth is inexorably tied up to his complicated relationships with women and the dynamics of his sexual addiction. The Moon in Taurus/Jupiter in Libra inconjunction is disposited by Venus. This interplay of planetary forces leads to a love of pleasure, sensuality, and luxury. It also contributes to an exaggeration of the qualities of the Moon in this chart, in this case, an incessant insecurity where women are concerned in Clinton's life. I need only mention in passing that as a boy, Clinton received a very mixed message about the nature of women, sexuality, power, and abuse. Pluto is square the Moon and through this placement is drawn even closer to the Sun.[8] This particular combination of Pluto/Sun/Moon is very challenging and leads to an obsession for personal power as well as strong compulsive impulses regarding women. As the tone of the chart is clearly dominated by the Venus/Neptune/Mars conjunction on the Ascendant in Libra, we should not be surprised about the scandals concerning the personal history of Clinton's private sexual life. The fact that women figure prominently in terms of the difficulties that he has had in his financial scandals is also revealed through this chart. (The American moral code sees financial misconduct as being less immoral than sexual indiscretions; thus financial misconduct usually results in less publicity and milder punishments. The reverse is true in Asia and Europe.)

From the psychological perspective, we can see the compulsion toward women and finances from the position of the Moon. She basically stands alone, without support from the other planets. The emotional message to Clinton from the Moon's position is: "You can never have enough!" (And a Taurus Moon is certainly concerned with substance, form, and quantity.) This lunar message is due to the difficulty that the Moon has in containing and sustaining Clinton's sense of identity, stamina, and well-being (the position of the Sun in Leo). Pluto and the Sun result in a tremendous urge for power, procreation, and self-expression. The Moon's job in any horoscope is to bring form and psychological support to one's efforts at creative self-expression. In effect, this is the archetypal mother's role in a person's life. The Moon in Clinton's chart gives strong women: his mother, Hillary, Jennifer, and certainly Monica, but Clinton's inner woman, his inner mother, his anima, in effect, gives him the message that he will not be supported (Moon square Pluto) or that such support will come only at the risk of giving himself away totally (Pluto/Moon/Sun and the fear of death).

From the point of view of astrological analysis, it may be difficult to determine if the Mars/Neptune conjunction is the ruler of the horoscope (as it stands within a degree from exactitude to the point of the Ascendant), or is Venus the ruler (as she is the dispositor of the Libra stellium in the First House and is in the First herself). They are both powerful influences and each is made even stronger by the sextile from Mercury to Mars/Neptune and the sextile from Pluto to Venus. The fact that sexual scandal would (almost) topple Clinton from office (destruction) is seen from Mars/Neptune *and* Venus square to the Midheaven, the point of personal achievement and position in a natal chart. Only the sustaining and regenerative power of Pluto/Sun/Moon in the fixed signs has kept him from total annihilation.

Returning to the question of the ruler of the chart, my sense is to go with Venus, as she stands potently behind Mars and Neptune (as well as disposits the Moon), and dominates the Sun in her influence on Clinton's life. Although Venus is not the final dispositor in this chart (there can be no final dispositor here as the Sun is also in its own sign), she is the ruler of the Ascendant and the dispositor of the Mars/Neptune conjunction. As she is in her own sign, she disposits herself. Venus also receives a "wounding" conjunction from Chiron, who is also inconjunct the Venus-ruled Moon. One can only hope that Clinton's wound is healed in time and that he himself can use the potential of his Eleventh House Leo heart, to help humanity move forward.

1. Data source: Rodden, Lois M., op. cit., p. 28.
2. This approach to astrology is found in the author's book, *Soul-Centered Astrology*, op. cit.
3. Data source: Rodden, Lois M., op. cit., p. 316.
4. The other two prime factors of consideration were discussed in the previous chapter: the sign and house positions of the ruler.
5. A more detailed discussion of planetary compatibilities is found at the end of this chapter.
6. Source: Private authority that confirms the author's own research data material.
7. In esoteric, soul-centered astrology, the qualities of the First Ray (Will/Power) are ascribed to the influence of Pluto. The astrology student can gain a great deal in his or her appreciation of the fundamental energetics of the planets and signs by becoming aware of the Ray dynamics that are also an inherent part of their makeup. For further research into the Seven Rays as they relate to human psychology, please refer to *Esoteric Psychology*, Vols. I and II, *Esoteric Astrology* (Alice A. Bailey, The Lucis Trust, Pub.), as well as the author's previous work, *Soul-Centered Astrology* (The Crossing Press, Pub.).
8. At first view, some astrologers may not allow for the square between the Moon and Pluto, thinking that it is too wide. But look again! The orb is only 8.28°, well within a 9–10° standard orb for squares between Moon and any other planet (a 10–11° orb is allowable for a natal conjunction, square, opposition, or trine between the Sun and the Moon). There is also a very important and ancient technique of planetary affinity in bringing planetary influences together. This is called "translation of the light." Translation occurs if there are three planets, two of which are out of orb for a major aspect, but the third is in aspect to the other two. In this case, Pluto and the Sun are too wide to be in conjunction (they are some 14° apart), but both the Sun and Pluto receive squares from the Moon. As this is the case (and the Sun is the *dispositor* of Pluto), one can say as I have in the above passage, that Pluto "is drawn closer to the Sun."

Summary of Rulership
and Planetary Compatibilities[1]

The following is a brief list of comments highlighting the most important effects of each of the planets especially *when functioning as the ruler of the chart* in relation to the other planets in a given nativity. There is a major principle that the astrology student must keep in the forefront of his or her analysis in this respect, as this will apply to all the planetary rulers:

When any of the signs rise, the character of the nativity will be highly affected by the quality of contact *of the closest major aspect from any of the other planets to the planetary ruler of that sign.* Let us say that Cancer is rising and the Moon is in Pisces with an exact conjunction to Venus. This Moon/Venus contact will greatly color the direction and attitude to life. This is even more clearly delineated (and this should be well noted by the astrologer) *if there is a potent contact between the ruling planet and its own dispositor.* Thus, if Leo rises and the Sun is in Capricorn square Saturn in Aries, this Sun/Saturn aspect will definitely dominate the natus. Should Scorpio rise in the chart, for example, and Pluto is in Virgo trine to Mercury in Taurus, this trine will be a primary vehicle for the expression of the native's personality. Look for it to govern over many other features of the horoscope. If you can find the major threads of the chart, the horoscope will reveal the hand of the Weaver.

Leo Rising (Sun as Ruler)

The function of the Sun is to energize and vitalize any planet that it disposits. What is important for us to note here is that when Leo rises the Sun sign will play an exceptionally important role in the horoscope.

The astrologer should observe the nature of the elements and qualities of the signs involved in the pairing of the Sun and rising signs, assessing the level of their compatibility. Also take note that if this is a "Double Leo" chart (Sun and Ascendant in Leo), is the Sun in the First or the Twelfth House? The former will tend to produce a roaring "King" (or at least a person with aspirations and pretensions to such a position), while the latter yields a Lion who prefers to rule while remaining more quietly in his den.[2]

In general, when in harmonious aspects to the other planets, the Sun as ruler is usually a good influence, giving life and strength. But should the Sun be in an inharmonious aspect with any of the other planets, the tendency is to "over-vitalize" the other body, and its effects on the horoscope then will be too strong.

Sun/Moon: The Moon can shine much more brightly and one's emotional nature will consequently be enlivened when the rays of the Sun fall harmoniously upon the lunar surface. The square or opposition of the Moon to the Sun can strongly diminish the ability of an individual to find the magnetic energy needed to bind and hold the solar creative drive. Thus, when there are positive aspects between the Sun and Moon, the individual can give formation and sustaining power to his or her creations. The opposite is true when the Sun and Moon are in inharmonious aspects. A Leo-ruled person is always involved with the focus of his or her creative drive. If this is supported by the Moon, the Lion is much more apt to feel nurtured and accepted by life. But when the Moon challenges the light of the Sun, the Lion struggles in a world that is not particularly safe psychologically or supportive creatively.

Sun/Mercury: When the Sun is too close to Mercury (and they can never be more than 28° apart), it overstimulates the mind, creating a false concept that what the person thinks, is *who he is*. The sense of self, then, is seen to identify with the mind and there is little conscious separation between a person's mental activities and the intrinsic nature of that self. A good rule to follow is the further away Mercury is from the Sun, the more objective one's thinking process is likely to be.

Sun/Venus: As the point of greatest elongation between the Sun and Venus is 48°, there can be no major aspect between these two bodies other than the conjunction. Yet Venus loves to be bathed in sunlight and the conjunction to the Sun in any of the signs will lend a magnetic, charming, and artistic nature to the Leo personality. The semi-sextile (30°) between the two is helpful in harmonizing interpersonal relationships, adding a positive touch of the "muse" to one's character. The semi-square (45°) can lead to too much pleasure seeking and the need to conform one's relationships to one's inner ideals and personal values.

Sun/Mars: Some planets may overreact from the solar rays, no matter if the aspect is harmonious or otherwise. Mars may be too strong when in trine to an Aries or Sagittarius Sun, becoming too assertive, but has less chance to go into overdrive when in sextile from the Sun in Gemini or Libra. Mars conjunct the Sun in Leo as the ruler can be too overwhelming an influence for other people to handle peacefully, or at least passively, unless the energy from the Sun is "Soular," as the light of the personality can be too bright. This will inevitably force the more sensitive and conscious among us to leave the room and take shelter from the dominating fiery ego (unless of course we are dealing with that huge number of unconscious beings who love to bathe in the maya of other people's stardom).

Sun/Jupiter: Essentially, Jupiter and the Sun work very well together, adding creative potency and robust health to one's nature. Even a square or an opposition will not thwart the basic optimism that comes when these two planets are joined by aspect and/or dispositorship. Yet a strong Sun/Jupiter combination can give the tendency to overexaggerate self-importance and underestimate the abilities or capabilities of others. This would be especially the case when Leo rises in the chart and/or the Sun and Jupiter are strongly connected through Leo, Aries, Sagittarius, or Capricorn.

Sun/Saturn: An otherwise gloomy Saturn will perk up considerably with a nice, healthy trine from the Sun as ruler of the chart. But Saturn conjoined, square, or opposing the Sun, for example, diminishes the potency of the Sun's vitality and opens a person to fretful pessimism as well as an incessant unhealthy urge to control life's circumstances. This is strongly underscored should the Sun be the ruler of the chart.

Sun/Uranus: Uranus and the Sun add will (or willfulness!) to the personality. The need to express one's creativity and sense of self in unusual ways is enhanced with the harmonious aspects. Less than successful results occur when the aspect in question is of an inharmonious nature. Remember that Leo rising likes to shine and should the Sun be in a strong aspect to Uranus, this sunlight will be very unique in nature. The challenge here is always one of how a Sun-ruled individual can integrate his or her creative self-expression within a larger social context (Uranus/Aquarius) without necessarily ruling that social context.

Sun/Neptune: Depending on the nature of the contact, the Sun either will add more fuel to Neptune's glamour, self-denial, and illusions, or burn away the elusive veil, leaving true compassion and love. Sometimes Neptune in strong aspect to a ruling Sun can void the sense of personal identity, giving rise to either a psychologically troubled person or one who has contact with all of life, without any personality boundaries. A complex situation arises, for example, if one has Leo rising and Sun conjunct Neptune in Libra. Here we have a constant leonine theme of "I am the emperor and lord and seek to be recognized as such," right alongside the incessant urge to melt or diffuse personal identity within the context of intimate relationships. This would be modified by the Lion rising with Neptune conjunct the Sun in Sagittarius—then the urge would be to personify and totally melt into some idealistic ideology or spiritual path. Neptune in Scorpio square an Aquarius Sun-ruled chart would tend toward the urge to transform a facet of the collective, drastically altering the social patterns and activities into which one was born. This could give rise to a form of political martyrdom when expressed in the extreme, or it may be merely the need to find a place in society in which one could offer oneself through service. As in all these examples, much depends on the other factors in the chart, especially *the position of the dispositor of the chart ruler.*

Sun/Pluto: The Pluto in Leo generation (1938–1957) is composed of a group of people who have the tendency to renew and "reinvent" themselves through the focus of their creativity. This would be the case especially for those people in that generation born with Scorpio rising. The Sun as the dispositor of Pluto in Leo gives power and intense regenerative and restorative abilities. This power can be abused, denied, or inverted when Pluto and the Sun are inharmoniously configured. It is very common to find people in the Pluto in Leo generation with Pluto square, opposed, or even conjunct the Sun who continuously repeat non-regenerative patterns of creative self-expression.

The most challenging scenario in this case would be found in the following *line of energy*: Scorpio rising, Pluto in Leo, Sun in Scorpio square Pluto in Leo. People who have this configuration in their horoscopes tend to enter into very deep battles with themselves. Their inner struggles are based on repetitive and non-regenerative activities. The tensions build up to a point that eventually leads to a crisis of transformation. But instead of "dying" and allowing the transformation to take place, they insist on doing the same thing once again. This results in yet another crisis of the same quality, diminishing vitality and inhibiting evolutionary growth. In this case, it is a question of the alignment of the will of the personality with the intent of the soul, or higher self. The fact that these aspects occur in fixed signs only makes the transcendence of this conflict more difficult. It does, however, make the results of the successful overcoming of such a conflict that much more powerfully rewarding.

A nativity with Leo rising and the Sun in Scorpio conjoined Pluto in Scorpio (very frequently found in Scorpio births between 1984 and 1995), yields a person whose need to dominate and transform others according to his or her personal desires will be amazingly strong. One should note that in this planetary pattern, the dispositor of the Sun in Scorpio as the ruling planet (Leo rising) is Pluto in its own sign. It will be very interesting to see how this coming generation uses or abuses its power. We already know through the frequent and horrifying American middle and high school murders, that this is a generation that has to confront death in a most brutal and imminent manner. They will require both the generations before and after them to look at death and the instruments of death (handguns, for example) in a new way.

Cancer Rising (Moon as the Ruler)

The function of the Moon is to bring *formation, cohesion,* and *emotional/instinctual awareness* to any planet that it disposits. When the

Moon as ruler of the chart is in aspect to any of the other planets, *especially to its dispositor*,[3] the effects highly personalize the nature of the planet with which the Moon is in aspect. This is especially the case if, in addition to the Ascendant being in Cancer, the Moon is also in this sign, or the planet aspected by the Moon is in Cancer. The tendency is to use the energy of the planet in question either in its most subconscious or personality-centered sense. In effect, the energy of that planet will be functioning at its most subjective/unconscious level. Let us say that Cancer rises in the horoscope and the Moon is in Gemini square to Mercury in Virgo. In this scenario, the individual in question tends to create highly self-protective methods of communication. Relating, especially in terms of work-oriented relationships (Virgo), would be uniquely reflective of that individual's subjective views and opinions (Gemini). Naturally, as the level of consciousness develops into a more objective focus, such subjective, self-centered patterns of communication would also develop and mature.

Moon/Sun: In a Cancer-ruled chart, if the Sun is in major aspect to the Moon, motivation for one's creative self-expression and lifeforce is stimulated, or can be totally dominated, by the early psychological conditioning of the native. This would be the case, for example, if the Moon was in Capricorn as the ruling planet. Here the urge for personal security could easily obscure the creative potentials available in the present moment. This would be especially so if the Moon in Capricorn was afflicted by an aspect to Saturn in a Cancer-rising chart. The nature of this theoretical person's past history and biological karma could diminish the ability to objectify the present moment without projecting his past conditioning. The Capricorn influence instinctively leads one to structure the *present* in terms of the *conditioning factors of the past.*

Moon/Mercury: Mercury and the Moon work well together when harmoniously configured. This combination not only can add a highly imaginative quality to memory (especially when in the air and water signs), but also lends compassion and understanding through the written and spoken word (especially if in the water and earth signs). When Mercury and the ruling Moon are in square or opposition, there is some difficulty aligning and synthesizing the emotional and mental aspects of the personality. In this case, a duality occurs in the personality, as the individual ever seeks to rationalize his emotions or tries to give emotional support to his thoughts. This dilemma is certain to be exaggerated if the Moon and/or Mercury is in one of the mutable signs or in Libra.

Moon/Venus: Venus and the Moon are usually quite compatible, as they give the urge for both material and emotional comfort. This tendency would be emphasized should either or both of these bodies be in the earthy or watery signs. The emotional dynamics of life, of course, are always prominent with Cancer on the Ascendant. Moon/Venus contacts always give personal magnetism, as well as a sincere, profound urge for intimacy in relationships. Difficulties that may come about when these two are in square or opposition arise from an imbalance in the dynamics of nurturing that are in any close relationship. The individual might choose partners who are not capable of giving the type of emotional support the Moon-ruled person requires. Also, some people with difficult aspects between Venus and the Moon (especially if one or both of these planets is found in Scorpio, Aries, or Capricorn) are not capable of giving others the type of emotional or material support and comfort that *they* need.

Moon/Mars: Mars and the Moon are not usually compatible. While the Moon seeks to retain, sustain, and contain the emotional and physical forms of life, Mars endeavors to project and create new opportunities for the expression of the personality. A Cancer-rising chart is concerned with the creation of situations that sustain, maintain, or support the past, or at the very least, the status quo of one's life. Mars, when positive in a nativity, is an influence that tends to push life forward into new directions. This movement into new avenues of experience is not in keeping with the nature of the Moon, especially in a Cancer-dominated chart, which is a far more conservative influence.

Therefore, aspects between these two bodies tend to create anxiety unless they are well aspected, and in the horoscope of an emotionally mature individual. If that is the case, Mars opens the door for the Moon to embrace new situations that are in keeping with what *has already been established as a safety zone* of expression for the individual. A trine or a sextile between Mars and the Moon, especially in earth signs, gives an increase in the formative abilities of a Cancer-rising chart. The

Moon is the "glue" that attracts form to any creative impulse. If she is in an earth sign, this ability to manifest ideas and emotions into physical form is increased. Mars stimulates and accelerates this process. Thus the individual can enter into new experiences and formulate the circumstances of such experiences into shapes that support that person's sense of what is or will be, safe and secure. The Cancer-ruled person is consistently at work creating those situations in life that are protective and supportive. Challenging aspects between Mars and the Moon *abort and sever* life situations and emotional contacts, inhibiting such goals from taking place.

Moon/Jupiter: The Moon and Jupiter are essentially compatible influences because Jupiter is exalted in Cancer, the Moon's natural sign. When Cancer rises in the chart with the Moon in either Sagittarius or Pisces, and in harmonious aspect to Jupiter, the individual tends to be fortunate in terms of the house positions of both these planets. Expansion and well-being results from the person's ability to embrace himself and, therefore, life in general. One cannot correctly nurture and support others if one does not know how to do this for one's own self. Benefits come to a Moon-ruled horoscope when the individual is inclusive of others and compassionate toward them. In effect, the world then becomes one's family. This is one of the primary reasons why Jupiter's exaltation in the Moon's sign is so auspicious. Difficult aspects between these two bodies lead to an exaggeration of personal needs and excessive emotional responses to the most ordinary situations in life. This often manifests in a personality that displays too much caring and concern over one's (and others') emotional security with a tendency to exaggerate the importance of most events. Disappointments tend to follow when emotional situations are over-dramatized.

Moon/Saturn: Saturn and the Moon are both complementary as well as antithetical in their significance. In a Cancer-ruled chart, any major aspect between the Moon and Saturn leads to an extraordinary preoccupation with security issues. If the Moon is in a mutable sign, and in a challenging aspect to Saturn (including the conjunction), fretting about the smallest details of life is an integral part of the personality. When in fixed signs, there often is an obsession about gaining mother's love and support. This is infused into one's way of being a woman/mother or into the relationships one has with women in general, regardless of the individual's gender.

When in the cardinal signs, Moon/Saturn afflictions become the driving force behind all emotional encounters. Hard aspects between the Moon and Saturn frequently indicate a person who is highly insecure and thus can be quite manipulative and controlling. When in trine or sextile, the individual is more able to learn from past experiences and thus more capable of structuring events, circumstances, and resources into forms that support and aid his or her security. Very often, family help is forthcoming, which is certainly not the case when these two bodies are in square or opposition. One exception: if the family of a Moon-Saturn person holds him in "financial ransom," or economic dependency, this security is very emotionally costly. There is certainly no "free lunch" when Saturn and the Moon collide in a Cancer-ruled chart, even if there is a lot of food to go around!

Moon/Uranus: We come to another pair of fundamentally incompatible influences, especially in a Cancer-dominated chart—the Moon and Uranus. The Moon, unless found in Aquarius or Sagittarius, is normally conventional. She wants to preserve, not innovate. Uranus, of course, is the most original and innovative of planetary influences, doing all it can to initiate the birth of new experiences and archetypes of relationships into an individual's life. A Cancer-rising, Moon-ruled person is far removed from this freedom-oriented experience. A Moon person is the type of individual who is most satisfied and secure by eating the same food that mama used to make. She is definitely not prone to trotting off to try the latest in south Bolivian or north Mongolian cuisine (unless mama were from either of these two countries).

A true Uranian, of course, is just the opposite. He is the kind of person who brought those original menu delights to New Jersey in the first place!

The Moon is incredibly sentimental, Uranus is definitely not. The Moon is instinctive, while Uranus is intuitive. The Moon is intimate, while Uranus is impersonal. The Moon holds and preserves, Uranus abandons the past and opens the door to a very unpredictable future. Although this combination of planets may work much better in an Aries-ruled chart, they are certainly challenging to a Cancer-ruled one. One of the benefits of this combination, however, is that it does add a breath of objective vision to the Moon's sensitivity, removing the individual from home and into a wider and far more exciting world. When harmoniously activated in the horoscope of an emotionally mature individual, Moon/Uranus aspects allow him or her to explore a great many relationship possibilities and open the door to more variety in friendships—certainly some interesting ones will come to the open-minded Moon/Uranus person!

Moon/Neptune: Like Jupiter, Neptune is also exalted in Cancer. Therefore, positive aspects between the Moon and Neptune tend to be very supportive of a deep and gratifying emotional life. But this is the case only when an individual has achieved some level of emotional growth and spiritual development. Such contacts can stimulate the urge to be helpful to poor and less fortunate members of the human family. It leads one to seek out the disenfranchised and the oppressed, bring comfort, succor, and spiritual upliftment. At the very least, it indicates an unprejudiced, protective, and universal approach to others. The difficult aspects between the Moon and Neptune, especially when Cancer rises, speak about a mother who was emotionally wounded. It can indicate alcoholism or other forms of drug addiction in one's family. As an adult, the individual has a difficult time with emotional boundaries, being unsure how far one's feelings extend or how deep one's emotional involvement should be in most relationships.

Moon/Pluto: Pluto with the Moon tends to intensify all emotions and emotional situations. Pluto conjunct the Moon in Leo in a Cancer-ruled chart, for example, indicates a person who overly dramatizes and exaggerates the importance of his or her feelings. Pluto in Cancer trine to the Moon in Scorpio can be highly effective in eliminating any opposition to one's sense of personal safety and security, although in the emotionally mature and spiritually evolved, this same aspect is a potent tool for healing. Cancer rising with the Moon conjunct Pluto in Sagittarius opposing Saturn in Gemini can reveal a strong need to overthrow and transform one's family religious or philosophical beliefs before evolving one's own way of walking the spiritual path. In all and every instance where Pluto and the Moon meet in a Cancer-ruled horoscope, the past must be incorporated into some large frame of reference. The process of individuation may thus continue beyond the context of the individual's psychological and physical inheritance—his or her "biological karma." If such an effort at personal regeneration does not occur, the individual becomes even further entrenched in old family patterns.

Gemini or Virgo Rising (Mercury as Ruler)

If the Twins rise, the function of Mercury as the ruler of the horoscope is directly linked to the communication of ideas, thoughts, and opinions. There is also a need to be a liaison, a link between people and their ideas, or to bring people together as a result of one's own personal knowledge and views of life. The latter would be especially the case should Gemini be rising with Mercury in Libra. If Virgo is rising, then Mercury is less concerned with communication for communication's sake, but is more involved with finding a practical form and outlet for one's ideas. Work will definitely dominate the life, and relationships are viewed as they relate primarily to the individual's ability to get things done.

Mercury/Sun: The Sun with Mercury as the chart ruler stimulates and adds energy to the mental potency of an individual who has a sign ruled by Mercury on the Ascendant. Unless the Sun and Mercury are too close together, say a conjunction of less than 5°, the solar force supports the individual's drive towards establishing his or her social and/or practical relationships and goals. If the conjunction between these bodies is too tight, and especially if this conjunction occurs in one of the fire or air signs, the mental nature tends to become overactive, adding a definite nervousness to the person's general character.

Mercury/Moon: In a Mercury-ruled horoscope, the primary orientation to life is mental. The Moon adds magnetism to Mercury and the thinking process. When these two planets are in harmony, the individual is helped to put his or her thoughts together in ways that add support to the individual's plans, goals, or basic urge to communicate. When in hard aspect, there is often confusion between what is thought and what is felt. If Virgo is the ruling sign, for example, and Mercury is in Taurus trine the Moon in Capricorn, it would be fairly easy and quite natural for the individual to organize and structure his or her resources into successful work-related projects. Gemini rising with Mercury in

Aquarius and the Moon in Libra would facilitate the process of coming together with like-minded groups to advance and circulate one's own social agenda, ideas, and concepts.

Mercury/Venus: Positive aspects between Mercury and Venus when either of Mercury's signs rise (or the mutual reception of Mercury in Libra and Venus in Virgo, for example) add to artistic talents and an ability to bring harmony (Venus) and verbal content (Mercury) together into esthetically pleasing packages. This combination also contributes to being able to bring other people together in some mutually beneficial commercial or artistic venture. Very often, harmonious contacts between Venus and Mercury add graciousness to speech and social interactions. The only inharmonious geometric contact that can occur between these two is the semi-square. Should this be the case, the individual has to learn how to blend, integrate, or communicate his ideas more effectively into proper social or work-related contexts. In any event, this should not be a major challenge to one's life.

Mercury/Mars: These two planets can work quite well together if they are harmoniously configured with one another. If Gemini rises and Mercury is trine Mars, a boost is given to the individual's ability to be direct, rather than diffused in her efforts at communication. If Virgo rises and there is a trine between Mercury and Mars, the ability for the individual to grasp and quickly synthesize the circumstances in his environment—especially the working environment—meets with success. The conjunction between these two bodies can make one's movements too quick and jumpy, while the opposition and especially the square, lead to a snappy tongue and a tendency to premature and ill-conceived judgment. If Virgo dominates and these two planets are in difficult aspect, there can be a tendency to try to dominate all work-related situations, while being dissatisfied with the results of one's own efforts. Harmonious aspects between Mercury and Mars with Virgo on the Ascendant will often lead to precision and accuracy as well as the ability to focus the mind on the challenge at hand.

Mercury/Jupiter: If Gemini dominates a horoscope with aspects between Jupiter and Mercury, look for an individual who is always on the move, one who is a natural-born traveler, teacher, and communicator. Should these aspects be inharmonious, then planes are missed, trains are stalled, and cars tend to break down, thus inhibiting such movements. Stalled travel plans are the result of afflictions between these two bodies in the fixed signs. A person tends to make too many conflicting travel plans when Mercury and Jupiter square or oppose one another in the mutable signs. When Jupiter or Mercury find themselves afflicted in the cardinal signs, one is challenged through one's *motivations* for traveling, teaching, or communicating. When Virgo rises, all the above-mentioned mercurial dynamics are geared towards practical aims. These goals can be successfully accomplished when the contacts between the two are harmonious or, conversely, can be thwarted in design, execution, or their results, when in mutual affliction. In all cases, when either of the signs of Mercury rise and Jupiter is in major aspect with the ruler, Mercury, one must widen one's mental horizon through either work (Virgo) or through more direct intellectual means (Gemini).

Mercury/Saturn: These two planets are natural "friends." In soul-centered astrology, we see Saturn as the ruler of the mental plane, influencing the entire structure of the mind and all its faculties. Mercury is viewed as the communicator between various facets of the mind. Metaphorically, we could say that Saturn is the entire beehive while Mercury represents all the interchanges, contacts, and communications between the individual members and classes of the bees themselves. Saturn, in this respect, gives the overall structure and purpose of the hive while Mercury carries out this purpose. This more practical application of the contact between these two planets would be more in evidence should Virgo rise and Mercury and Saturn be in the earthy signs. With the Twins on the Ascendant and harmonious aspects between these two planets, look for a person gifted in design, drafting, and architecture. This architectural orientation could also extrapolate into social planning or the design of a business enterprise. Difficult aspects between Mercury and Saturn, especially in a Virgo or Gemini chart, lead to overanalysis, confusion between the purpose of an idea and the communication of that idea, or to a mind that tends to think pessimistically.

Mercury/Uranus: When Uranus is in harmonious aspect to Mercury and Gemini is rising in the chart, the individual can be gifted with a quick, intuitive mind. The ability to grasp many facts at one time along with the capacity to categorize such data into logical sequences is high, aiding one immeasurably to communicate with many types of people on a variety of subjects. Similarly, the mental process tends to be inventive and original. When spiritually developed, the individual with such a placement can use her mental faculties for the benefit of society. When Mercury and Uranus are afflicted with Gemini rising, especially if either or both of these planets find themselves in the mutable or airy signs, there is a tendency to be nervous and jumpy. This jumpiness can result in a conflict in which intuition and logic are all ajumble. Then the individual can formulate all the right reasons, only to arrive at the wrong conclusion! When Virgo rises and/or these planets are in the earthy signs, mistakes are more likely to be made in methodologies, processes, and techniques. There can be too much experimentation with too little practical result.

Mercury/Neptune: One of the most antithetical planetary contacts takes place when Neptune is in aspect with Mercury. Even the harmonious placement of these two bodies may lead to idealistic (Neptune) rather than logical thinking (Gemini), or a lazy and "otherworldly" attitude to work (Virgo). At their best, Neptune and Mercury work well together in certain forms of laboratory research or other kinds of healing-related endeavors (Virgo), or in the artistic realm as the creation of novels, poems, as well as in psychological counseling (Gemini). Mercury requires logic and precision to perform at his best and Neptune is not a planetary power that supports such qualities. The dream state is often much more of a reality than the waking one when these two planets collide. Check for muddled thinking and action (or certainly *evasive* action), when Neptune afflicts Mercury with Gemini or Virgo rising. On the personality level, the avoidance of telling (or even *seeing*) the truth is a frequent characteristic. It is very difficult for such an individual to walk a straight line or to think in a logical manner. This does not mean that this person is mentally deficient; it just means that a logical sequence of thought or activity should not be expected. Sometimes, a Neptune/Mercury person can be a great illuminator of spiritual truths, but in the spiritually immature, such a planetary contact often leads to spiritual self-deceit.

Mercury/Pluto: This combination of planetary influences creates a bond that deepens the mind, making it more penetrative. Yet when afflicted, especially if either of these planets are in Scorpio, Pisces, or Cancer, suspiciousness and jealousy may easily result. I like to think of a person with this combination has having a "spy mentality." The tendency is to look deeply into a subject or a person and perceive any and all hidden factors in the situation or the relationship. This is the Gemini-rising individual who says, "You are not telling me everything you know." It is the Virgo-rising person who states, "You are holding back from doing your best in this situation—I know you have more to offer!" When afflicted, Mercury and Pluto create a mind that is overly suspicious, and when taken to the extreme, paranoid (this would be especially true if Neptune were also involved in this planetary combination). When harmoniously configured, especially if Virgo rises or Mercury or Pluto is in that sign, no little detail escapes the eye.

Taurus or Libra Rising (Venus as Ruler)

Venus is representative of what is magnetic or attractive about a person. When in Taurus, she magnetizes and attracts form and material abundance, whereas in Libra she performs her function in the realm of relationships. In both cases, Venus will add a sense of aesthetics and a love of the beautiful, or deny this sense if debilitated. An individual with a Taurus-ruled chart is therefore more conscious of the material facets of life than if the chart is ruled by Libra. If Libra is rising, the life then is centered on one's social contacts and the externalization of one's ideals of attractiveness.

Venus/Sun: The Sun with Venus adds vitality and personal magnetism to an individual's general character. The Sun conjunct to Venus in a Libra-ruled chart (especially if that conjunction also takes place in Libra), indicates idealization of relationship and a certain degree of narcissism (the latter is also present if the conjunction is in Aries or Leo). In a Taurus-ruled chart or, if the conjunction takes place in that sign with a Venus-ruled sign on the Ascendant, this can result in an extreme sense of self-righteousness. The individual with this placement would be unusually attached to his or her sense of personal values and self-worth. All human beings are attached to their values, but the degree of intensity of this connection is emphasized in Taurus, a fixed sign that personifies self-worth, especially when expressed through money and material forms. In all cases with the Sun and Venus intimately linked, the love of the arts will be a dominant factor in the life.

Venus/Moon: In a Libra-dominated horoscope, the Moon's aspects to Venus add an instinctual, gut feeling about relationships. An individual with a Venus/Moon aspect in a Venus-ruled chart has a definite "feeling" about people, giving instant likes and dislikes, attractions and repulsions, and a sense of safety or danger concerning relationships. In Taurus, the Moon helps with the formative dynamics of attractiveness, and depending on the nature of the aspect, makes it that much easier or difficult to attract money and material support. Thus, if Taurus rises and Venus is in Capricorn trine the Moon in Taurus, it will be relatively easy for the individual to build capital or to find himself in relationships with people who are economically supportive. Should Venus be in Capricorn in opposition to the Moon in Cancer, the need for financial security will dominate one's orientation to relationships, often leading to poor choices which threaten the very same security one is seeking to build. This would be further emphasized if Neptune were conjoined or square to either of these planets.

Venus/Mercury: These two planets are usually friendly with one another. See the explanations given about these two bodies under the previous heading, "Gemini or Virgo rising." When Libra rises, this combination of influences will aid in the ease and grace of one's social interchanges. Should Taurus rise, the conjunction or sextile between Mercury and Venus will more easily allow the individual to picture her ideas as they may result in form. This adds discrimination, precision, and practicality to one's creative endeavors as well as balance and beauty to their eventual outcome.

Venus/Mars: When these two planets are combined, they increase the focus on the libido. This especially is the case when any of the four signs ruled by these two planets (Aries, Scorpio, Taurus, and Libra) are on the Ascendant (see the next heading, "Aries or Scorpio rising," for additional comments about Mars). A Taurus-ruled chart with Venus in positive aspect to Mars gives drive for the successful attainment of material or sexual goals. This same drive exists when in square or opposition, but the urge for financial or sexual encounters may be over-stimulating, creating an imbalance or even obsessiveness. The conjunction of these two planets in any sign tends to intensify the sex drive and if in inharmonious contact with Uranus or Neptune, for example, can lead to irregular or compulsive sexual activity. The square or opposition from Saturn to this conjunction indicates sexual frustration, or the thwarting of financial objectives. The intensity of one's sexual or financial desires remains the same, but the outcome leaves much to be desired. These indications are basically the same for a Libra-ruled horoscope as they are for a Taurus-ruled one, but the orientation of the energies of Mars and Venus is geared to the relationship factors of life. Afflictions from Neptune to Mars and Venus in this sense lead to addictive behavior in relationship and romance, giving the tendency to deceive oneself or to be deceived by others with whom one is in intimate contact.

Venus/Jupiter: This planetary combination leads to fun and good times. When in mutual, positive aspect, hedonism reigns. If Taurus predominates as the ruling sign, look for a trine or sextile between Venus and Jupiter to increase the possibilities of material abundance as well as increased spending. This is especially the case when either or both of these bodies are in the earth signs. The water signs add resourcefulness to the personality. The air signs give fecundity in the realm of ideas and social contacts, while if Venus and Jupiter trine in the fire signs, good times are even made better. The difficult aspects between these two planets do not necessarily take away from their potential abundance, but they do bring about waste and foolish excesses. When Libra rises, the combination of Jupiter and Venus adds to the benefits one is able to give and receive from relationships. Difficult aspects between Jupiter and Venus with Libra on the Ascendant create an imbalance in partnership as idealism dominates over practicality. If either or both of these planets are afflicted in the mutable signs with Libra on the Ascendant, look for complications to arise from having too many conflicting relationships taking place at the same time. When Jupiter and Venus are afflicted in the fixed signs, there is the tendency to hold on to relationships long after they have proven their true value. The cardinal sign difficulties between Venus and Jupiter point to an incessant creation of relationships based on false or erroneous ideals, values, or concepts.

Venus/Saturn: This is not the most compatible of planetary energies no matter what the nature of the aspect that links them. Although Saturn and Venus can be beneficial in terms of long-range monetary (Taurus rising) or sentimental (Libra rising) relationships, Saturn does take away a lot of the pleasure that is so much a part of the Venusian nature. Look for strong Saturn and Venus aspects in horoscopes of people who marry for money or social position. Success in lucrative marriages may be indicated by the trine or sextile between these two planets. Venus and Saturn can also work well in relationships with people older than oneself. When harmoniously linked together in fixed signs, long-term commitments are easy to maintain. The trine or sextile can indicate that the individual wants relationships to continue, knowing that time only brings out their greater value. The square, opposition, and often the conjunction of Saturn and Venus in the chart can indicate that such lengthy ties are burdensome rather than pleasurable, more a fulfillment of debt than a bringer of reward. In any event, Venus/Saturn contacts certainly bring about a sense of responsibility where financial (Taurus rising) or romantic (Libra rising) relationships are concerned.

Venus/Uranus: This planetary interplay is a most interesting one. The resulting energies and consequent events are more suited to Libra rising than Taurus. Let us remember that Uranus is in its fall in Taurus, as the Bull never likes to be upset or moved about against its will, and Uranus can never leave things in status quo. Uranus is much better behaved in a Libra-ruled chart for several reasons. In the first place, Uranus rules Aquarius, which, like Libra, is an air sign. This gives Venus and Uranus a strong elemental affinity. In the second place, although Venus rules personal relationships and Uranus impersonal ones, they are connected through their effects on the general social dynamics of life. Thirdly, from the esoteric perspective, Uranus is the ruler of Libra, and the intention of the soul is to evolve the personality into a unit capable of loving all and everyone equally, which Uranus and Libra can both do well.[4]

In terms of aspects, I have discovered that Uranus/Venus aspects (and most especially the square) are a common significator of male homosexuality in the natal chart. This does not mean that everyone who has a Uranus/Venus contact in his chart is gay. It does mean, however, that a large percentage of gays do have such a contact. At the very least, a strong Venus/Uranus aspect in the horoscope leads to the need to explore many variations on the theme of sexual and emotional partnership. Should Libra (or Aquarius) be rising, these indications seem very strong. The same connection in a Taurus-rising chart can urge one to experimentation in financial investing or even financial irregularities, because no person with their ruling planet in strong aspect to Uranus is likely to follow any rules but their own.

Venus/Neptune: Combinations of these planets require a lot of emotional maturity if one is not to fall into addictive traps in their relationships. There is no doubt that this combination produces a great love of beauty in all its forms, yet when in difficult aspect (including the conjunction), there is a tendency to fall in love only with beauty—one's own or one's partner's. When Libra rises, blindness to the more practical realities of life is definitely an issue in relationships. Addictions occur that lead to co-dependency and obsessive needs in one's intimate partnerships so that the individual is never comfortable when alone. It can become easy to create a drama of romance around a totally inappropriate partner, the inner message being, "I would rather have a bad relationship than no relationship at all."

When Taurus rises and there are difficult aspects between Venus and Neptune (or even positive ones in the horoscope of a soul who is young in evolutionary terms), many of the same relationship tendencies are present, but also look for subterfuge and deceit where financial matters are concerned. A positive response to Venus/Neptune combinations can be uplifting and wonderful. It is, after all, a poetic combination, one that refines the senses and the sensibilities. Combined, Venus and Neptune can bestow a universal and self-sacrificial love nature, and when in Taurus yield an individual who is capable of finding and distributing collective resources to those in need.

A person with Taurus on the Ascendant and Venus in Aries in the Eleventh House trine to Neptune in Sagittarius in the Seventh, for example, may work as a catalyst to unlock social or governmental resources that can be distributed for humanitarian purposes. Yet this same Venus/Neptune individual may precipitate herself into a series of relationships with many false starts and unfulfilled promises. After more than three decades at this craft, I have observed and still see that people have the most difficulty in their private lives when the energies of Venus combined with Neptune are not lived out on the highest level. Perhaps this is a holdover from the Neptune-ruled Age of Pisces (the sign in which Venus has her exaltation), but all too often, people with strong Venus/Neptune contacts in their charts tend to project their idealized, romantic drama and fanciful inner yearnings onto the surface of their relationships, no matter how many warning red flags are waving in the wind.

Venus/Pluto: Like one would expect, the combination of Venus and Pluto brings intensity into relationships. Jealousy and possessiveness occurs with great frequency when these two are inharmoniously linked by aspect, especially if one or the other is in a fixed sign. When Libra rises, there is the tendency to destroy the very people or relationships one loves the most. Yet should these two planets be harmoniously linked, or the lessons of the square or opposition finally learned, the Venus/Pluto individual can be a vehicle for bringing out all sorts of hidden talents that have laid dormant within the partner.

When handled impersonally through a profession, for example, this combination can make for a great psychologist, or a vocational or human resource counselor. This is a person who not only heals relationships — both one's own as well as others' — but who also is capable of transforming relationships into a deeper level of connectedness. When Taurus rises in a horoscope in which this combination is harmoniously situated, Venus/Pluto allows for the discovery of hidden or buried treasure. There is an ability to invest in little-known enterprises that eventually yield great results; this more likely would be the case if Pluto were in Virgo in trine to Venus in either Taurus or Capricorn. Remember that Pluto takes a long time to reveal its true treasures, whether this is in the realm of finances or in terms of human relationships.

The following horoscope shown in the chart on the next page bears

Example 13: The Horoscope of Dylan Klybold[5]

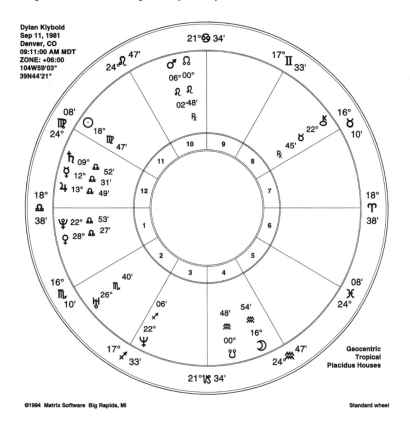

Dylan Klybold
Sep 11, 1981
Denver, CO
09:11:00 AM MDT
ZONE: +06:00
104W59'03"
39N44'21"

21°♋ 34'

24°♌ 47'

♂ ♌
06° 00°

♌ ♌
02'48'

℞

17° Ⅱ 33'

08'
♍ 24°

☉
18°
♍
47'

16°
♉ 10'

♂ 22°
45' ℞

♄ 09° ♎ 52'
☿ 12° ♎ 31'
♃ 13° ♎ 49'

18°
♎
38'

♇ 22° ♎ 53'
♀ 28° ♎ 27'

11   10   9   8

12   7

1   6

2   3   4   5

18°
♈
38'

16°
♏
10'

♅ 26° ♏
40'

06'
♐
22'

48' ♒   54' ♒

00° ♒   16° ♒

☊   ☽

08'
♓
24°

17° ♐ 33'
♆

21°♑ 34'

24° ♒ 47'

Geocentric
Tropical
Placidus Houses

©1994 Matrix Software Big Rapids, MI

Standard wheel

examining, as it is a prime example of Libran imbalance and also addresses many of the issues present in a Libra-ruled chart.

This is the natal map of one of the two boys responsible for the April 20, 1999 massacre of fifteen people at Columbine High School in Littleton, Colorado. In spite of this event, one which took a perverse courage to perform, this is fundamentally a weak horoscope. The chart reveals very little in the way of a firm sense of self, and much in the way of deeply internalized self-destructiveness that externalized in a most horrendous fashion.

The Sun has a great deal to do with the focus of selfhood and the sense of personal identity. When square to Neptune and not supported by any other major planetary forces, the Sun's vitality, and as a result, this contact with one's creative center, is weakened. There are only two major aspects to the Sun in Dylan Klybold's chart: Neptune square and the Moon inconjunct. This young man's sense of personal identity is thus diffused and muddled and not reinforced by other aspects that would add a more positive self-image. The Eleventh House influence on the Sun indicates a need for him to establish himself in society and be supported by the social collective of which he was a part. Indeed, it is only through a clandestine group possessed of totally antisocial ideals, dressed in a veil of black to mask individuality and reinforce a specialized, collective identity (Neptune in Sagittarius square the Sun), that such support came to this misguided youth. The problem of social ostracism is accentuated by the inconjunct from the Moon in Aquarius (the natural ruling sign of the Eleventh) to the Sun in Virgo. Here we have a person in great need of being embraced by society in order to anchor a sense of himself. The Moon rejects this need, by not allowing a clear and firm sense of social embrace. Furthermore, the Sun as ruler of the Eleventh is disposited by Mercury in the Twelfth conjoined to Saturn, adding to the restrictive social dynamics that are a prevalent theme in this chart.

The social complexities underlining Klybold's life are further emphasized by the position of the ruler of the horoscope. Let us analyze these associated placements according to the method outlined in this work, and then we will see just how very powerful such rulership factors are in the outworking of the chart.

Libra rises in the natal map with Venus in close conjunction to Pluto. The only other aspect that Venus makes is a 7.35° square to Mars in Leo in the Tenth House. Thus the only planetary contacts to the ruler of the Ascendant are the two planets of death and destruction: Mars and Pluto. In addition, Pluto in Libra can be said to be the ruler of the horoscope as it is conjoined the Ascendant by a little over 4° in the First House. This placement of Pluto and its conjunction to its dispositor, Venus, is made even stronger by house affinity and rulership. Taurus is on the cusp of the Eighth House of death and is therefore also ruled by Venus natally.

Consequently, we can see that the natal and the natural rulers of the Eighth (coruled by Mars) are conjoined in another house also naturally ruled by Mars (the First) with the Red Planet square to the natal house ruler of both these houses, Venus.

This factor of planetary relationship brings us to another important procedure of delineation: determining the significance of a planetary ruler of two or more houses. This analysis may be undertaken as follows:

1. Assess the nature of each individual house with special reference to how each house is affected by the natal signs on each of their cusps.
2. Combine the influences of both houses.
3. Note the position by sign and house in the horoscope of the natal planetary ruler.
4. Note the position of the *dispositor* of the planetary ruler and see if there are any aspects between these two bodies.

Using the above procedure as our guide, we come to the following conclusions:

1. The First House is about the moment-to-moment contact the ego has in relation to its environment. It also reveals a great deal about a person's physical appearance, presence, comportment, and the general way we are perceived by others. In Klybold's case, we have Libra rising with Venus in the First House. The young man is good-looking, mild-tempered on the surface, with a strong need to make social contacts and to be in strong partnership relationships.

The Eighth House with Taurus on the cusp is also ruled by Venus in the First. The Eighth is the house of death, but it is also the house of sexuality and regeneration. Regeneration here is a most important concept. If a person cannot properly circulate their energies, if these energies become bottled up and frustrated, then we can expect the more brutal and destructive energies of Mars and Pluto (the natural rulers of this house) to come forward with great potency. It is clear that frustrated sexuality, inhibited regeneration of personal vitality, leads to violence and war. This is human nature.

The nature of the Eighth House and its associated array placements gives Klybold a strong, but highly frustrated sexuality. His horoscope signature adds to the normal need to meet young women as well as be part of a generally accepted, teenage social scene. The romantic urge as seen in his horoscope is thwarted from any release in a number of respects.

Firstly, the ruler of the Fifth House of romance is Uranus, highly charged in Scorpio but integrated into the horoscope only by two afflicting aspects: an opposition from Chiron in the Eighth and a wide square from the Moon in Aquarius in the Fourth. This opposition from Chiron reveals a need to be an individual, but that the process of individuality is "wounded." Uranus disposits the Moon and is afflicted by her. This means that the wound from Chiron does not have a chance to be healed too easily because the socializing characteristic of an Aquarius Moon squares, and therefore, does not embrace Klybold's normal urge to be sociable in a general sense—and more specifically, inhibits releasing sexual tensions. Also, as previously pointed out, the Moon is inconjunct the Eleventh House Sun. Secondly, Venus is square to Mars, natural ruler of both houses of which Venus is the natal ruler! This square only intensifies sexual tensions without a clear path towards their discharge in an easy, healthy manner.

2. The energies and principles of the First House (Aries) and the Eighth House (Scorpio), when harmoniously combined, lead to the regeneration of the ego and the consequent release into the environment of new creative potentials of the developing self. Death occurs to previous forms of self-image so that, hopefully, newer and better facets of the personality may emerge. This process is totally inhibited in Klybold's chart. We can state this very simply in astrological terms as follows: the natal and the natural ruler of the First and the Eighth houses are square in the primary angles, the First and the Tenth. The urge for self-projection within a social context (Libra) is stymied from a more intimate personal level (the ruler of the First square to the ruler of the Seventh), as well as from a more social level (Mars is in the Tenth square to Venus in the First). Sexual potency is frustrated

in its normal course of release (Eighth House ruler and its various afflictions both from the natal and natural planetary rulers), only adding to the potential for violence and self-destruction, the latter already seen as a theme in the chart.

3. The natal planetary ruler of the chart is Pluto in Libra conjunct the Ascendant and Venus, its own dispositor. Pluto in the First only intensifies the sense of loneliness and social alienation that Klybold experienced. Let us keep in mind that this is a very socially oriented horoscope: group affiliation is essential to Klybold's sense of well-being.

But his horoscope shows that he did not feel well in society. Among the many astrological factors that reveal this position are: Mars in the Tenth square Venus; the Sun in the Eleventh square Neptune (Klybold was a member of a "public" secret group), the South Node in Aquarius with Mars conjoining the North Node and Venus squaring this entire combination; Libra rises with Venus in the First House in that sign conjunct to Pluto, and last but not least, the Moon is in Aquarius inconjunct the Sun and widely opposing the Tenth House Mars.

Let us continue now with our summary of rulership and planetary compatibilities. From this point on, many of the implications of the various planetary combinations have been covered in previous headings. For example, some of the primary implications of the combination of Mars and the Sun can be found in that section dealing with this planetary pair. Likewise, with Mars and Mercury, please refer to Mercury and Mars under the paragraphs outlining the effects of "Gemini or Virgo rising (Mercury as ruler)," etc. I will, however, be making some additional comments in the pages that follow, in order to elucidate the effects on the horoscope of the *ruling planets of the various Ascendants* with greater specificity while avoiding needless repetition.

Aries or Scorpio Rising (Mars as Ruler)

Mars definitely is the personal ruler of these two signs, even though Pluto is the ruler of the deeper and more profound effects of Scorpio and thought to be by many astrologers the co-ruler of Aries. In the day-to-day outworking of these two signs, the Red Planet definitely reigns over Aries. Although the effects of Mars open doors and present new opportunities to people (as well as killing and maiming them), the nature of this process is so different in each of the signs it rules that I am choosing in the following passages to deal with Mars/Aries and Mars/Scorpio in separate sections under this heading.

Aries Rising (Mars as Ruler)

Mars/Sun: When Aries rises, the astrologer should take note that the vitality and energy of the solar force will be directed by the individual to very specific personal goals of egocentric behavior. The ego, or "lower self," can be positive in nature, seeking to do good in the world and advancing the humanitarian causes that can profoundly interest an Aries-ruled person. Let us remember that Mars is very much a defending warrior who seeks to mess up the bad guys who invade his territory; thus, he is not always the villainous pirate out to rape and pillage. Yet should this not be such a virtuous Martian, the skull and crossbones are indeed hoisted atop Aries' prominent mast and the Sun's involvement only adds fuel to Mars' destructive fire.

Mars/Moon: When the Ram dominates the horoscope, look for Mars to overpower the Moon. When these two bodies are afflicted, the individual is in a constant war with his mother. Very often the maternal energies are seen as castrating, or at the very least, as a threat to one's ability to do his own thing in his own way. In a man's chart, this often leads to psychological wars with women. What complicates the issue is that there is often a very intense sexual drive towards conquering the very women whom the individual at the same time fears. In most cases, this war is played out on deep subconscious levels, resulting in botched marriages and severe problems with the opposite sex. Positive contacts between Mars and the Moon, especially with the latter in an earthy sign, gives the man or woman a sense of profound support from the mother and consequently from the women in one's life. Please note that this is true when any sign rises, but if Aries is on the Ascendant, the astrologer needs to give tremendous weight to the implications of this combination because it will dominate the life rather than be simply another facet of the personality.

Mars/Mercury: The primary effects of this combination in an Aries-ruled chart focus on the importance of the individual's ability to communicate his message—and there is always a message in need of communicating! The person is intensely aware of his ability or inability to say what he really means in such a way that convinces others of his intent. The harmonious contacts between these two bodies allows for ease and success in the expression of one's ideas; while the square or opposition can create diffusion (in the mutable signs); frustration and inhibition (when in the fixed signs); or confusion in intent and purpose of communicating (when in the cardinal signs).

The conjunction always intensifies one's need to bring forth ideas and images and this aspect will require further analysis regarding any other planetary aspect to the conjunction. For example, Saturn trine a Mars/Mercury conjunction will benefit long-range and well thought-out plans and projects, while Uranus square the Mars/Mercury conjunction will only make the Aries-ruled individual think and act that much more impulsively and prematurely.

Mars/Venus: Mars will always dominate over Venus in an Aries-ruled chart. This means that there is a tendency for the "green light" to overpower the "red." In other words, the individual is much more likely to see "Go!" signals in personal relationships rather than heed the warning to "Stop!" The person with Mars opposed Venus in such a chart will be totally oblivious to the cautionary yellow light and will definitely get his or her social signals confused. There is a tendency to project one's desires onto the energy field of the other person, who more than likely is seen as a sexual or social objective. The more harmonious contacts between these two planets results in ease of contact with others, and a more integrated balance between the romantic and the purely sexual (or power-oriented urges to conquer).

Mars /Jupiter: When these two planets combine in an Aries-ruled horoscope, they yield an adventurous person, one who is always seeking to expand his horizons. This can be expressed in a highly cavalier, idealistic, and foolish manner, complete with a trumpeting of bravura "full of sound and fury and signifying nothing" when these two planets are inharmoniously aspected. Should the signs Sagittarius or Leo also be strongly significant in the horoscope, this dramatic tendency will be even further exaggerated. Yet when combined in a positive geometric angle, look for a really noble man or woman, one who is very eager to help people in distress with a tempered sword and an honesty of aspiration. A goodly dose of positive Saturn and/or the more mature presence of Capricorn will only help to bring out a sense of responsibility and orderly behavior in the nature of that person.

Mars/Saturn: These two planets when joined in an Aries-ruled chart must be in a positive aspect in order for the individual not to feel inhibited or otherwise frustrated in his or her attempts at self-expression. Mars is exalted in Capricorn, but Saturn is in detriment in Aries. This means that while Mars is on his absolute best behavior, working to create positive structures and patterns that will evoke social rewards while in Saturn's sign, Saturn is a lonely law unto himself when positioned in the Ram. In an Aries-ruled horoscope with Saturn also in this sign, the individual has to learn how not to control every event and person with whom he or she comes in contact. The conjunction, square, or opposition between the two can be like a person driving with one foot on the accelerator and the other on the brakes. The trine or sextile gives one a quiet power of persistence as one tackles the objectives and goals of life, no matter what the level of difficulty may be.

Mars /Uranus: The combination of Mars and Uranus in an Aries-dominated horoscope can indicate a person who is ahead of his time. This can be an innovator of great talent—one who fearlessly puts forth ideas or inventions out into the world that aid and support the evolution of humanity. I am, of course, speaking here of a highly gifted genius, one with a mature outlook on life, who has overcome the need to be the first for the sake of dominating or shocking the immediate environment. In most cases Mars and Uranus, especially when Aries rises, results in a person who has a profound urge to be different. This can be expressed through antisocial means and methods. Uranus in Cancer square to Mars in Aries, for example, will tend to result in a person who must rebel against the collective social mores of his family or even his own generation. "I must be myself under all and every situation, even if this means that I will be a political party of one!," is this person's avowed declaration. The more positive linkages between these two bodies definitely gives courage and the urge to be different. This is not for the sake of pure dramatics, but for a very definite need to more highly individualize one's essential nature. There may be an inner calling that requires this person to follow his own isolated path in life, resulting in meeting up with other highly gifted, but often quite eccentric men and women.

Mars/Neptune: This is not the easiest combination of influences to harmonize. As Mars seeks to go forward, giving the Aries Ascendant the space in which to project itself, Neptune obscures or dissolves such projections. The square and opposition between the two are especially pernicious, as the individual attempts to write his name on the blackboard with one hand while the other holds a water-soaked eraser! Mars and Neptune infuse a sense of mission and devotion into the life. This missionary zeal needs a practical purpose in order for the person's goal not to be shrouded in false idealism and self-aggrandizement. A good Saturn and/or some strong placements of planets in the earthy signs will help a great deal to anchor a sense of reality. The more positive aspects between Mars and Neptune fuel the need for the person to find a deeper truth about the nature of life. As a result, such geometric angles (even the more difficult ones in a horoscope of a spiritually mature man or woman) produce philosophers and spiritual seekers. Those with a more scientific bent can find that Mars and Neptune are good for research and unlocking nature's secrets. An Aries individual is a soldier in his or her attitude to life. When Mars is with Neptune, such a person may become a martyr to a greater cause or sacrifice himself needlessly as he battles a cloudy set of aspirations with blunted weapons.

Mars/Pluto: The combination of Mars and Pluto is a powerful one. It adds resilience, consistent regeneration, vitality, and drive to the horoscope. In an Aries-ruled chart, it endows one with a "never say die" attitude to life, giving one the stamina to face any set of challenges. And you can be sure that with a strong Mars/Pluto aspect in such a horoscope, there will be many challenges to face! The Aries individual has to map out new territory for herself. She is not one to follow in anyone else's footsteps but her own. In fact, she has to create the very path on top of which her feet will travel. The constant need to make her own way through life is given added potency with Pluto in close contact to her Mars ruler. The urge to dominate one's own life and to overcome any opposition to self-expression is highlighted when these two planets are together.

If in square, opposition, or conjunction, especially in the fiery or cardinal signs, the urge to dominate may be overpowering. The person can create conflicts where none exist or, most likely, engage in a constant battle with himself. Often there is a war between the lower and the higher self, one in which the lesser ego is asked to sacrifice its desires and intent to make way for some more impersonal and transcendental goal. Resistance to this evolutionary process results in a great sense of inner tensions. This is especially the case when either or both of these planets is in a fixed sign.

Scorpio Rising (Mars as Ruler)

The nature of Mars in a Scorpio-ruled chart as it combines with the other planets should be seen in much the same light as the definitions offered above. Yet there is one major difference. In a chart with Aries rising, the theme of the life has much to do with blazing new territory. In this respect, the effects of Mars are to bring the individual forward, helping him or her to invent a sense of self based on a continuous confrontation with life. One has to push oneself forward, advancing through life via a constant projection of personal intent. This underlying principle in the horoscope of most individuals takes the form of desire: "I go forward into life where my desires take me and do battle when such wishes are not openly met and embraced." The more highly evolved Aries-rising person stands ready to do battle for those beliefs and ideals that seek to open self *and* others into new territory. The battle usually takes the form of the advancement of consciousness for the benefit of humanity.

The Scorpio-ruled individual is constantly seeking to recreate himself. Confrontations take place that result either in a repetition of old patterns, and as a consequence their further entrenchment into the substrata of the personality, or to deal a death blow to such patterns and thus release vital energy so that new and more refined patterns of self-expression may come about. Therefore, we should view Mars in the light of a planetary force which brings death so that true regeneration may occur. Mars is then acting in one of its most evolved capacities—as the vehicle for the regenerative objectives of its higher octave, Pluto. Mars as Scorpio's ruler may also work through its negative polarity. In this case, Mars becomes a stimulus for the generation of those life situations that serve no positive evolutionary function. Mars then acts as an agent for the involution and inversion of the life process, robbing vitality through the perpetuation of the obsessions of the lower desire nature. The determination of which way Mars is acting is based on the level of soul growth within the individual and cannot be readily determined from the natal chart. This is another instance when the intuition of the astrologer serves to reveal the nature of a planet's activity and role in one's life.

To summarize these principles: *When Scorpio rises*, Mars and the Sun either regenerate or degenerate the life/vitality principle. Mars and the Moon either destroy instinctual emotional responses that inhibit psychological growth, or stimulate such negative emotional habit patterns, making them more powerful. Mars and Mercury either disrupt old patterns of thinking, allowing for the refinement of the communicative process, or reinforce such communicative patterns, thereby robbing mental vitality. Mars and Venus either rupture old ways of relating, allowing love to become harmonized with sexuality, or increase the desire nature to such a point that love is sacrificed. Mars and Jupiter either bring out a deeper or hidden truth from one's travels or philosophical goals, or make one an exile to all beliefs and faiths, save the theology of the lower self—"I am the master or mistress of my own mini-universe." Mars and Saturn either create opportunities to reinforce mental and physical structures and discipline, thus refining the use of creative energy, or stimulate serious blockages to personal or other people's success. Mars and Uranus either become a vehicle for the advancement of the process of individuation, or make one wildly rebellious to the point of self-annihilation. Mars and Neptune either serve to unlock the mystery of the universe, deepening one's contact and identification with the whole of life, or act as a source of powerlessness as one becomes increasingly addicted to self-destroying habits. And finally, Mars and Pluto either work as a tremendous fount for the regenerating will-to-good, or act as a weapon of war against the evolving self.

Scorpio Rising (Pluto as Ruler)

This theme of regeneration and the constant recreating of oneself is prominent in a Scorpio-ruled life. It is as if the Scorpio-ruled person is walking on a tense boundary between glory and defeat, evolutionary growth and cessation of vitality, the refinement of the life urge and the apparent ease of long periods of stagnancy. The result is a never-ending tension with the added pressure of an attitude towards sex. Not such an easy path! In no other sign is the potential for living in an evolutionary testing ground greater than it is when Scorpio rises. So what is the purpose of a Scorpio Ascendant? A life directed by the Scorpion is one in which there is an inner need for a series of devastations so total that one can only survive (indeed if one does survive!) through starting all over again. This succession of "mini-incarnations" gives one the opportunity to surge through the barriers of the lower self and assume one's greater destiny in service to humanity. An incarnation spent dominated by Scorpio rising is one that presents some incredible spiritual opportunities—and whoever said evolutionary growth came cheaply and without tears?

Mars is the more personal ruler of this sign. Mars shoots the gun and "bam!," you're dead. That's it, swift and easy. Pluto is apparently not so merciful. If you have ever gone through a long—and there is no short—Pluto transit by square, opposition, or conjunction, you know that it exhorts a long and involved death agony before the final coup de grâce. Yet if you did the job well, if you let go of what Pluto was demanding, if you released what was inhibiting the higher nature of the planet or point over which Pluto was passing, after a certain time of recovery from the process, you are stronger than you have ever been before. That planet or major focus of your chart is now renewed, refined, and regenerated.

Pluto's effects on the other planets in the chart when Scorpio rises involve a profound, intense, and intricate process in order to release the highest good from all combinations. If the aspect is a harmonious one, the means will be a lot easier to effectuate this distillation of high-octane planetary petrol. The results are well worth the effort and, besides, Pluto gives us little choice: transmute or die. Should there be a square, opposition, conjunction, or inconjunction between Pluto as the ruler of the horoscope and any other planet in the chart, look for a constant battle of destruction without necessarily the promise of a bright horizon. It may come, but it will require the individual to soul search in the deepest and truest sense of the term.

Pluto/Sun: This intense planetary combination either regenerates or degenerates physical vitality and the ability to use the power of the will correctly. When these planets are inharmonious, and especially if in the fixed signs, it is possible to reach a certain level of achievement only to fall flat on one's bottom. Then you have to wait a bit in order to recuperate—pick yourself up and try again. The fixed signs always bring about a test of will, and the cardinals ask you to examine your motives, while the busy mutables challenge direction, means, and methods of operation. The more harmonious aspects, especially if either Pluto or the Sun is in a fire sign, give a never-ending font of life force. Pluto sextile or trine the Sun is a very fortuitous factor in a Scorpio chart, as one is constantly in the process of intense birthing or dying.

Pluto/Moon: The Moon and Pluto have to do with breaking away from biological karma inherited through the physical qualities of one's genes and chromosomes, and the psychological factors surrounding one's birth and early family life. We have to keep in mind that a person with Scorpio rising is one who is in an incarnation destined to end one cycle or level of self-expression in order to release yet another. Pluto's aspects in such a horoscope are vital from a distinctly evolutionary perspective. The Moon in difficult aspect with Pluto shows the need to regenerate the relationship not only with one's mother, but with the entire instinctual approach to life. This requires the individual, if possible, to transform the instinctive or subconscious into the conscious. This is usually accomplished through a series of very difficult emotional experiences. The goal here is to become mentally objective to the emotionally subjective. The positive aspects between Pluto and the Moon makes this evolutionary objective that much easier to do. If Mercury is also strong in the horoscope, there is the ability to say: "Oh, *that* was the lesson I was supposed to learn from that experience!"

Pluto/Mercury: Please refer to the comments on page 135, under the heading "Gemini or Virgo rising (Mercury as ruler)," keeping in mind that the emphasis with Scorpio rising in the chart is on Pluto and the theme of regeneration. Thus, the astrologer should look for an intensification of the mental process, a deep and intricate mind, one easily given over to research and development of ideas, products, and services. As with Mercury in Scorpio, do not look for an individual who easily reveals his innermost thoughts and ideas. Do not be surprised if there are no outermost thoughts—every idea is deep and personal to a Scorpio-rising individual with a strong contact between Pluto and Mercury. Difficult aspects between the two, especially if in the fixed signs, give what is called in French, "les idées fixes." This is the kind of person who obsesses over certain thoughts and opinions and who cannot or will not let go of such ideas long after their usefulness is over (if they were at all useful in the first place). At the very worst, Mercury/Pluto contacts lead to close-mindedness that does not permit the circulation of mental energy unless it is the ceaseless repetition of the same thought in one's mind.

Pluto/Venus: In the case of Pluto and Venus, I refer the reader back to page 144 where the essential nature of this contact is mentioned. As we are speaking here about Scorpio's rulership, Pluto's potency is emphasized. The square, opposition, and sometimes the conjunction (especially if in Leo or Scorpio) intensifies the attraction the person has for his or her love object (which is all too often confused with an object of desire). This intensification leads to obsessive/compulsive behavior. There is no letting go of the other person, even if the Scorpio-ruled individual is no longer in love with that individual. In the more positive contacts, what is loved is loved deeply and truly, no sacrifice being too great, no gesture too small.

Pluto/Mars: The battle is on for the regeneration and reorientation of the lower self. Please refer to the comments about the relationship between these two planets on page 153 (Mars/Pluto); pages 154–156 (Scorpio rising/Mars as ruler); and pages 156–157 (Scorpio rising/Pluto as ruler).

Pluto/Jupiter: One of the most outstanding features of a more highly evolved person with Scorpio rising is their need to deepen their contacts to their higher self. The search for the true meaning of life is augmented when there are positive contacts between Pluto and Jupiter. As a rule, the individual will have abandoned his or her family's religion or philosophical beliefs. The individual feels confined by any orthodoxy or conventional ritualized worship. If the family is atheistic, then atheism will be the creed that is released. The urge here is to find a way of approaching the higher life that is deeper and ever more fulfilling than was presented in childhood. The positive combination of these planetary influences may actually have an expansive effect on one's finances. Look for the personality to express an enterprising nature, one which seeks to widen the reach of personal power through the acquisition of a greater material status. The latter is also true when Jupiter and Pluto are in square or opposition, but the methods used to achieve such goals may be rather ruthless. It is also possible that Jupiter and Pluto in one of the harder aspects may indeed precipitate a surprising advancement in one's economic status, only to be followed by some equally great loss. This polarization can be applied as well to one's religious or spiritual life: great breakthroughs in belief followed by "the dark night of the soul," only to be followed once again by another expansion of understanding.

Pluto/Saturn: The interplay of Saturn and Pluto is one that is often expressed through the use — rightly or wrongly — of the will. Both of these planets are connected to power and authority. When they are harmoniously joined in a Scorpio-ruled chart, the individual is capable of making the most out of the least. This is a person who can restructure his or her resources in ways that allow a small expenditure of energy to produce extraordinary results. The danger with this combination lies in the urge to control. If such a need is sincerely geared to the well-being of others, then the Saturn/Pluto person can assume increasingly more potent executive positions without harm either to himself or to anyone else. Yet should the urge for power be based on an emotional need to dominate, then severe challenges are bound to enter the life from either those over whom one dictates, or from others seeking to usurp the individual's power. The difficult aspects between Saturn and Pluto may indicate a definite ruthlessness in the application of power. This can manifest passively, i.e., the individual himself may have been the victim of a tyrannical father or other authority figure. Should the Eighth House be involved, Saturn or Pluto be in Scorpio, or either Saturn or Pluto be configured with Mars, sexual or other forms of physical abuse are common.

Pluto with Uranus or Neptune: The next two combinations, Uranus/Pluto and Neptune/Pluto, are generational in effect. Literally hundreds of millions of people will have either or both of these contacts in their chart. The great majority of persons born between late 1942 and mid-1945 have Uranus sextile Pluto *and* Pluto sextile Neptune. In fact, about 80 percent of all people on the planet born in the twentieth century have Pluto sextile Neptune in their natal charts. An entire generation born between August of 1962 and September of 1969 have Pluto conjoined Uranus, while the overwhelming majority of a more recent group, born between January 1994 and January 2000, are gifted by the presence of another Uranus/Pluto sextile in their charts.

There are only two factors that can personalize such subtle contacts:

1. A level of consciousness that can respond in an individualized manner to these "higher-octave" planetary connections.
2. The fact that the ruling planet (in this case, Pluto) is being conditioned by its proximity to one or the other with certain predictable results upon the personality.

The first consideration is beyond the scope of the present work but underlies the foundation of esoteric, soul-centered astrology. I would only like to say at this point that it is the astrologer's intuition that can assess the level of consciousness of a given individual and the resulting effects of the planets. If neither of the above-mentioned factors are present in the individual's life, then such aspects between Pluto and Uranus or Neptune will go fairly undetected by the conscious mind or the sensory organs.

Should the Scorpio-ruled individual be able to respond consciously to this interplay of the higher-octave planets, look for such an individual to be ever working in ways that enrich his or her spiritual and/or community's life. The function of such planetary contacts is to increase

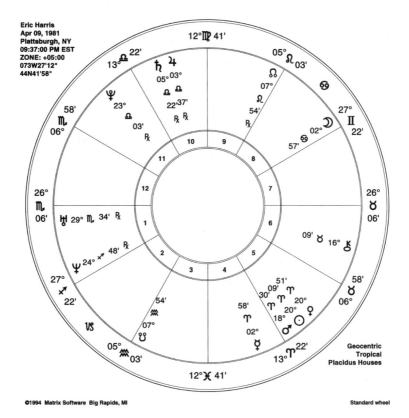

Eric Harris
Apr 09, 1981
Plattsburgh, NY
09:37:00 PM EST
ZONE: +05:00
073W27'12"
44N41'58"

12°♍ 41'

Geocentric
Tropical
Placidus Houses

12°♓ 41'

©1994 Matrix Software Big Rapids, MI

Standard wheel

a sense of universality or inclusivity within the consciousness of the individual. In this respect, Uranus will bring about the need to be part of a large, communicative network or participate in groups of other relatively enlightened men and women for the purpose of advancing personal evolution or, at the highest level, the evolutionary development of humanity. In terms of Neptune and Pluto, they convey a constant urge to pierce the veil of material existence. A subtle "knowing" that the invisible world is indeed a more sizable reality than the visible will also impress itself upon the consciousness. In the lives of those individuals still enchanted by the glamour of the emotions, the tendency to join cults and sects that promise immortality or sudden enlightenment is a definite common generational thread.

Harris is the stronger of the two Littleton, Colorado assassins. His

Scorpio-rising chart is certainly on the surface much more prone to violence than is the natal map of his Libra-dominated partner. Yet the interplay of the planets and signs in the horoscopes of both of these boys is remarkably similar. The reader may wish to refer back to Dylan Klybold's chart on page 145, as I will later briefly compare the two, outlining the most important contacts, but first let us concentrate on the Harris chart shown on the preceding page.

Uranus in Scorpio is close enough to the Ascendant to be considered the ruler of the natus. It is posited in an interesting combination of aspects: a trine from Mercury in Aries and a sextile from Jupiter in Libra. I use the word interesting, as the combination of these three planets yields a strong philosophical orientation. Yet the signs do not all match. A very harmonious grand trine connection for these planets would occur if Uranus was in Sagittarius and Mercury and Jupiter stayed where they are. This sign change would have lessened the bombastic quality of the philosophy to which Harris was attracted. As it stands the belief system and attitude to society which dominates this horoscope engages Harris in an interesting personal and also a social vendetta. He feels like an outcast and is determined to go to war. This can be seen astrologically through the following set of aspects:

1. Uranus conjunct the Ascendant with Jupiter in the Tenth in Libra which is opposing Mercury in the Fourth in Aries. This, in short, implies a belief system that serves to individualize and singularize through a sense of being personally challenged by the prevailing social and religious beliefs of society.
2. Jupiter conjunct Saturn in the Tenth opposed to Mercury in Aries in the Fourth, and both are square the Moon in Cancer in the Eighth. This means that the prevailing social structures, rules, and regulations oppose the individual's own thoughts and opinions and do not make him feel that he is at home in any social setting.
3. Moon in Cancer in the Eighth inconjunct Uranus in Scorpio in the First combined with the astrological factors stated above in point 2. This results in great insecurity and a sense of isolation

and social ostracism—the urge to get back at and go to war with the oppressors.

Uranus as the chart ruler is disposited by Mars and Pluto which, although making no aspect to Uranus itself, do oppose one another. Pluto's position is especially potent and difficult, as it is in Uranus natural house, the Eleventh, and opposed to the natal ruler of that house, Venus. Venus is in Aries in a tight conjunction with the Sun and Mars and is disposited by Mars in its own sign. Thus, we have an alignment of planetary forces that bring Harris into immediate conflict with society.

The urge for his personal creative self-expression (the triple conjunction in the Fifth House) will be at odds with the larger social world of which Harris is a part (Pluto in Libra in the Eleventh). The fact that Pluto's dispositor (Venus) is in a sign of Mars and conjoined to Mars in the sign of its dishonor (Aries) only adds tension to an already tense and highly charged planetary grouping. Pluto/Mars and Venus rule the Ascendant/Descendant axis and their oppositions make it that much more difficult for Harris to create positive relationships. Once again we see sexual frustration in the horoscope of a highly libidinous teenager.

The fact that there is a Venus/Mars/Sun conjunction in Aries in the Fifth House of romance on a Scorpio-ruled horoscope is a clear indication of a very powerful sexual drive. Yet the opposition from Pluto in the sign of relationships (Libra) to its own dispositor, which is also both the natal and natural ruler of the Seventh House of partnerships (Venus), certainly tells the astrologer that an easy and clear release of healthy relationship potential is strongly challenged in this horoscope. Venus is also the ruler of the Eleventh House of society. It would appear to me that a great deal of sexual/Martial frustration is transferred from the more acceptable one-to-one contacts of the Seventh House to the larger arena of the Eleventh. It is as if the chart were saying, "If I cannot make love with one girl, then screw society!"

Sexuality plays a dominant theme in any horoscope with Scorpio rising and strong Venus/Mars/Pluto contacts. If the Eighth House is also involved, then the focus upon sexual dynamics is very much augmented.

We have seen this both in terms of the events triggered by this chart as well as in human nature in general. If appropriate sexual contact between human beings is not possible, violence, abuse, and death frequently take their place. There is no coincidence that Mars and Pluto, Aries and Scorpio are the rulers of war, death, sexuality, regeneration, and resurrection, and Harris, along with Klybold, played this darker side out. An Aries Sun with Scorpio rising is a very challenging map. It requires absolutely that the individual rise above his or her baser instincts and urge to violence and destruction, and move forward as a Warrior for Light. Unfortunately, Harris fought the wrong battle and lost the war, taking many others with him.

The ruler of the Eighth House is Mercury. Mercury is in Aries, disposited by Mars in opposition to the Eleventh House Pluto, which is itself disposed by Venus in Aries conjoined Mars. In addition, Mercury is also in opposition to Saturn and Jupiter as well as square Neptune and square the Eighth House Cancer Moon. To say that this boy was sexually confused, that he had more Martial, Venusian, and Plutonian energies than he could successfully and normally channel, is obvious. In addition, the conflicting Mercurial aspects on top of a secretive Scorpio-dominated chart made it impossible for him to communicate his subjective difficulties with anyone other than a partner, Klybold, who would agree with and support him. His internal drama gets played out in a public arena. The focus is on a highly afflicted Pluto in the Eleventh House—and he cannot regenerate himself, so Harris sets out to kill society. Scorpio inverts and Aries goes to war.

These two charts also make a fascinating study in synastry. In this respect, let me point out some significant astrological indicators that show how these two boys found themselves in such a sad, murderous partnership. Space does not permit me to explore their deadly symbiosis in detail.

In the first place, Klybold is Venus-ruled and Harris is dominated by Mars and Pluto. Both boys have strong contacts and afflictions between these planets. Klybold has Pluto conjoined Venus in Mars' natal house (the First) square to Mars. Harris has the rulers of the Ascendant (Mars and Pluto) in opposition to each other while Mars is also conjunct Venus opposing its dispositor, Pluto. This makes for some very intense antisocial behavior. Let us also not forget that even though Klybold has a Libra Ascendant, Pluto conjoins this point and is conjunct to Venus, which is square to Mars. This combination of planetary contacts underscores the fact that in addition to being the sign of partnership, Libra is also traditionally called the sign of "open enemies." Such a theme certainly balances the more obviously Mars/Pluto-dominated Ascendant of Eric Harris. In addition, there is a very potent problem involving the Moon, Cancer, and Uranus, which works out as his feelings of being an alien in society.

In Harris' chart, the Moon is in the house of Scorpio (the Eighth) in Cancer inconjunct Uranus in Scorpio. Klybold has the Moon in the Fourth House in Aquarius square Uranus in Scorpio. Finally, Harris has the Jupiter/Saturn conjunction in Libra in opposition to Mercury and square the Moon, while Klybold has a conjunction of Saturn/ Mercury/Jupiter in Libra trine the Moon, pointing to high intelligence and an interest in social issues. Had these boys been nurtured or fated otherwise, I believe that Klybold would have probably gone into the legal or teaching profession, while Harris could have been an outstanding computer scientist or mechanical engineer.

Let us now continue with some further comments about the remaining planetary/sign rulership contact.

Sagittarius Rising (Jupiter as Ruler)

The Centaur on the Ascendant is always seeking to expand the horizons of the person in question. As a dual sign, this urge to enlarge the scope and meaning of life usually takes two directions: through the senses and/or through the mind. It is only when the Sagittarius-ruled individual has learned to become one-pointed in purpose and direction that the higher nature of this sign manifests. It is then that the individual can find his or her path through the chaos and tensions of duality. A Sagittarius-dominated chart will seek to widen its scope of life experiences. The planet most closely aspecting Jupiter will definitely point to the primary direction of such expansion. In all instances, when dealing with the delineation of a ruling planet, much has to do with that ruler's sign placement. Sagittarius rising with Jupiter in Aries trine the Sun in

Leo, for example, will heighten the urge towards creative self-expression in highly innovative and personal ways. With Sagittarius on the Ascendant, life is always an adventure, and must be explored through self-initiated challenges. With Jupiter in Taurus, many of the deeper lessons of life come through the need for expansive self-valorization. In Gemini, expansive growth and development take place through travel and education, and so on through the signs.

The reader is asked to refer back to the appropriate passages in this chapter that deal with the interrelationship of Jupiter with the Sun, Moon, Mercury, Venus, Mars, and Pluto to understand the nature of this ruler when placed with each of these other planets. What should be pointed out here is that we are dealing with Sagittarius on the Ascendant and therefore the main emphasis in life is on the principle of expansion. This characteristic expansion can range from the inflation of one's ego (Jupiter and the Sun), the fattening of one's waist (Jupiter and the Moon), the padding of one's pockets (Jupiter and Venus), the opening of one's mind (Jupiter and Mercury), or the growth and dimensions of one's spiritual aspirations (Jupiter and Neptune, Jupiter and Pluto).

Jupiter/Saturn: When these two planets are in harmonious aspect, this is a helpful combination for an individual with Sagittarius on the Ascendant. The urge to structure and create proper boundaries for self-expansion is highlighted and can be easily integrated into one's life. This allows a person to make long-range plans and to balance the idealistic, Jupiterian influence with the realistic and pragmatic energies of Saturn. A square between the two gives a genuine conflict in achieving this goal. Saturn (structure, order, responsibility) has to be integrated within the Sagittarian/Jupiterian expansive outlook, but how to go about doing this? Blind, emotionally polarized expansion without obtaining "permission" from Saturn will only lead to enforced limitations and a deep sense of personal restriction. The opposition between Jupiter and Saturn usually results in periods of life that are very expansive followed by other cycles that are far more limiting in their effects. The objective balancing and harmonizing of these two influences, then, has to be a major factor in a Sagittarius-dominated life. The adage "put a dollar away for a rainy day" is most appropriate here. The conjunction between Jupiter and Saturn intensifies the need to blend and synthesize these two rather opposing energy fields. I have often found that in the horoscopes of the intellectually gifted, the conjunction of Jupiter and Saturn leads to an interest in history, jurisprudence, and the science of economics.

Jupiter/Uranus: This is a combination that is bound to bring surprises into one's life. It is related to those unexpected social situations that serve to widen a person's understandings of life. Often it is found in the horoscope of people drawn to unusual intellectual or spiritual interests. With Sagittarius rising and Jupiter in close affinity with Uranus, the individual tends to see life as one big school. If Uranus and Jupiter are in square or opposition to each other, or relate strongly to the individual's Third and/or Ninth houses, or are in Gemini and/or Sagittarius in the natal chart, quite often the person has a hard time in any type of formal education. This is the type of person who would prefer to take all electives at college rather than following the proscribed program for freshmen and sophomores. Perhaps this is why many Uranus/Jupiter people never graduate. Intuition can be a highly developed tool in the chart of a Sagittarian with this combination, as the Centaur's mythic propensity for prophecy is certainly given a boost when the ruler is in a strong aspect with Uranus.

Jupiter/Neptune: The combination of Jupiter and Neptune is one of the least practical in a horoscope. If well aspected in a Sagittarian chart, it can give deep compassion and a tremendous urge to be of service. If poorly configured, the same compassionate nature is present, but the direction of its release can be too "otherworldly" and unrealistic. This would be especially the case if Jupiter and Neptune were in the fire or water signs. This combination definitely adds to the desire for a spiritual life, although afflictions between the two, especially if they relate to the luminaries, can give an aversion for the things of the earth along with a deep need for solitude and contemplation. When taken to the extreme, this influence adds to a person's escapist urges, as the world may be too harsh a place for one with such a sensitive disposition.

I have noticed also that the sense of smell is highly stimulated by this planetary contact and that the individual can be overly sensitive to anesthetics, drugs, or even strong detergents and toxic cleansers. On the other hand, there is a definite nose for perfumes and wine. Sometimes this combination, especially if Leo or Pisces is involved, wears too much of the former and drinks too much of the latter!

Jupiter/Pluto: In the Sagittarius-rising chart, the emphasis is on Jupiter. Pluto's aspects in this respect create a constant urge to transform the philosophical belief systems upon which the individual bases his or her life. In many instances, the combination of Jupiter and Pluto give the urge to propagate highly obscure, esoteric doctrines and religious creeds. For additional information, please refer to page 159 in the text.

Capricorn Rising (Saturn as Ruler)

In Greek, Saturn is known as Chronus, coming from the word *chronos*, meaning "time." To the philosophically and more eastern minded, time is cyclical, female, illusionary, and infinite. To most Western minds, time is conceived as being linear, masculine, defining, and incremental. This latter view of time is, of course, more prevalent in our culture, and gives to Saturn an authoritarian aura. Even in esoteric astrology, Saturn is known as the "Lord of Karma," requiring a person to have mastered a sense of responsibility of how one spends one's time (on Earth), before being allowed to move onwards to the more transcendental time frame of the soul.

When Capricorn rises, time and the boundaries of mortality play a major issue in the way an individual manifests his or her methods of creative self-expression. There is a sense of limitation about life in general and about the possibilities for success in one's own life in particular. People with Capricorn rising and a strongly afflicted Saturn feel like the characters in a 1930s horror film when Bela Lugosi pressed a button and the library walls began to close in upon our hapless hero and heroine. Such Saturn-afflicted people have all they can do to keep from feeling that they are daily being squashed by life and they are often tense, fearful, and depressed as a result.

On the other hand, a Capricorn-rising chart with a strong and positive Saturn reveals an individual with a firm mastery of time. This is an efficiency expert, one who knows what to do and when to do it, as well as how much to invest in terms of time and energy in any given project.

My first esoteric teacher was such a wise Saturnian and he taught me that the keys to success on the earth plane are the mastery of "process, order, structure, and form." A poorly aspected and weak Saturn in a Capricorn-dominated chart signifies an individual who does not have a mastery of these four dynamics, while when Saturn is acting from its more harmonious side, these four qualities are indeed an integrated part of the personality.

Saturn/Sun: In terms of combining planetary influences when Saturn rules the chart, please refer to the appropriate passages in this chapter that apply to the relationship of the Sun, Moon, Mercury, Venus, Mars, Jupiter, and Pluto with Saturn. Keep in mind that when dealing with the Mountain Goat on the Ascendant, there is a change of emphasis in the definitions cited in the referred passages. In other words, a square between the Sun and Saturn in a Leo-rising chart will weaken vitality. The sense of limitation will come through not having enough energy for one's creative plans and urges. Although this may also be the case when Capricorn rises, there is a shift in perspective and experience. The Capricorn-ruled individual is more likely to create his or her own limitations with Saturn square the Sun by being overbearing and controlling. Such a person will seek not to make a friend with time (as would a Sun trine Saturn person), as much as to try to dominate time and people, and life circumstances in general. In both instances, problems with fathers and authority figures will play an important role in one's life.

In the case of Capricorn rising with the Sun in difficult aspect to Saturn, this will be even more of a struggle because one of the most important factors in such a life is to be an authority figure. One would have to defeat the inner parental figure while at the same time try to recreate that archetype within oneself. This dilemma would be emphasized in a chart when Saturn is opposed, square, or inconjunct the Sun in a Capricorn-ruled chart.

Saturn/Moon: Where the Moon is concerned, we have to realize that in a Capricorn-rising horoscope, the Moon is the ruler of the Seventh, as Cancer is always on the cusp of this house. Here we see that the individual is trying to give order, structure, and form to one's partner in ways that assure his or her personal emotional security. This means that there is a repetition of the early patterns that a person experienced with his or her mother and in the early family environment. In addition, a square, opposition, inconjunct, or conjunction between Saturn and the Moon is neither a favorable nor a supportive planetary contact for a sense of emotional integration and wholeness.

Thus, we have a person who is attempting to control other people so that the relationships that occur are patterned after unsuccessful and unnurturing earlier contacts. This repetition gives a sense of security in that it is familiar, but it certainly does nothing to resolve the Capricorn-rising individual's emotional needs. In a man's chart, such a contact will speak about the women he attracts into his life. These are often older, emotionally injured, and quite capable of fulfilling the space he has subconsciously created for them within himself. In other words, these relationships are sure to fail! Unless and until the man has objectified and transformed his initial emotional life content, he will be sure to marry "a girl just like the girl that married dear old dad."

When this combination appears in a woman's chart, she will tend to shape herself to fit into those non-regenerative emotional patterns and then will wonder how come the man in her life is so emotionally controlling and/or why she feels so inadequate to fulfill his or her own emotional needs.

No matter the gender, such situations will be aggravated if the Moon or Saturn is found in Cancer, Capricorn, or Scorpio, and if Pluto is also configured with either or both of these two other bodies. When there are positive aspects between Saturn and the Moon in a Capricorn-ruled chart, look for benefits to come from the family and from older women, especially the grandmother (or grandmotherly types) in particular. This planetary combination also tends to bestow upon a person an inner sense of emotional dignity and refinement. In addition, there is often an instinctual "knowing" about how to behave in society—especially when elders or people in authority are concerned. Marriage can be made with someone older or who is in a well-placed social position. Look for "old money" or a richness of family tradition, especially if the Saturn/Moon sextile or trine involves the earthy signs.

Saturn/Mercury: In terms of Mercury and Saturn in a Capricorn-ruled chart, the emphasis is on creating long-range plans and the concurrent ability to work out details *within the context of a structured plan of action*. The emphasis on wholeness and longevity is much less present when Saturn is with Mercury in a Gemini- or Virgo-ruled horoscope. Here the focus of activity is centered much more in terms of immediate needs and goals. Capricorn-rising people are always involved in life with a view to the long-term repercussions and results of their actions.

Saturn/Venus: Saturn seeks to make socially acceptable relationships or partnerships that improve one's social or professional status when it is in aspect with Venus in a Capricorn-dominated horoscope. This social orientation is either thwarted or aided depending on the aspect between these two planets. Should there be no aspect between the two, study the position of Venus and then integrate its meaning into the general relationship theme of the natus.

Saturn/Mars: In a Capricorn-rising chart, a good Mars/Saturn contact aids in the ability to achieve one's goals and ambitions. The individual's willpower is increased, and personal magnetism is added in terms of his or her capacity to control life's circumstances. A difficult planetary connection between the two inhibits all of the latter, leading to frustration in the achievement of one's goals. Remember that Mars is the natural ruler of the Ascendant, while Saturn is the natural ruler of the Midheaven, so that conflicts between these two planets challenge the integration of these two major points in the chart, while harmonious angles between Mars and Saturn add to the integration of who one is with what one does.

Saturn/Jupiter: Jupiter in a harmonious contact with Saturn will open the doors and widen the portals to the success orientation that is always present when Capricorn is on the Ascendant and Saturn is the chart ruler. Long-range plans are easily conceived and implemented. There is a clear understanding of how to extend oneself in terms of one's creative plans and projects through structuring correct boundaries. Jupiter square or opposed Saturn in such a nativity tends to evoke aspirations that are too impractical or idealistic, especially if the water or fire signs are involved.

Saturn/Uranus: Saturn and Uranus are not particularly "good friends." In brief, Saturn represents the old order, while Uranus is the progenitor of the new. In a Capricorn-rising chart, Saturn will always be the predominant influence. When Uranus and Saturn are in a harmonious aspect in such a chart, the individual will utilize new social contacts or innovative ideas to reinforce his or her established position. The positive joining of these planets also allows a person to be a bridge between generations, or between people of very different social, national, or racial backgrounds. This would be especially the case if the signs Gemini or Libra were involved and if Venus were also harmoniously configured with these two planets. The Capricorn-ruled person may indeed be of a highly evolved state, and thus his or her orientation may be so traditional that it is universal in nature and therefore very inclusive in intent. If I have Capricorn rising, for example, and I seek to build an organization whose purpose is to structure food supplies to feed a hungry world, my focus is on service and helping humanity. If I have Saturn trine to Uranus in my natal chart, I may find it very simple to use the latest in computer technology to aid me in my noble and selfless cause. Should Saturn and Uranus be in a difficult aspect, look for a conflict between the new and the old and a difficulty in coming to grips with the collective mindset of incoming generations. This would be a Capricorn-rising person who refuses to modernize or change with the times. The result would indicate that this individual would be left behind by time. In essence, a prime candidate to become a typical "old fogey." If Cancer, the Fourth House, the Moon, or the planetary ruler of the Fifth House were also involved, look for a person who refuses to accept his or her children's point of view, or who finds such opinions as being very personally threatening.

Saturn/Neptune: These also are not the most naturally aligned planetary forces. Saturn is very practical, while Neptune is the least pragmatic of the planets. Saturn is very structured and time-oriented; Neptune is the least organized and the most universal in nature and orientation. Saturn is very demanding, while Neptune is quite permissive. Saturn insists on self-discipline and control, while Neptune rules over hallucinogenic drugs and other addictive substances that loosen control.

In a Capricorn-ruled horoscope, the effects of a difficult aspect between Saturn and Neptune are pernicious. An individual with the square or opposition between the two enters into a relationship or business situation with a tremendous fear of being trapped. Thus, the first thing he would look for upon entering a situation that has any hint of responsibility is the location of the way out! It is only when this type of Capricorn-rising person knows where and how he can leave such a position that he feels safe enough to hang around for a while.

There may be also a constant battle with addictions, as the individual is prone to creating habit patterns, as all Saturn-dominated people are habitual by nature, but such habits may often be quite deleterious in their effects. The opposition between Saturn and Neptune is often indicative of a person who alternates between highly self-destructive life periods and other times when he or she is engaged in a deep dedication to self-discipline and personal order. The harmonious contacts between these two planets support the tendency to be highly strategic. It gives the ability to engage in behind the scenes planning and negotiation. When the earth signs are highlighted in this combination, it lends itself to the blending of the real with the ideal, often producing a person who by some special gift or magic is able to find the solution to a very difficult and highly complex problem. The trine or sextile between Saturn and Neptune is also excellent for the construction (especially if Uranus is also being helpful) of special effects on film, television, or in the theater. It is a fine combination (along with a good Mercury) for the creation of secret codes and the construction of computer games.

Saturn/Pluto: Finally, we come to Saturn and Pluto. In addition to what was mentioned about these two planets on pages 156–157, under the heading "Scorpio rising (Pluto as ruler)," we should note that here the emphasis is for the refinement of the use of willpower. This is a very potent planetary influence, and to be used correctly, the Capricorn-ruled individual has to be pure in terms of the intentions of the heart. No matter the nature of the aspect between Saturn and Pluto, this is a combination that in an already power- and will-oriented Capricorn chart, only serves to increase the tendency to control the circumstances in one's environment. When harmoniously activated, Saturn and Pluto will serve to refine a person's ways and means for getting things done. This combination of energies allows a person to harness the very best (or the very worst) from within himself. It can give rise to an utterly ruthless disposition (especially if the signs Aries, Leo, Capricorn, or

Scorpio are involved), one that obeys no law but its own. Yet when in the horoscope of a more selfless and perhaps soul-centered individual, Saturn and Pluto tap a tremendous power of healing, overthrowing past patterns of harmful or wasteful behavior, opening a gateway into a positive and potent use of one's life energy.

Aquarius Rising (Uranus as Ruler)

It is the Uranian force in the horoscope that allows for (or if afflicted, inhibits) the unfolding of the personal path of individuation. The older reader may already have noticed the effects of the transit of Uranus in opposition to natal Uranus that occurs sometime between the thirty-seventh and the forty-second year of life, depending on Uranus' sign. It is at that time in one's life that a person is asked to create a more defined sense of oneself in ever more individualized terms. Such questions are asked: Do I break away from what I have established and go forth into a completely new line of work, new type of relationship, or new ideo-logical goals? Do I, in effect, release my past or do I, if it is possible, take the past along with me into an unfolding set of challenges that create a more refined sense of who I am and what I do on this planet? No won-der that this Uranus/Uranus opposition occurs at the time of one's midlife crisis. It is that crisis!

When Aquarius rises in the horoscope, a life is indicated in which a person either struggles to defend his or her ways of thinking and doing no matter what the external social circumstances may bring into life (and with a Uranus-ruled horoscope there are always surprises!), or that individual is hard at work breaking the bonds of the status quo. Any planet in close contact with Uranus will serve to define the focus of the nature of these challenging and/or innovating life circumstances. The intense urge to be different and to go one's own way is very Uranian. Even the planet itself is physically unique. Uranus is the only globe in the solar system that rotates on its equator and from east to west. Therefore, when you see Uranus in the sky, you are looking at its pole, and its retrograde revolution on that pole.

Uranus/Sun: The reader is asked to review those passages in this chapter that speak about the nature of Uranus when with the other planets, bearing in mind that the weight and emphasis of the effects of Uranus when in an Aquarius-ruled chart predominate over the nature of the other planets in question. Uranus/Sun aspects always heighten the nature of the individual, leading one to experiment in terms of one's creativity. Difficult aspects between the two always lead to the diffusion of vitality and a need to rebel for the sake of rebelliousness. The harmonious contacts add strength, direction, breadth, and originality to one's personal creative drive. These qualities may also exist when the square, opposition, or inconjunct exists between the Sun and Uranus. The difficulty comes in the person's often chaotic and "I'll do my own thing in my own way!" attitude of self-expression.

Uranus/Moon: Uranus with the Moon when Aquarius rises can bring further detachment to the emotional nature, indicate a very eccentric mother or family life, or bring about a distinct avoidance to sentimental, emotional intimacy. Friendships and a sense of deep commitment to group ideals (a "family of friends") may, however, be quite strengthened when the Moon and Uranus meet in the horoscope. The author has a Moon/Uranus conjunction in Gemini in the Seventh House square to Venus in Pisces in the Fourth. As a child, I always felt like, and was usually treated like, an outcast from the other children. My friends were few but very special eccentric or gifted children like myself, and I frequently used to invite them home for lunch. One day my mother said to me, "Alan, I'm glad that you bring friends home and I am happy to feed them, but can't you bring any normal kids home once in a while?" I replied, "Mother, I am not a normal child!" End of discussion.

Uranus/Mercury: Now this is a pair of great astrological friends. When harmoniously combined in an Aquarius-ruled horoscope, they give rise to all sorts of wonderful inventive and innovative ideas. If either or both of these two are themselves in the airy signs, a spark of genius can be found to flourish. If in difficult aspect, especially in the mutable signs, look for the person to display a great diffusion of mental energy and exhibit ideas that just don't quite fit into the prevailing social trends and circumstances. A nervous and high-strung disposition will tend to predominate no matter what the aspect. It is the person's ideas and the way they communicate them that set them apart and indicate the nature of the urge to individualize.

Uranus/Venus: When Venus is with Uranus in an Aquarius-ruled nativity, she shares a common personality trait with Uranus and the Moon—a need for excitement and social stimulation. We see with Venus and Uranus the urge for a wide range of interpersonal contacts. This is especially the case if either or both of the planets are in the mutable or air signs. Look for an individual who is artistic or bohemian in temperament and one who feels most comfortable with people who are the same. There is also the tendency to be involved with groups whose common focus of interest is highly specialized. Such groups are often "alternative" in nature and represent people whose hobbies or interests place them outside the mainstream of society.

Uranus/Mars: The combination of the effects of the Red Planet with Uranus can be very volatile. There is no doubt about it, when Mars is in close aspect to this planet, the urge to be a unique person is strong indeed. When joined by major aspect, Mars and Uranus bestow a courageous nature, indicating a person who challenges life and the status quo. If taken to an extreme (and Mars/Uranus people often like to live on the edge), this aspect leads to experimentative sexual activities and stimulates what one could call an "alternative" lifestyle. It is best exemplified by such sports as bungee jumping, hang gliding, and other activities that seek to stimulate adrenaline (ruled by Mars) under very risky and highly individualized activities (ruled by Uranus). It is no wonder then that the highly risky genre of sports known as "X" (for "extreme") was innovated by the Uranus in Scorpio generation (1974–1981). By risking one's own and other people's lives, and in the testing of personal boundaries, one comes in contact with the path to individualization with Uranus/Mars types.

Uranus/Jupiter: This is a planetary union that can blend beautifully and yield a fascinating approach to the higher mind, religion, sociology, jurisprudence, and other forms of philosophy. If Uranus and Jupiter are strongly united in a chart with Aquarius on the horizon, look for the individual's major interest to be colored by an idealized humanitarian perspective on life. When afflicted in an Aquarius-ruled chart, the person is often found to be a "church of one" or at the very least, to be attracted to unusual cults and sects. If Mars, especially when in hard aspect or a conjunction, is involved in this combination, look to fanaticism and ideological zealotry because the path to personal individuation takes place through belief systems.

Uranus/Saturn: As has been pointed out in the previous passage on the effects of Saturn and Uranus in a Capricorn-ruled chart (see page 171–172), these two planets do not have the easiest time in blending together harmoniously. When they do, they invent new social systems that benefit great masses of people. In the Capricorn chart, Saturn seeks to blend the new (Uranus) into an established sense of personal or collective order. When Aquarius rules and these two planets are linked by major aspect, the urge is much more to evolve what has been established into what is being envisioned. In effect, the past becomes either an impediment to the future (the square or opposition) or it becomes a steppingstone to a more advanced way of integrating one's ideals, groups, or even singular personality, into the collective social environment in which one lives (the trine or sextile). The path of social evolution and one's role within that orientation becomes the way of individuation.

Uranus/Neptune: This is a nonpersonal, collective combination of planetary forces. In the horoscope of most people, the afflictions give a sense of discomfort with the prevailing social trends and environment. Sentiments such as "I know that there is something better I have to do with my life, but I just do not know what that is," can be said to characterize the generation of people with Aquarius rising who have Uranus square Neptune (1951–1959). The sextile between the two (mid-1965 to end-1968) makes finding that place or function in society that much the easier. The conjunction or close approximation of Uranus and Neptune in an Aquarius-rising chart (1989–1997) is productive of a very special generation, one whose function will be to act as the collective seed for unfoldment of a large cycle (+/- five hundred years) of social evolution. On an individual basis, such individuals will possess some very interesting ideas about how people should interact with one another and will themselves be quite fascinating in terms of their concepts and ideas. I would say that this will extend into this entire group of people and not be limited to only those with Aquarius on the

Ascendant. The latter, however, will be more decidedly sociological (or sociopathic—depending on other influences) than their generational "compadres" with any of the other signs rising. The path to individualization takes place through a distinct challenge to the collective status quo of humanity.

Uranus/Pluto: In terms of the generational and personal implications of the combination of Uranus and Pluto, I ask the reader once again to refer to the appropriate passages under the heading of "Scorpio rising (Pluto as ruler)," found on pages 155–156. The implications of having Aquarius rising with the combination of these two planets is wider in its urge for disseminating new doctrines and other types of social reformations. The path towards individuation is geared toward joining those organizations and groups that seek to change society. In this way, one might find a path to further one's ideals.

Pisces Rising (Neptune as Ruler)

When Neptune rules the chart, there is a distinct devotional urge. This can manifest as a need to sacrifice oneself for the sake of some lofty or idealized religious, social, or philosophical belief, or conversely, in the lives of the more egocentric and less mature, it can lead to the loss of self through any number of addictive urges and practices. A question arises about the object of such devotion. Is it a type of devotion geared to the exploration of the senses, or is one's devotion to the exploration of higher ideals and principles? Service will be a major part of one's orientation to life. But once again, because Pisces is a dual sign—one Fish swimming upstream towards the spiritual life and the other Fish downstream into the world of the personality—is this selfless service to humanity, or a type of self-serving disposition that leads to total self-indulgence?

In terms of other personality characteristics, Neptune as the ruler of the horoscope will intensify one's general emotional sensitivity (especially to the immediate environment) and heighten one's psychic sensibilities. There is very often a distinct attraction to art, music, dance, theater, and films. The astral nature is very potent and consequently the dream life will play a major role in life. But this same trait can lead also to a dreamy disposition and the tendency to be somewhat vague and absent. A true Neptunian is someone who is not entirely "here." An aspect of themselves, a facet of their consciousness, seems to be off in some other, often undefined reality.

This is a person who will rebel at being pinned down and who will avoid any type of self-discipline that impinges on his or her fragile sense of boundaries. This is because of the Neptunian tendency to be easily penetrated by surrounding emotional forces. Compassion, empathy, and the urge to merge (either voluntarily or involuntarily) with the energies in the immediate environment is a prevalent trait. A person with Pisces rising is often overly sensitive to others and requires a great deal of time alone so that he or she may "wring out" their psychic sponge.

Neptune/Sun: All of the possible planetary contacts with Neptune have already been covered in previous sections of this chapter. The astrologer only has to note that should Pisces rise, the emphasis on delineating its ruler with any of the other bodies is on the effects of Neptune on that planet rather than the other way around.

Thus, the Sun with Neptune in a Pisces-rising chart adds strength and vitality to the psychic nature. In a heart-centered individual with this combination, look for the urge to be present for other people when they are in need. Sun/Neptune in this case can be a source of strength for people in distress. Yet should Neptune and the Sun be in a square or opposition, the Pisces-rising individual may lose him or herself in the urge to bring aid and comfort into other people's lives. This could manifest as a tendency to giving one's own power away by focusing on the ideals of helping (Neptune) rather than on the degree of personal vitality (the Sun) that one has available for such assistance. The Pisces-rising person would be the one to pay the price for such a miscalculation.

Neptune/Moon: In terms of the Moon when the Fish are on the Ascendant and Neptune is in strong aspect, the emotional and subconscious natures are very close to the surface in this combination. The individual will tend to see his or her personal emotional drama as the universal play. Everyone will have a part in the show and the individual with this placement will take on a role in everyone else's play. Emotional discrimination is thus very important. To the more spiritually mature, this is a combination that will heighten a person's understanding of others, thus making it easier to be of succor and service.

Neptune/Mercury: Because the emphasis is on the emotional and not on the mental when Neptune rules the chart, any aspect between this planet and Mercury has to be seen in this light. If one has Pisces rising and Neptune square, opposed, or conjoined Mercury, it is very difficult to achieve clear and logical thinking. The mental nature is often inundated by the waves from the subconscious that tend to flow into the mind. Yet this contact can produce some great poetry or theater pieces, and if the soul is of a high order, create a wonderful avenue for the channeling of intuitive insights and messages. If the individual is enchanted by a glamorous figment in his or her astral nature, such a Mercury/Neptune combination leads to the channeling of "Master Boo-Bah from the Zilch Nebula."

Neptune/Venus: This combination is as lovely as it can be potentially dangerous in terms of self-deceit in relationships. When the emphasis is on Neptune and its aspect to Venus is a harmonious one, look for a compassionate and helpful individual. The tendency is to love all and everyone and to use one's personal charisma and magnetism as a vehicle for healing in all interpersonal dynamics. Should the aspect be a difficult one or should the individual not be clear about where he or she stands in terms of one's own relationship needs and self-esteem, look for love addictions to people who are both self-destructive and harmful.

Neptune/Mars: If Neptune is a stronger influence upon one's life than Mars, such as in a Pisces-ruled chart, great care has to be taken in the integration of this combination of planetary influences because of what they may bring to the person. The astral life is very strong, leading to any number of false battles and difficult sexual entanglements. This will be true no matter what aspect links these two planets, but certainly the situations will be a lot more serious when the aspect is a conjunction, square, opposition, or tight inconjunct. If the Pisces-ruled individual is emotionally mature, this is a combination that may yield well-earned spiritual progress. Within a strong Neptune/Mars contact, there is the potential to confront and be victorious over the dark forces in life that seek to obscure the Light of Love. Such an individual may develop into a true spiritual warrior only after first conquering his or her lower nature.

Neptune/Jupiter: This is a very idealistic combination. Because Jupiter and Neptune corule Pisces, there is little difference in effect between Neptune and Jupiter in aspect when Sagittarius rises or when Pisces is on the cusp of the First House. However, in a Sagittarius-ruled horoscope, the tendency is for the idealism experienced by this combination to be more mental in expression, while in a Pisces-rising chart, such devotion to one's higher nature is realized more through the emotional nature. The tendency for self-deception in terms of one's belief is equally present in both, as the possibility of sharing some profound philosophical or spiritual truths. As with all aspects of Neptune, the nature of the effects of this planet depends on the level of a person's emotional maturation and level of spiritual evolution.

Neptune/Saturn: Whenever there is a tight aspect between Neptune and Saturn in a Pisces-dominated chart, there will be an emphasis on the dissolution of structures and boundaries. It must be determined whether such boundaries *need* to be in place. Dikes are very necessary to keep the ocean back from inundating the land, and fields cannot be properly watered if the irrigation canals are not structured properly. If a person needs to be consciously creative of this kind of protection in his or her life, then the inharmonious effects of Neptune or Saturn can be very deleterious. Let us say that Pisces is rising and Neptune is in Libra in the Seventh House in a trine to Saturn in Gemini in the Third House. This is a very healthy combination that allows for the continuous refinement and structuring of the mind through one's partnership associations. This planetary contact endows the individual with the ability to be in relationship with people who constantly support and inspire her. Such partnerships and close friendships allow her to easily structure her methods of communication so that she may share her understandings, ideas, and opinions with others.

As has been noted, the Neptune/Uranus and Neptune/Pluto contacts are so long-lasting that they affect and color entire generations. It is important to see in both cases if these combinations contact the Sun and/or the Moon. If this is the case and the individual is sufficiently developed to recognize them, then there is an ability to be in conscious contact with collective waves of evolutionary movement that sweep through our planet, touching all and everyone. Individuals with Pisces rising who are capable of such an attunement to these universal influences are our advanced thinkers, spiritual leaders, and healers.

---

1. As the current work is designed for students who have completed their basic training in terms of their astrological studies, the author assumes that the reader is already conversant with the fundamentals of the astrological language and is therefore quite familiar with the sign compatibility of the planets. Even so, a brief review and summary of this information can be found in Chapter 1 of the present work. It is also understood that the reader is acquainted with the nature of the six major geometric aspects (conjunction, sextile, square, trine, inconjunction, and opposition). The author's comments and observations here are geared towards bringing forth some of the more essential dynamics of planetary interchange specifically connected to the position of the ruler of the horoscope. These facts deserve to be highlighted, as they are not always available or readily found in other astrological sources. This listing is not meant to be an extensive treatise on all the thousands of planet/sign/aspect combinations possible, as we then would run into a work of encyclopedic length. Readers are always welcome to study the Recommended Reading List at the end of this book for works that further elucidate the compatibility of the signs and the nature of the interplanetary geometric angles.
2. A "double" Leo (or any other sign for that matter) could also see the Sun in the Second or the Eleventh House as well. For a fuller description of the rulers in their houses, please refer back to the appropriate passages in Chapter 4.
3. Examples: Cancer rising, Moon in Sagittarius square Jupiter; Cancer rising, Moon in Aries trine Mars, etc.
4. See the author's earlier work, *Soul-Centered Astrology,* op. cit.
5. Source of data: Colorado Department of Birth Records.
6. Source of data: Colorado Department of Birth Records.

The Placement of the Rulers in the Astrological Houses

Having focused on the Ascendant, its rulers, powers, and significance, we can now concentrate on the meanings and positions of the ruling planets of the other eleven houses in the natal chart. We are touching here upon the real art of astrology and that is the *art of synthesis*. The ability to synthesize energy patterns and their relationship as expressed through the symbols and geometry of astrology is one of the greatest gifts that our ancient science is able to bestow on its practitioners. When one can truly synthesize, the person within the horoscope emerges along with all of his or her talents and traumas, potentials and propensities. The dynamics of personal destiny reveal themselves, and the astrologer can be a helpful vehicle of support for the individual sitting on the "opposite side of the desk."

This chapter is a guide to a general understanding of the implications of each of the rulers of the houses when placed in the various astrological domiciles. It is impossible to list all the tens of thousands of possible variabilities of planet, sign, house, aspect, and dispositor relationships that exist in natal astrology. It does help to simplify and accelerate the process of delineation if we keep the primary astrological keywords in mind. The houses, planets, and signs have fundamental definitions. This "astrological alphabet" is found throughout astrological literature and is no doubt quite familiar to the reader. I add the following suggestions to this existing compendium with a special emphasis on life in this initial phase of the Aquarian Age.

Use the following Summary of Astrological Keywords and Phrases to flesh out the meanings of any of the specific planetary placements.

For example, if Mars is in the Second House, by consulting the keyword phrases you would be able to say that the individual's attitude toward the use of money and the expression of his or her self-worth would be assertive. The ability to prosper would be linked to that person's energetic potency. If we add a sign factor to Mars in the Second House, let us say Cancer, the keyword formulas taken from the Summary of Astrological Keywords and Phrases is: The need for acquiring and using individual resources is connected to the establishment of personal security and an anchoring of one's own psychological foundation. The reader is urged to experiment in this way with all the planet-sign-house combinations.

As you move through the various ruler-house combinations that follow, it would be good to keep in mind this *rule of delineation*: If a planet in a given house is in aspect with another planet in the natural sign rulership of that house, it emphasizes the importance of that planetary placement for good or ill, depending on the nature of the aspect. Example: Moon in Virgo in the Second House in trine with Mercury in Taurus.

Summary of Astrological Keywords and Phrases

The Planets

Sun: vitality, creative potency, link to life essence
Moon: instinctual nature, emotional responsiveness, form-sustaining, link to biological karma
Mercury: communicative nature, general mental activity, link to language
Venus: values, esthetics, nature of relationship urge, link to society
Mars: assertiveness, nature of sexual urge, sense of personal territory, link to energetic potency
Jupiter: expansion, aspiration, enterprise, generosity, link to nonjudgmental understanding
Saturn: boundaries, structure, responsibility, link to maturation of the personality

Uranus: urge for individuality, intuition, link to the Internet of the collective mind

Neptune: sense of universality, spiritual sensibility, illusion, devotion, link to the collective heart

Pluto: regeneration, transmutation, transformation, link to immortality

The Signs Through Their Positive Polarity of Expression

Aries: being, projection, immediacy, the awakening of opportunity, self-assertion

Taurus: having, holding, magnetism, the anchoring of opportunity, self-valuation

Gemini: communicating, objectifying, connecting, multiplying opportunity, self-connecting

Cancer: feeling, subjectifying, integrating, personalizing opportunity, self-securing

Leo: expressing, enlarging, embellishing, enhancing opportunity, self-creating

Virgo: discriminating, practicalizing, learning, particularizing opportunity, self-synthesizing

Libra: relating, stimulating relationship, engaging, idealizing, sharing opportunity, self-reflecting

Scorpio: transmuting, refining, enhancing life harmony through conflict, inheriting, redefining opportunity, self-transforming

Sagittarius: aspiring, path orienting, searching, generalizing, idealizing opportunity, self-expanding

Capricorn: willing, goal orienting, patterning, constructing, planning, shaping opportunity, self-structuring

Aquarius: networking, categorizing, archetyping, collectivizing, inventing opportunity, self-individualizing

Pisces: healing, including, flowing, spiritualizing opportunity, self-fulfilling

The Signs Through Their
Negative Polarity of Expression

Aries: dominating, conquering, invading, other-denying, the killing of opportunity, self-inversion

Taurus: possessive, denial of circulation, "black hole"—no light escapes, parched, the denial of opportunity, self-devaluation

Gemini: prevaricating, confusing, unresolved duality, cold and unfeeling, diffusion of opportunity, self-deceiving

Cancer: traumatized in the past, fixated in survival, fearful, the non-nurturing of opportunity, selfish

Leo: egocentric, energy vampirizing, shadow producing, blind to opportunity, self-dramatizing

Virgo: cluttering, non-discriminatory, promiscuous, non-integrational, incohesive response to opportunity, self-deprecating

Libra: wavering, flighty, noncommittal, polarizing, manipulative, reluctance to seize opportunity, self-repudiating

Scorpio: life absorbing, energy consuming, degenerative, destroys opportunity, self-consuming

Sagittarius: wasteful, opinionated, indiscriminate expansion, overly opportunistic, self-indulgent

Capricorn: prisoner of form, abuser of resources, dictatorial, controlling, manipulates opportunity, self-crystallizing

Aquarius: disruptive, superficial, detached from the heart, incohesive, diffuses opportunity, self-opinionated

Pisces: unconsciously responsive, indiscriminately sensual, addictive, dissolves opportunity, self-destructive

The Houses—from a More Socially
Evolved Perspective

First: What I am to myself and project to others.

Second: What I have and value within myself and offer to others.

Third: What I think and seek to communicate to others.

Fourth: What I stand upon as my foundation so that I may give to others.

Fifth: What I create and enjoy sharing with others.

Sixth: What I integrate within myself so that I may serve others.

Seventh: What I seek to harmonize within myself that externalizes through my relationships with others.

Eighth: What I need to transform in myself so that I may better heal others.

Ninth: What I expand in myself and thus may teach others.

Tenth: What I achieve through my efforts so that I may be supportive of others.

Eleventh: What I envision as truth and how I may distribute this vision with others.

Twelfth: What I believe about life so that I may inspire others.

The Houses—from a More Traditional, Astrological Perspective

First: ego in action, initial contact to the world around oneself, primary personality characteristics, physical appearance

Second: money, self-worth, possessions, values, esthetics, ability to prosper

Third: method of communication, early education and environment, brothers and sisters, close friends

Fourth: psychological roots, one's family and especially the mother, domestic issues, homes

Fifth: pleasures, children, method or area of creative self-expression, romance and lovers

Sixth: work and job, health, pets, employees, techniques of self improvement

Seventh: relationships in general, marriage or business partners in particular; what I seek in others

Eighth: sex, death, and taxes; inherited or shared wealth coming from partnerships, methods of regeneration; dream life

Ninth: higher education, religious or philosophical beliefs, foreign travel, publishing

Tenth: career, status in the world, the father, culmination of professional activities

Eleventh: groups and organizations; friends and associates; hopes, wishes, and aspirations

Twelfth: all things hidden or obscure; secret lovers, hidden treasure, concealed strengths and weaknesses

The Nature of the Second House

There are two primary meanings associated with this astrological realm. The first is literal and physical: our money, personal possessions, material wealth and substance. Though it manifests physically, it is relatively unformed, more like the o re in a mine, a potential waiting to be processed and shaped into its various forms and uses. The sign on the cusp of the Second House and the condition of its ruler symbolizes our natural orientation toward money in general, and our own financial state in particular.

The second meaning of this house is figurative and psychological because it deals with our innermost feelings about what we most (or least) treasure. In this way, it describes our self-worth, self-esteem, and sense of personal value. In a broader context, the Second House indicates where our financial support comes from and where it goes. If the Second House and its ruler are afflicted, this orientation to our personal cache of riches can be stunted. The result is a poverty of consciousness, lack of money, and a consequent sense of lacking something fundamental within ourselves.

When the ruler of the Second House is in the First, it can be said that we "wear our self-worth on our sleeve." The closer the ruler is to the degree on the Ascendant, the more obvious this association between what we value in ourselves and what we physically own, and what we project as our self-image. If one's self-esteem is very low (indicated by the Second House ruler afflicted by Saturn and/or a poorly placed Venus, for example), then the individual is likely to present a poor physical image of him or herself to the world. The ruler of the Second in the First points to an urge to project what we possess to the forefront of life. In effect, this is another way of saying, "I am what I have." Sagittarius on the cusp of the Second House and Jupiter in the First, for example, can indicate a gambler, a person who "plays games" with his or her financial resources. This same contact from a nonmaterial sense can reveal a personality who is a teacher by nature. This is someone who in his or her moment-to-moment contacts with life is saying, "My wealth is in my knowledge. What I believe about myself is who I am and this extends into my worldview." Should such a perspective be limited by the level of the individual's psychological or spiritual maturity, we may easily encounter a very self-righteous person. This would be especially true if the ruler of the Second were afflicted in a fixed sign and located in the First.

When the ruler of the Second House is in the Second, there will be great emphasis on the affairs of this domicile. The individual must use his or her resources, financial and otherwise, in a most personal way. If this is the Sun, for example, (Leo on the cusp of the Second), the individual is strongly identified with what he has or has not. It is very important for this person to use his resources in ways that clearly indicate the nature of one's own talents and abilities. The statement one is making is: "What's mine is so much an expression of my identity that it always bears my personal stamp". If Saturn is in Taurus and square the Sun in Leo in the Second, look for a person who has been wounded in his or her sense of self-worth and feels limited in the ability to let the "Sun shine" in this facet of life. Most likely this limitation has come through a materialistic father (Saturn in Taurus) who may himself have had problems in the area of his own self-worth. This aspect is particularly strong, as the Sun in Leo is in the Second House square a planet in Taurus, the natural sign ruler of that house. An examination of the nature of the Tenth and Fourth houses (family, parents, psychological roots) would help to substantiate this indication.

When the ruler of the Second is in the Third, the nature of one's self-worth or the actual substance of value (money, for example) has to be communicated. The need to connect with people or with life situations that amplify one's opportunities is essential. Any planet found in the Third House is used to make connections. When it is the ruler of the Second, then such connections are sought that may increase the potential uses of one's personal talents and resources. If that planet is afflicted, then there is a limitation or difficulty with the connection-making process. Let us say that Virgo is on the cusp of the Second, and Mercury is in Leo in the Third, square to Saturn in Scorpio. In this case, the individual has a strong urge to communicate the wealth and worth of his or her ideas and opinions but is blocked from doing so by Saturn. This may be a result of the inability to move beyond the original patterns of communication learned in childhood. The square from Saturn in Scorpio indicates that Mercury is inhibited from regenerating these early thinking patterns (fixed sign/Third House combination). In general, when the Second House ruler is in the Third House, there is a natural orientation to experiment in a multiplicity of ways in the experience and discovery of one's self-worth and the use of personal resources. This tendency definitely would be increased if the ruler of the Second were in the Third in a mutable sign.

When the ruler of the Second is in the Fourth, it indicates that the sense of self-worth is especially linked to the values of one's parents. There is a need to use one's resources as a foundation for building greater potentials for opportunities in order to anchor personal security in the world. If Cancer were on the Second House cusp, and the Moon as the ruler of the Second were in Virgo in the Fourth, there would be a strong need to find the right kind of job that would allow full use of personal talents and resources. For example, if the Moon were in trine to Jupiter in Taurus from its position in the Fourth House, then a good source of investment for such an individual might be in commercial real estate or a job in this area might turn out to be quite profitable. This is seen in terms of astrological symbology as: Moon = houses; Fourth House = domestic associations, foundations; Virgo = commercial enterprise, practical use of land; Jupiter in Taurus = expansion in things of the earth and in fixed goods such as real estate; trine = sustained opportunity.

This is an even more opportune aspect because Jupiter is exalted in the Moon's natural sign, Cancer, and Jupiter's position in Taurus emphasizes this positive planetary interchange. In addition, Taurus is the sign of the Moon's exaltation, and the Moon is in its own house here and therefore very comfortably posited in the chart. The astrologer would need to caution the client to move slowly in his or her investments, carefully building one upon the other because Virgo is the sign of Jupiter's detriment, but the positive dynamics of this combination far outweigh the negative connotations.

When the ruler of the Second is in the Fifth, the individual would be prone to use his or her resources for pleasure. This position seems to say: "I have it, I earned it, and now I will enjoy myself." There is also a tendency to see one's self-worth and riches in terms of one's children, because the Fifth House rules children. Afflictions to the ruler of the

Second in the Fifth may indicate that one feels that children are costly to raise, or that one's sense of self-worth is not validated by the activities and lives of one's progeny. Positive aspects to such a placement would reverse these indications and give validation to self-worth from one's children or from any other form of one's creative self-expression.

When the ruler of the Second is in the Sixth, the indication is that the individual has to work for his or her money, using personal skills, tools, and techniques to bring a feeling of self-improvement in his sense of self-worth. If the ruler of the Second is well situated in the Sixth, earning one's livelihood may indeed come about under very pleasant circumstances. The individual in question can find that his or her experiences on the job offer good ways to cultivate an increased or more refined sense of self-worth and consequent economic gain. Such a set of positive opportunities could occur, for example, if Venus were the ruler of the Second (Libra on the cusp) and in Aquarius in the Sixth in a sextile to Mercury. Increased financial returns on one's efforts and the development of an improved sense of self-worth come about through social contacts (Venus as the ruler of Libra/relationships in positive aspect with Mercury, ruler of connection making). In this example, the individual would then tend to experience a great and uplifting camaraderie (Aquarius = groups of friends or equals) on the job (Sixth House).

When the ruler of the Second is in the Seventh, partnership will be essential to the expression of self-worth and the increase of personal wealth. No matter what the planetary ruler might be in this case, the astrologer should look carefully at the placement of Venus in the natal chart. This is because Venus is the natural planetary ruler of *both* the Second and the Seventh houses. Any aspect that Venus makes to the ruler of the Second in the Seventh would thus be a major conditioning factor describing the financial (Second) and social (Seventh) circumstances of the individual. One difficulty that could arise from this position could be because the individual in question is highly reliant on his or her relationships for self-valuation.

Should there be an affliction to the Second House ruler in the Seventh, such validation may not be easily forthcoming. If the Second House ruler is afflicted in this house position especially by the

Seventh House ruler, then the tendency is for the individual to have financial difficulties in partnership in general. A good example of this situation would be if Libra were on the Second House cusp and Venus were in Pisces in the Seventh in opposition to Neptune in Virgo. In this instance the message is very clear: The individual has a distinct tendency to fool herself (Neptune in the First) about her financial dealings (opposing the Second House ruler) with partners (in the Seventh House).

When the ruler of the Second is in the Eighth, there is an indication that personal resources are inherited or that one's sense of self-worth is connected to values that have been handed down through generations. The latter case would be especially true if the Fourth House and its rulers and/or the signs Cancer or Capricorn were also intimately involved. The following example horoscope illustrates these principles perfectly.

Christina Onassis was the only surviving child of one of the richest men in Europe, Aristotle Onassis, the second husband of Jacqueline Kennedy Onassis. Her natal chart shown on the following page reveals that the ruler of the Second House, Mercury, is in Capricorn in the Eighth. Mercury is in opposition to Uranus in Cancer in the Second and this position makes a T-square with Saturn in Libra. This difficult position shows the many conflicts in her personal life that such wealth brought upon her. It also reveals the family orientation of this money (the signs Cancer and Capricorn are prominent) as well as the focus on the father (Saturn at the apex of the T-square). Christina inherited her father's entire estate (himself a Capricorn) upon the accidental death of her brother. This can be traced by examining the nature of the Third House (brothers and sisters). Here we see that Cancer is on this cusp and that its ruler, the Moon, is conjunct to Mars and square to Neptune. These aspects point to the potential death of a sibling (with the possibility that alcohol or other drugs were involved). Such indications are reinforced, however (the astrologer should always look for additional astrological reinforcements to major conclusions), when we examine the house of death of siblings, the Tenth. The Tenth is the Eighth House (death) from the Third (siblings). Here we find that the ruler of the cusp is Aquarius. The primary ruler of this house is therefore

Example 15: The Horoscope of Christina Onassis[1]

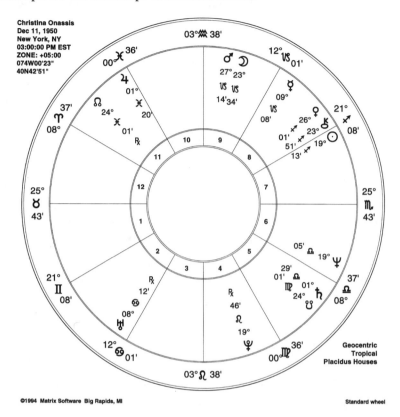

Christina Onassis
Dec 11, 1950
New York, NY
03:00:00 PM EST
ZONE: +05:00
074W00'23"
40N42'51"

©1994 Matrix Software Big Rapids, MI

Geocentric
Tropical
Placidus Houses

Standard wheel

Uranus, and the secondary ruler is Saturn. These two are in square with Uranus in Christina's Second House of personal wealth and Saturn is the dispositor of Mercury in Capricorn, ruler of the Second, placed in the Eighth and square to Saturn in its own right.

The fact that money dominated her life is also seen by the fact that Taurus is the ruling sign of the Ascendant, and its ruler, Venus (natural ruler of the Second), is also in the Eighth conjoined to Chiron (she was wounded both by love and money) as well as the Sun. The Sun is the ruler of the Fourth House of family and is also an indicator, especially in a woman's chart, of one's father. But we can also take the "official" house of the father, the Tenth, and see that its ruler, Uranus, lands right back in Christina's Second House of personal resources.

When the ruler of the Second is in the Ninth, the individual's sense of self-worth is intimately related to what he or she believes. Religion and philosophy will play an important role in determining the direction of personal development, especially the establishment of personal values. If the Moon were the ruler of the Second (Cancer on the cusp), the orientation to self-worth and money in general would be connected to how deeply one was influenced by the family. If the Moon were in Aquarius in the Ninth House and square to Saturn in Scorpio, it would be extremely challenging for the individual in question to develop his or her own set of beliefs relative to Second House affairs. The tendency would be to believe one's self-worth was in accord with one's family's opinion—which in the case of this astrological example would not be particularly positive. Another implication of the presence of the ruler of the Second in the Ninth is that one could use one's talents and resources through the other facets of life connected to the Ninth: foreign travel, publishing, and teaching, to cite a few examples.

When the ruler of the Second is in the Tenth, the individual has the opportunity to make the most out of what he or she possesses. Let us remember that the Tenth is the house of *culmination and fruition.* The Second House supplies us with raw materials, but the Tenth allows us to put our potential out into the world (the function of this potential having been refined through the Sixth House) and reap the consequent benefits from our efforts. There is a natural, positive link between the Second and the Tenth because the natural ruler of the latter, Saturn, is exalted in Libra, one of the two signs ruled by Venus, natural planetary ruler of the Second House. In addition, both the Tenth and the Second are "earthy houses," as they deal with the material dynamics of life and are ruled by earth signs. If the ruler of the Second is afflicted in the Tenth, especially by the planet ruling the sign on the Tenth House cusp, it will be challenging for a person to capitalize on his or her natural talents. Should Saturn be the afflicting planet, even if there is success, the individual is likely to feel shortchanged in some way, believing that her full potential is somehow limited or restricted by the circumstances of life. Should the ruler of the Second be well supported by any of the other planets in the chart, the likelihood of extracting the gold out of one's ore and selling it for a good price is strongly emphasized.

When the ruler of the Second is in the Eleventh, one's talents and abilities are linked to friends, associates, and the groups or organizations to which one belongs. The Eleventh House is the arena of the collective social values of the society in which one lives. An individual with this placement of the Second House ruler indicates that personal values and self-worth are either supported or refuted by this larger surrounding social collective. In this respect, the relationship between the individual and his or her social environment is thus of major importance in one's life. Additional wealth may come through public approval of one's talents; inhibitions to material growth can occur when what one values is not in keeping with society. Material losses can occur if the Second House ruler is afflicted in the Eleventh and one lends money to friends and associates. The old adage, "Neither a borrower nor a lender be," is very appropriate when such afflictions are present. On the other hand, if there is a well-placed Second House ruler in the Eleventh, the individual can expect material and moral support from friends and the various social groups to which he or she belongs.

When the ruler of the Second is in the Twelfth, one's personal resources often are hidden. But, if well aspected, the Twelfth House ruler may indicate the ability to ferret out buried treasure, valuables that are tucked away in such obscure sources as garage sales, attics, or thrift shops. This position can also mean having a "financial guardian angel," that is, the tendency to receive money and other support from clandestine or unknown people or circumstances. If the ruler of the First House (paternal aunts and uncles) is well aspected to the ruler of the Second in the Twelfth, for example, a person may receive a surprising legacy from a relative. In some cases, this position points to a person who can be rather unaware of his true talents and abilities, only to find that under duress or extreme conditions, such unknown richness within himself rises to the surface. An afflicted Second House ruler in the Twelfth may also indicate the squandering of personal resources or that poor investments can be the source of one's financial undoing.

The Nature of the Third House

This is a full and busy house because it concerns a multitude of factors.

Primarily, this is the house of relating in terms of our immediate environment. It speaks about our verbal skills and the way we communicate our thoughts, ideas, and opinions through the written or spoken word. Our mental framework is conditioned by our early learning circumstances, and it is not until we enter the larger world, outside our neighborhood, that we come in contact with a wider and higher education that serves to expand our horizons (the nature of these experiences will be found in general in the houses above the horizon of the chart). The Third House, then, deals with short journeys, elementary schooling (up to high school), and the people in our family that are closest in age to us: brothers and sisters, cousins, and close, lifelong friends who are like siblings.

When the ruler of the Third is in the First, our opinions and ideas are out in front. Who we are is linked to what we think and how we communicate those thoughts to others. Often the condition of a Third House ruling planet will describe the nature or appearance of a sibling or close friend who plays an important role in our life. Saturn as the ruler, for example, could indicate an older brother or sister, one who helped to condition or structure our early life. The Moon in this position could easily indicate a sibling that acted as a mother figure to us as we were growing up and who maintains this position of importance in terms of the way we project our self-image.

When viewed from the perspective of our methods of communication, the planets tell us yet other things. Saturn, in this position (especially in Cancer or Capricorn), indicates that we have been strongly conditioned by the traditional thinking of our family or early social background. The Moon here points to the fact that our thinking and communicative processes have been highly influenced by our mother and that it may be quite challenging to "come up to date" in our thinking process and move out of these past conditioning factors. Mars in this position points to a person who is prone to dominating the environment and immediate social contacts with his or her thoughts and opinions. An afflicted Mars as ruler of the Third in the First can indicate a sibling with whom we have many conflicts. This is a person who does not accept other people's ways of expressing themselves when they come in conflict with his own. Such a Mars-ruled person will fight to maintain his or her opinions no matter what the cost, and therefore encounters frequent challenges to his own ideas.

When the ruler of the Third is in the Second, it gives us a person who places tremendous value upon what he or she thinks. In some cases, this individual's personal riches reside in her mind and therefore she tends to use her mental abilities as the primary source of both her talents and debilities. A well-aspected Venus in this position, for example, can indicate that the person has a "wealth of ideas," and can use this mental treasure trove in order to advance herself in life (especially if Venus is trine the Midheaven or its ruler). A strong Saturn in this position speaks about a person who will carefully use his or her ideas, does not waste words, and who is rather cautious about what she reveals. Rather like an author who may write several books in order to make the most use (and gain the most profit) out of her thoughts, rather than condensing these ideas into one volume. An afflicted Saturn (especially in Taurus or in difficult aspect with another planet in this sign) in this same position can point to an individual who feels constricted about the value of his thoughts. It gives the inner message, "My thoughts are worthless."

When the ruler of the Third is in the Third, brothers and sisters can play a significant role in one's life. This ruling planet will describe the person and any special circumstances surrounding the relationship. If Mars is the ruler in the Third, afflicted by Uranus, for example, look for a sibling who is rebellious or accident prone. If this planet is a well-aspected Venus, especially in Libra, Taurus, or Pisces, an artistic and often physically beautiful brother or sister is likely. *Planets are people* and no matter where they appear in the chart, they often describe the people whom the individual is likely to meet or be with in relationship, according to the house in question. In terms of an individual's attitude and scope of communication, when the ruler of the Third is in its own house, look for a mind and method of expressing personal ideas and opinions that is described by that ruling planet and its astrological conditions by sign and aspects. If we take the same planets we just used in speaking about siblings, we can also interpret them in terms of their importance as significators of the individual's mental focus. A rebellious Mars square Uranus as ruler of the Third will not create a peaceful, rational mind, nor an attitude eager to communicate any but its own opinions. The individual is prone to anger in response to ideas that challenge his own. He is liable to say things that offend others (on purpose!) or to take personal offense at issues of an impersonal nature. "As this situation has nothing whatsoever to do with you personally, why are you angry?", would be a question one could ask such a Mars Uranus/Third House person. Lovely Venus in Libra as the Third House ruler would indicate a peacemaker, a person who brings harmony into all conversations and who seeks to be an agent of accord in his or her relationships. This position would also indicate an artistic turn of mind and reveal an individual with many ideas linked to the muses.

When the ruler of the Third is in the Fourth, the nature of one's ideas and opinions are highly subjective. This position also indicates a person who may go through life with the sense of "I keep my ideas to myself." This would be true especially if the ruler were in any of the water signs or in Taurus. Neptune, Saturn, or the Moon in strong aspect to the ruler of the Third in the Fourth House, could either restrict or further subjectify the communicative process. This definitely is a person who is a deep thinker but those thoughts are very personal in nature.

The astrologer should keep in mind that several of the planets will rule more than one house in any given horoscope. Let us say that Aries is on the cusp of the Third. If this is the case, then in moderate latitudes, Scorpio will be on the MC. If Mars, as ruler of the Third *and* the Tenth, is in the Fourth, then there just might be a way for the subjective nature of this person's method of communicating to serve his or her career interests (Tenth). In terms of other Third House matters, there is often something uniquely important with relationship to the individual's siblings. This position of the Third House ruler may also indicate an individual who likes to live near, or even with, his or her brothers and sisters.

When the ruler of the Third is in the Fifth, the mind tends to be highly creative with strong urges to do something intellectually important. "How can I turn what I think into something of practical use?", is the question one would have if the ruler were in the earth signs. "How can my ideas be fully representative of myself (Aries or Leo) or what I believe (Sagittarius)?" "How can I use what I know to further my creativity towards communicative ends?", is the question should the ruler be in the air signs. "How can I be more emotionally supportive of myself and others or use my creative talents more resourcefully?", asks the person with the Third House ruler in the Fifth in the water signs. When well aspected, the Fifth House position of the Third House ruler is also indicative of the ability to communicate well with children, and young people in general.

When the ruler of the Third is in the Sixth, the mind and thoughts are usually geared to the practical issues of life. There is an ongoing need to acquire additional skills and methods of communication that can be applied and integrated into one's job and work area. If the individual is an employer and the ruler of the Third is Mars afflicted in the Sixth, that person is likely to have a number of altercations with his or her employees. If the Third House ruler in this domicile is the Moon, for example, and the latter is well aspected, the individual is likely to communicate in a protective, motherly fashion to his or her employees. In addition, people with a strong and well-aspected ruler of the Third in the Sixth House will be able to communicate well with pets and animals in general. In fact, a pet may often be treated like a beloved brother, sister, or good friend. The planet itself may even describe the personality and appearance of such an endeared animal. Using the keywords and phrases as they apply to all the planets and signs will reveal the nature of one's communicative abilities in all cases. Almost everything can be read in the horoscope providing we know how to read it.

When the ruler of the Third is in the Seventh, it denotes a person with a strong need to intimately communicate with people. Aquarius on the cusp of the Third House with a well-aspected Uranus in Gemini in the Seventh, for example, speaks about a person whose spoken and written words have the ability to reach a large number of people. This is an individual who can create a personal sense of contact with others, even if those others are strangers. On a more intimate level, the ruler of the Third in the Seventh indicates an individual who has a strong need to communicate with his or her partners. This can be the kind of person who has to talk about his relationship with the person with whom the relationship is taking place. We could call this the urge to "process relationship." It is also important for such an individual to find an audience for his ideas, as this person needs to have what he knows be reflected back to him through the minds and opinions of others.

When the ruler of the Third is in the Eighth, the individual has the urge to change the way other people think, so that they conform to his or her own opinions and ideas. In a negative sense, this can give rise to manipulation through communicative opportunities. This would be especially the case if the ruler of the Third were Mercury in conjunction, square, or opposition to Pluto or vice versa. In the mind of the unscrupulous, the sextile or trine between Mercury and Pluto in this case would only facilitate the ability for such manipulations to happen. Positive aspects do not indicate a positive moral character, just an ease of expression of the planetary energies so configured.

In the horoscope of a positive and helpful person, such Mercury/Pluto-type aspects serve to refine, redefine, and reorient other people's thoughts and ideas so that they are productive and increase the other person's creative potentials. Hard aspects between these planets would only indicate that such a well-meaning individual would find herself in ideological conflicts with others, and thus the orientation toward a transformational process would be difficult to achieve. Third House rulers in the Eighth aid psychologists, psychiatrists, and counselors in general. When in the water or earth signs, they also can indicate a person who is prone to giving investment advice. A strong Neptune, as the ruler of the Third in the Eighth, can point to an individual with a powerful dream life. Third House rulers in the watery signs in the Eighth, especially in aspect to Jupiter, give a psychic and prophetic nature.

When the ruler of the Third is in the Ninth, the door is wide open to education and learning. This is a person who seeks to widen his or her mental horizons and will usually do this through abundant travel and exploring his or her never-ending thirst for knowledge. The sense of movement associated with the Third and the Ninth (and their natural signs, Gemini and Sagittarius) is supported and augmented in the horoscope if the ruler of the Third is in the mutable, fiery, or airy signs. Look for less activity but better abilities to concentrate upon what one is learning when the ruler of the Third in the Ninth is in the fixed signs. The urge to capitalize in a practical way upon what one is studying is likely to be successful when the ruler of the Third is in the Ninth House in one of the earth signs. One problem that may come about from this position, especially if the Third House ruler is afflicted in the Ninth by either Jupiter or the natal ruler of this house, is if the individual thinks that his personal thoughts, ideas, and opinions are universally true, or are more inclusive and comprehensive than they actually may be.

When the ruler of the Third is in the Tenth, the individual is likely to use his or her communicative abilities for career purposes. With this position, there is a need to bring one's ideas and opinions out into the larger world. A badly afflicted Third House ruler in the Tenth in the air signs, for example, may indicate a person who must communicate for a living, but who has a horror of public speaking and/or is very bad at it. (Look for an afflicted Moon and/or difficult position of the Second House ruler to support this supposition.) A strong Third House ruler in this position indicates a person who likes to be heard and feels comfortable and happy when other people act upon his or her ideas. The Tenth is an executive placement. Saturn or the Sun as ruler of the Third in the Tenth is definitely someone who enjoys giving orders. The nature of how these orders are heard and acted upon is indicated by the aspects from other planets aspecting the Third House ruler in relationship to the houses they rule in the natal chart. If Capricorn is on the Third House cusp, for example, and Saturn is in the Tenth House in trine to Mars, ruler of the Sixth (Aries on the cusp), the horoscope would show that this is a person who will command respect (or fear) from his or her employees and "an order is an order is to be carried out!"

When the ruler of the Third is in the Eleventh, the urge to communicate seeks a larger audience in terms of the groups, organizations, and general social contacts in a person's life. If Venus is the ruler, the person can use his or her natural charisma to bring people together for mutually beneficial purposes. When the ruler of the Third is in the Eleventh, the primary impulse for communication is to create a forum for the sharing of ideas. There also may be the need to find new and original ways to facilitate communication, not only of one's own thoughts and opinions, but also of the collective ideology or larger frame of reference that is usually so much a part of one's life. This is definitely one of the better placements for the Third House ruler in terms of personal evolutionary possibilities for growth, as it allows

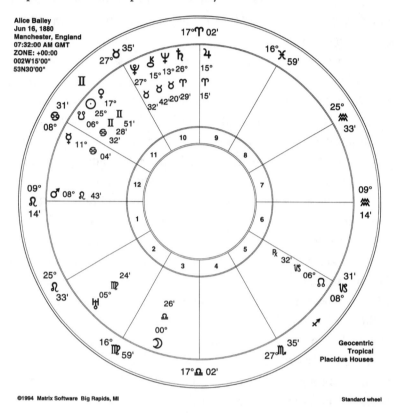

Alice Bailey
Jun 16, 1880
Manchester, England
07:32:00 AM GMT
ZONE: +00:00
002W15'00"
53N30'00"

©1994 Matrix Software Big Rapids, MI   Standard wheel

one's individual ideas to merge with a larger collective. One can only hope that the right group has been chosen.

When the ruler of the Third is in the Twelfth, the mind is given over to hidden, secretive, or possibly esoteric and occult matters. When well aspected, this is an excellent position for research and investigative work. The individual's natural urge is to look behind the scenes and explore that which needs to be discovered. If poorly aspected, especially by Neptune or when in this position in the sign of Pisces, there is the tendency to agree with everyone else's opinion, but to not have one's own mental attitudes clearly defined. This is a position that adds to the psychic abilities of a person, especially if the planet is in the watery signs. This is certainly the case in the example horoscope that follows, the chart of Alice A. Bailey. Mrs. Bailey worked for thirty years as the amanuensis for the Tibetan Master, Djwhal Khul, with whom she had a direct intuitive contact. Together, they produced a prodigious and incredible body of work, which are the clearest treatises on the Ancient Wisdom Teachings produced in this century.

In this horoscope we see that Virgo is on the cusp of the Third (her writing was done completely in the spirit of service) and Mercury, its ruler, is in Cancer in the Twelfth with Gemini on the cusp. This makes Mercury the ruler of both these houses. Mrs. Bailey's psychic sensitivity is clear. Mercury, ruler of the Twelfth, is in a water sign in the Twelfth House and sextile to Neptune, and square to Jupiter. In addition, Mercury is disposited by the Moon in the Third, adding to the mental sensitivity and responsiveness. The Moon is disposited by Venus in the Eleventh, which itself is disposited by Mercury, and it is obvious from her lectures and writings that Mrs. Bailey's work was totally group-oriented. Mrs. Bailey was the founder of both a spiritual publishing house (Jupiter in the Ninth square to Mercury with the ruler of the Ninth sextile to Mercury) based on her writings (Mercury rules the Third). She was also the founder of an esoteric educational organization, the Arcane School. We can see in the chart by the various Mercury/Jupiter/Neptune aspects that her relationship to writing and teaching esoterica is a natural affinity.

The Nature of the Fourth House

Traditionally associated with one's mother and the domestic environment in general, the Fourth House reveals the emotional climate surrounding birth and the early years of life. This is the third component of the chart which, when assessed with the astrological factors associated with the First and Third houses, gives the astrologer a rather complete view of the primary conditioning circumstances constituting an individual's psychological orientation to life. Frequently referred to as the "nadir" or the "IC" — the abbreviated form for the Latin words *immum coeli*, meaning "at the lowest point of the heavens" — in astrological texts, the cusp of the Fourth House symbolizes the most subjective facets of our being. The Fourth House is definitely a key to the nature of our primary roots (what I like to refer to as the "biological karma") and deals with the psychological foundations upon which we build the rest of our life. Along with the Moon as the natural ruler of this domicile, the natal ruler of the sign on the cusp of this house, and the general nature of the house itself, the Fourth reveals a great deal about what we have absorbed from the past: our family, tribe, race, nationality, and inherited social patterns.

When the ruler of the Fourth is in the First, the early domestic circumstances and the relationship with one's family imprint the individual profoundly. If the ruler is the Moon itself (Cancer on the cusp of the Fourth), then there will be no doubt that the mother's role is the paramount force in the shaping of the individual's character. The personality of the mother and the individual's relationship with her dominates one's emotional orientation both to oneself as well as toward others. In a man's horoscope, if the Moon is afflicted in this position (especially by Pluto or Saturn), there can be confusion with women because he seeks to be in an emotionally intimate relationship with a woman in the same way that he was in relationship with his mother. Added to this difficulty is the fact that the man often may wish to play out the maternal role himself, and two cooks in the same kitchen only bring trouble!

The ruler of the Fourth in the First brings to the surface of life many of the surrounding issues of childhood. If this is a well-aspected Venus, for example, the individual is a harbinger of peace and a bringer of beauty into every situation that he or she touches (although one's values and esthetics may closely resemble those of one's mother). If the ruler is a discordant Mars, the person may have to prove him or herself at every turn. The competitive and survivalist attitudes of one's background will always be leaping into the foreground of one's immediate contacts with the environment.

When the ruler of the Fourth is in the Second, the early conditioning factors highly influence our values and most specifically, the way we deal with money. Our sense of self-worth, the opinions we carry about the nature of our inner resources, the way we deal with the sharing of our personal substance—all of these are dominated by what we inherited from our roots. Although the Eighth House is the primary indication of wills and legacies, if the ruler of the Fourth is well aspected and harmoniously placed in the Second, this is another indication of money and financial support received from the family. This would especially be the case if the ruling planets were Venus, Jupiter, or the Moon, and in the signs Taurus, Capricorn, or Cancer. In the case of the Moon, Cancer on the cusp of the Fourth with the Moon well aspected in Taurus in the Second, is a clear indicator of inheritance of real estate in general and family property in particular. Should there be hard aspects to the ruler of the Fourth in the Second and especially if the signs Cancer or Capricorn are involved and/or the ruling planet is Saturn or the Moon is in Capricorn, the individual is likely to have financial or emotional responsibilities for his or her parents.

When the ruler of the Fourth is in the Third, look to the parents and one's early environmental conditioning to have an especially strong effect in the way a person thinks and communicates. Let us say that Capricorn is on the Fourth House cusp and Saturn in that sign is in the Third in a particular individual's chart. This position would indicate the person would tend to have come from a traditional background where the energies of the father (Saturn in Capricorn) would have had a great deal to do with the shaping of the individual's thoughts and opinions.

Please keep in mind that the Fourth House is not always the house of one's mother. It often points to the father, if the latter were the more influential of the parents from a psychological perspective. If the astrologer has any doubt about which parent "belongs" in which house, look to the sign on the cusp of the house, or planets within that house, to describe the parent. If possible, refer to the horoscope of the parents themselves for a more complete astrological portrait.

In the case of the author's son, for example, he has Aries on the Fourth House cusp and Venus-ruled Libra on the Tenth. The author is an Aries with Scorpio rising with Mars in Cancer, and acted as the primary nurturer and caregiver. (In addition, the author's Moon is conjunct his son's Sun.) My son's mother has a chart clearly ruled by Venus (five planets in Taurus including Venus conjunct the Sun in the First House), and she definitely brought a sense of esthetics to their relationship. In this case, the parents are much better described by a reversal of the traditional house assignments. Sometimes the ruler of the Fourth in the Third indicates that as an adult the individual would tend to live near his or her parents because the Third House is also where we can find our neighbors.

When the ruler of the Fourth is in the Fourth. I love astrology! Sometimes the indications are so precise, so clear, that it is obvious that the dictum from the Ancient Wisdom Teachings, "God geometrizes," is beautifully apparent. Such is the case when we look at the meaning of the ruler of the Fourth in the Fourth and study it with Julia Child's horoscope as our example. If we take a home and assign various rooms or portions of that dwelling to each of the houses of the chart, we find that the First House rules the entrance; the Second rules safes, vaults, and storage places of things of value; the Third rules one's study as well as connecting corridors; the Fifth, the playroom or the children's room; the Sixth rules the garden, an office or shop in the home, broom and linen closets, as well as many parts of the bathroom (especially the medicine cabinets); the Seventh rules the living room, dining room, and any shared bedrooms; the Eighth rules the toilets, septic tank, as well as that portion of the house where material to be recycled is stored; the Ninth rules the library; the Tenth rules the structure of the house and the general way it functions; the Eleventh is the part of the house where the computer is placed and also the den, where friends come to gather; the Twelfth is the attic, garage, basement, and naturally the hot tub or the swimming pool. And the Fourth House? The Fourth House rules the hearth, the kitchen!

Julia Child is the most renowned of American chefs. Her cookbooks have sold in the many millions and her television shows have been the most popular programs of their genre for two generations of viewers. Is it any wonder that the ruler of her Fourth House is in the Fourth and that this ruler is the Sun in Leo? Julia Child is definitely the queen of cookery as she stands over six feet tall and *non-pareil* as the ruler of her domicile. If we look a little further into this map (see page 207), we will see that Saturn on the Ascendant adds authority and dignity to her presentations, while the conjunction of Mercury and Venus in Virgo in the Fourth, gives methodology and precision to her recipes.

From a more psychological perspective, when the ruler of the Fourth is in its own house, the individual has to be a master of his or her own home. The nature in which this is carried forth, and the nature

Example 17: The Horoscope of Julia Child[3]

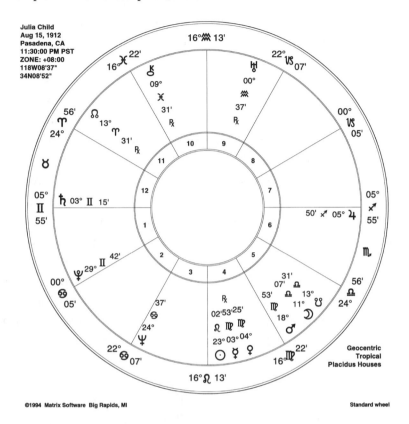

Julia Child
Aug 15, 1912
Pasadena, CA
11:30:00 PM PST
ZONE: +08:00
118W08'37"
34N08'52"

©1994 Matrix Software Big Rapids, MI

Geocentric
Tropical
Placidus Houses

Standard wheel

of the domestic life in general, is indicated by the sign on the cusp of the house and any planets found therein. Should this be the ruling planet of that sign, look to all the associated astrological indications to be exaggerated. Aries on the cusp of the Fourth with Mars in that house will definitely indicate a person who has to be "lord and master" of his own castle. Taurus on the cusp of the Fourth with Venus in that domicile indicates a person who needs peace, serenity, and beauty in his or her home environment and would tend to be a beautiful addition, an "agent of peace and positivity," to anyone else's home when he or she is visiting. Aquarius on this cusp with Uranus in the Fourth indicates a very unusual home, one that is far from traditional either in terms of one's parental background or in the way one creates one's own domestic relationship structures. Look for lots of friends visiting and many technological devices scattered throughout the dwelling. Should Uranus be afflicted in this position, especially in Aquarius, problems concerning electrical wiring and appliances are likely to be frequent and unwelcome surprises.

When the ruler of the Fourth is in the Fifth, one needs to take one's subjective life and give it form and focus to express one's creativity. If Libra is on the cusp of the Fourth and Venus is in the Fifth, for example, the individual holds within him or herself an inner sense of balance and an appreciation for all things of the muses. When in the Fifth, Venus has a chance to flourish artistically. The Fifth House will give this impulse an opportunity to express itself in ways which mark one's creativity with a personal stamp. One could also see this nascent artistry externalized through one's children. If Capricorn is on the Fourth House cusp and Saturn is afflicted in Capricorn in the Fifth, then the person would tend to hold back the more expressive dynamics usually indicated by Fifth House planetary placements. At the very least, the individual with Saturn in this position will have to wait until a certain age or stage in life, characterized by maturity and experience, before his or her creativity may truly emerge and flourish.

When the ruler of the Fourth is in the Sixth and the ruler is afflicted, the individual will seek methods and techniques that heal early family trauma. Should the ruler be well aspected, there will be an ease in finding conditions and circumstances that refine and reshape one's psychological roots and foundations. Here the indications are for a tighter, more synthesized integration of one's inner potential so what emerges in terms of work, job, and a general sense of well-being is moved forward and improved. If the Fourth House ruler in the Sixth is in the sign of Cancer, for example, then ways are sought for better self-nourishment. If the position of the Fourth House ruling planet is in Taurus, then the aim is for increased self-valuation and self-worth. The correct job and the right means of livelihood will go a long way to be helpful in this aspect of personal growth and development. On the lighter side, the ruler of the Fourth in the Sixth can speak about the nature of family pets and a strong connection between the individual and all domestic animals.

When the ruler of the Fourth is in the Seventh, the nature of the relationship between one's parents will have a lot to do towards conditioning the way the individual goes about creating his or her own partnerships. An afflicted planet in this house tells the astrologer that there is a strong possibility that there was dissension in the individual's childhood home and the nature of those difficulties are likely to be repeated in marriage or partnership. This is because the Seventh House is the Fourth from the Fourth, indicating the *home life of the parents*. On the other hand, a well-placed Fourth House ruler in this astrological domicile helps to prepare an individual for positive relationship contacts. It may also indicate that partnership can be a positive vehicle in nurturing and forming the individual's inner nature, thus deepening one's sense of personal security in the world. At the very least, it would show that an important facet of the native's urge for personality integration (Fourth House) will come about through relationship dynamics (Seventh). The degree of support or challenge to this process will be characterized by the nature and condition of the ruling planet of the Fourth in the Seventh.

When the ruler of the Fourth is in the Eighth, several important interpretations rise to the surface. First and foremost, we learn what the individual stands to inherit from the family. This can come in the form of emotional, psychological inheritance as well as in terms of purely material gifts and legacies. Should the ruler of the Fourth be in Taurus, Cancer, Scorpio, or Capricorn and well aspected in the Eighth—especially by Venus, Jupiter, Pluto, or the Moon—then look for an increased potential of financial inheritance. You know that this indication is reinforced—although there are no 100 percent guarantees in the cosmos—if the ruler of the Eighth is well connected to the individual's Second House planetary placements or its house ruler. If the positions indicated above are poorly configured in the natal map, there will be difficulty surrounding financial inheritances or no money is to be forthcoming from the family in this respect.

In terms of psychological inheritance, very often the ruler of the Fourth in the Eighth indicates the need to reorient the nature of the earlier conditioning of the personality. The Eighth always carries the energy of transformation and its subsequent lessons. The specific planet and its sign will indicate where the emphasis of such transformation is placed. Should this be Venus or a planet in Taurus, then the attitude towards money as a vehicle of self-worth has to be examined. If wellaspected, the family's values may be a beautiful steppingstone for the individual to find even greater moral and material wealth in both himself and in the world. If poorly aspected, then financial situations and standards relating to material conditions may inhibit or pervert the attainment of more refined personal values in this area of life. Working closely with the astrological keywords and phrases will unlock all the meanings of all planetary rulerships of this and all the other houses of the natal chart.

When the ruler of the Fourth is in the Ninth, the urge to anchor or enlarge upon one's religious beliefs or philosophy takes on great importance in life. One of the major pathways to the evolution of personal consciousness is the stage in our development when we awaken to the subjective motivations that condition so many of our responses to life. Once we awaken to our inner patterning and the psychological circumstances that condition our instincts, we discontinue leading our life from the "outside in." We cease being "karmic victims" and stop viewing the world around us purely as reflections of our own subjective, psychological conditioning. True individuation begins to take place. We begin to become objective to ourselves, learning to live from the "inside out." We gradually become aware of our "own movie," and are not just the unconscious stars of the film. When the ruler of the Fourth House is in the Ninth, the opportunity comes to us to enhance the scope of the foundational beliefs that conditioned our early environment. If well aspected (especially in a mutable sign, or in Aries or Libra) the ruler of the Fourth in this position will take us out of ourselves and into a much more amplified world of broader understanding.

Should the Fourth House ruler be afflicted in this position (especially in a fixed sign or in Cancer or Capricorn), we would tend to be more attached to these earlier belief patterns and natal family values. The challenges that come with such astrological circumstances can either provide a great stimulus in life to individual growth, or result in a firm adherence to our "home religion," no matter what the cost to personal development. Often a Fourth House ruler in the Ninth will point toward a tendency to make our home either in a foreign country or in a location far removed from our place of origin. A poorly aspected or otherwise afflicted Fourth House ruler in this position can indicate a person who is forced to move away from his country or place of birth against his will.

When the ruler of the Fourth is in the Tenth, there is a strong need to be successful in the world. Public approval will be an essential element of the personality. "I want to be accepted as I really am, as I subjectively conceive of myself as being," is the statement that is being made when the ruler of the Fourth is in this position. This can be very difficult to achieve because who or what one is subjectively (and often unconsciously) to oneself (Fourth House) may not be the public image that is projected in terms of one's social position (Tenth House). This urge for acceptance also can contribute to a certain kind of psychological vulnerability, rendering any criticism of who one is and what one does very deeply felt. It is hard to be thick-skinned in the world when you are always wearing your psychological underwear in public.

If the ruler of the Fourth in the Tenth is an afflicted Neptune or any other planet afflicted by Neptune, the individual more likely than not will encounter life situations in which he or she is misunderstood or deceived in some aspect of their career life. If the ruling planet is Jupiter and well aspected in the Tenth, look for the ability to succeed in convincing other people of what you believe (and *profit by it* if Jupiter is in an earth sign or in positive aspect with Venus or Pluto or most other planets in earth signs). Sometimes, the ruler of the Fourth in the Tenth indicates that the mother is the more prominent or influential of one's parents. Should the ruler be well aspected, the maternal influence could be extremely helpful in the individual's career or public standing. The reverse may be equally true. Especially if the ruler of the Fourth is afflicted in this position, then the psychological influence of the mother (or the family in general) could serve to inhibit or prevent worldly success.

When the ruler of the Fourth is in the Eleventh, the individual tends to make his home among his or her friends or in a social environment that is very nurturing or secure. There often is the impetus to share oneself with others and to be validated and approved of by friends, peers, or associates. If the ruler of the Fourth in the Eleventh is in a fixed sign (especially Taurus), one needs to find a group within which one's values are supported. Should the ruler be afflicted when in this condition, validation is hard to achieve and one's self-esteem is often challenged. If the Fourth House ruler is in Aquarius or is Uranus, look for a life in which one's choice of associates is *very different* from the type of people with whom one grew up. Because the Eleventh is traditionally associated with one's hopes, wishes, and aspirations, the Fourth House ruler in this position can indicate that the individual seeks to enlarge his or her subjective identification in the larger world. This gives rise to a set of circumstances that can be said to mean: "What I wish for myself, I wish for many others." Should this aspiration be self-destructive (Mars as the ruler of the Fourth in the Eleventh square to Neptune, for example, or Neptune as the ruler square to Mars), look for a life in which the individual provokes highly challenging social situations. Should the reverse be true and the individual's deepest subjective wish is for peace and harmony (Venus as the ruler of the Fourth trine to Neptune, the Moon, or Jupiter, or any one of these three planets trine to Venus), then such a person will project this positive, subjective orientation out into the Eleventh House world of larger public contacts and thus reap the rewards of this positive attitude.

When the ruler of the Fourth is in the Twelfth, there is a need for solitude and the urge to find a home that is far removed from the noise and intensity of modern life. Even if such a person lives in a large metropolis, he or she would search for a home that is in a relatively quiet or remote part of the city. If that is not possible, the person in question would seek an apartment in a part of the building that is furthest removed from the sounds of traffic, or a house in a cul-de-sac. If all else failed, then the individual would tend to select the quietest room in the apartment or house for his or her bedroom or study. The ruler of the Fourth in the Twelfth can also indicate that a person was strongly influenced by the family's "skeletons in the closet," or by a parent who did not live with the family but whose influence was far more subtle or clandestine. Many people with a mystical orientation to life can be characterized by having the ruler of the Fourth in the Twelfth, as this position points to an individual who identifies him or herself with inclusive ideas and beliefs. "The entire world is my family and my roots are universal," is the statement that such a person is making. Like

Neptune square, opposed, or conjunct the ruler of the Fourth House, this placement (especially if signified by an afflicted Moon or Saturn) can also indicate an orphan or an adopted person, whose parents and roots are unknown or difficult to trace.

The Nature of the Fifth House

As we know, the natural sign ruler of the First House is Aries and its ruling planet is Mars. Thus, in a word, we can say that the First House is directly connected with the "projection" of the personality. It is through the Fifth House, ruled by Leo and the Sun, that such projections take on coloration and vitality. The gift (and challenge) of the Fourth House experience is that it creates an anchoring or foundation for the integration of the personality into a cohesive unit. The Fifth takes this stage in our development to the next logical step — it shows both to oneself and others what one can do with one's personality, and all its talents and abilities. The Fifth describes not so much *who* we are but *how we express* our sense of personal identity in terms of what we create. This creative function has two primary forms: our children and our other, nonhuman "progeny." If I am a writer, then the Fifth House speaks about my books as my "children." If I am an artist, then the Fifth reveals my paintings. If I am an architect, then this house tells a lot about the way I express my architectural skills and what I create with them. The Fifth is also called the "party house," as it is associated with pastimes, hobbies, and the joys of life. It is definitely the house of romance and it is here that we find our lovers (our legal and contractual partners being associated with the Seventh).

When the ruler of the Fifth is in the First, the nature of personal creativity is greatly heightened. This is an individual who embodies her creative objectives in a highly personalized manner, a person who is usually quite preoccupied with making a name for herself in the world. The astrologer can therefore imagine the level of frustration in the life of someone with this position when an afflicted Saturn is the ruler of the Fifth in the First. This placement would indicate tremendous creative inhibitions and a holding back of the creative drive. Such would be especially the case if Saturn were afflicted either in a fixed or in any of the female signs. On the other hand, let us say that Mars in a male sign were the ruler of the Fifth in the First. We then would find an individual who strongly promotes his or her creativity. We would also find a person who is quite sexual in his orientation to himself and to life in general, in short, a person ever in search of romantic conquests.

This position would speak of an individual who identifies very personally with his or her children (or other created "offspring"). If a well-aspected Sun is the ruler of the Fifth in the First, then this indeed is the horoscope of a proud parent! Should an afflicted Neptune occupy this role, then we have either a parent with children who could have the propensity for addictive problems or a parent who does not understand his or her children very well. The pursuit of pleasure (or the restraint in this pursuit) also would be strongly marked when the Fifth House ruler is in the First in the natal chart. A person with Sagittarius on the Fifth and Jupiter in Leo well aspected in the First, for example, is certainly one who loves life (and him or herself) to the fullest. Capricorn on the Fifth with Saturn in Virgo poorly aspected in the First as the ruler, on the other hand, would tend to indicate a rather dour person, one with a poor sense of humor and a very restrained or even puritanical sense of fun.

When the ruler of the Fifth is in the Second, there is a strong connection between what one creates and one's individual, personal resources. If an afflicted Neptune were the ruler of the Fifth and located in the Second, the person could be the victim of financial deceit on the part of his or her children. A well-aspected Jupiter as ruler of the Fifth in the Second can indicate that the individual has abundant resources at his disposal to use for the higher education of his kids. It can also mean that the children act as a teacher to the parent, thus helping father or mother to expand his or her sense of self-worth, or may even be the source of wealth to one's parents. Naturally, the astrologer needs to look at the entire horoscope to lend support to this or any other supposition. A good rule to follow is: One should have three astrological indications for every major conclusion. If they are there, now we know how to find them! Basically we are seeking to answer the following questions when the ruler of the Fifth is in the Second: How will the expression of my creativity affect my personal resources and my sense of self-worth? How

Example 18: The Horoscope of H. P. Blavatsky

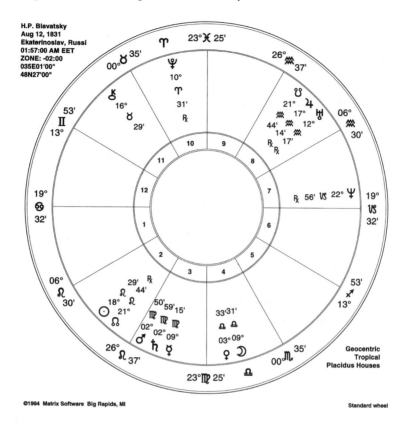

H.P. Blavatsky
Aug 12, 1831
Ekaterinoslav, Russi
01:57:00 AM EET
ZONE: -02:00
035E01'00"
48N27'00"

Geocentric
Tropical
Placidus Houses

©1994 Matrix Software Big Rapids, MI

Standard wheel

will my sense of self-worth and my resources support the expression of my creativity?

When the ruler of the Fifth is in the Third, look for writing and communication to be linked to the individual's creative self-expression. If you examine the horoscope of H. P. Blavatsky, you will see that the ruler of the Fifth is Mars in Virgo. The latter is in a tight conjunction with Saturn and Mercury in the Third House. Madame Blavatsky was the author of many esoteric texts, most notably among them was an extraordinary work entitled *The Secret Doctrine*. If you examine her Twelfth House, you will find Gemini on the cusp (indicating hidden, secret writing) and its ruler, Mercury, is with Saturn, the co-ruler of the Ninth (philosophy, religion, higher teachings) in the Third. H. P. Blavatsky also was known for her voluminous international correspondence in many languages. Letter writing is ruled by Mercury and the Third House. The ruler of the Fifth in her chart is in Virgo, a sign of Mercury and, as mentioned above, this planet is conjunct the ruler of the Fifth in its own natural house. Anyone who has read her writings knows that she was prone to giving out minute and voluminous details about her subject, and was also highly critical of those who did not share her opinions.

The nature of the way we communicate with our offspring also will be affected by the placement of the ruler of the Fifth in the Third. In addition, the relationship between the Fifth and the Third houses of the natal chart speak about the way we educate and travel with our children.

When the ruler of the Fifth is in the Fourth, our creativity is closely linked to our psychological roots and the nature of our relationship with our parents, especially our mother. This would be particularly so if Cancer was on the Fifth House cusp and the Moon was located in the Fourth. In general, this placement creates a highly subjective attitude in dealing with our creative self-expression. It may be hard for us to "come out of ourselves," as our creative inspiration comes from our personal life experience. This is not usually the horoscope of someone who travels widely and then writes, paints, or is in other ways inspired to express the nature of the countries or people one visits. Such experiences only serve to stimulate subjective viewpoints and opinions and do not lend objectivity to the world around ourselves. Such an individual would tend to use an event such as taking an espresso in the Piazza San Marco not to write about the habits of the Venetians, but to recall how his Italian mother or grandmother used to cook when he was a little boy.

When the ruler of the Fifth is in the Fifth, creativity, romance, children, and all other dynamics of this domicile are heightened for the good or otherwise, depending upon the nature and condition of the ruling planet. Leo on the cusp of this house with the Sun well aspected in the Fifth is an indication of a highly virile and passionate human being, one who takes great pride in what he or she creates. But should the Sun be afflicted in this house, especially by Saturn or Neptune, one may not have the stamina or vitality to sustain one's own creative expectations. In addition, children also may not live up to the standards this individual has envisioned or expects. Personal disappointments are bound to occur. Libra on this house cusp with Venus in the Fifth is a sure indication of a "born lover." This is a man or a woman who is not only artistic in their method of creative self-expression, but is also an artist in the art of love. If this individual has children, at least one of them (usually the first born) will be "fair of face and form" and an artist in his or her own right. Aquarius ruling the Fifth with Uranus therein is bound to produce unusual offspring who may challenge the parent's social views. A good factor to keep in mind when judging the nature of the ruler of the Fifth in the Fifth (or any house ruler in the house that it rules either natally or naturally) is *emphasis*. All events, people, and dynamics connected to the house in question are given definite and added importance by this double placement.

When the ruler of the Fifth is in the Sixth, look for rewards coming from one's own children or other forms of creative expression. The Sixth House is the Second from the Fifth, and as such it deals with personal resources (Second House keyword phrase) that are a direct result of Fifth House matters. Let us say Taurus is on the Fifth House cusp and Venus is well aspected in that sign in the Sixth. One assumption that the astrologer could make is that it would be easy for the individual to earn money from what he or she creates. The astrologer should then see if such a supposition is further supported by an examination of the individual's Second House, its occupants and ruler, and if there are any astrological relationships existing between the Sixth and Second houses.

The relationship between the Fifth and the Sixth houses also speaks about the nature of the individual's general health relative to his or her creative potential. If the ruler of the Fifth, for example, were Leo and the Sun was afflicted by Saturn in the Sixth, several possible interpretations would present themselves: 1. The individual would not have the stamina and strength to be as creative as he would want to be. 2. The individual would have a difficult time finding a job (Sixth House) in which his abundant creative drive (Leo on the Fifth House cusp) could be expressed. 3. The individual would set a standard of creative achievement for himself that could be above his current abilities (one indication of a Saturn/Sun square).

When the ruler of the Fifth is in the Seventh, in effect we have a symbolic conjunction of the Sun with Venus, which always bodes well for an artistic and romantically inclined person. But is this the reality existing in the life of the person whose chart is in front of us? The astrologer can rely on this: Should the rulers of these two houses be in harmonious aspect, the chances are that the individual will marry for love. Should the earthy signs also be harmoniously involved, then one is likely to marry for love *and* money and be successful with both! Let us give the optimum example of this and say that Libra is on the cusp of the Fifth House and Sagittarius on the Seventh. Then let us suppose that Venus is in Capricorn trine to Jupiter in Taurus. We should all be so fortunate! Here is the perfect example of heaven on earth for a person who has a deep romantic urge (Libra on the Fifth) and who seeks to expand and enjoy that urge through partnership (Sagittarius on the Seventh).

On a less romantic note, this same planetary combination can also indicate material success coming from business partnerships with one's own children. It also may mean that the individual has opportunities to come into contact with others who expand upon his or her creative potentials for their mutual benefit. If the opposite situation is the case and the ruler of the Fifth is badly aspected in the Seventh, look for disappointments in love, difficulties in romantic partnerships, and challenges to relationships with children.

When the ruler of the Fifth is in the Eighth, the romantic nature is highly sexualized. This is an individual who does not take his or her libido lightly! Should one of the planets be Mars or Venus, then the above indications are even further emphasized. The intense attitude towards the pursuit of pleasure through romance could become obsessive if the fixed signs were involved and/or the planet Pluto were strongly present in the configuration. Great difficulties would then be likely unless such indications were modified by other factors in the horoscope (or a little conscious, hormonal transcendence). Yet the creative dynamics of the ruler of the Fifth well aspected in the Eighth (especially by Mars, Pluto, or the Sun) are enormous. This positioning of the Fifth House ruler permits the individual to regenerate his or her creative possibilities, allowing for an abundant and profound source of vitality. However, any contact with the Eighth House must be observed carefully, because there is always a price to pay when this house is occupied or emphasized in a chart. That price is transformation.

In other words, in order for the individual with his or her Fifth

House ruler in the Eighth to be able to tap into the regenerative potential this position offers, the person must be prepared to undergo a transmutative crisis. This may mean a test of this evolutionary change so that the *instinctive procreative* urge becomes the *objectively creative.* Only then will the pursuit of pleasure be transformed into an intense dedication to the service or healing of others through one's creative drive.

When the ruler of the Fifth is in the Ninth and well aspected, great pleasure and creative possibilities occur through foreign travel and the pursuit of higher knowledge. A person's religious beliefs and activities also may be a source of enlightenment and joy. If poorly placed in this domicile, such Ninth House activities can present certain difficulties. We may also find when this combination is present in the horoscope that one's children may challenge our belief system and turn away from the religion or spiritual background we have offered them. This conclusion has to be corroborated by an examination of the person's First House, as this is the Ninth from the Fifth, and therefore speaks more specifically about the nature of one's children's beliefs. On a lighter note, when the ruler of the Fifth is well aspected in the Ninth, there is the possibility of taking much pleasure and enjoyment in foreign travel. If the ruling planet happens to be Venus, one may possibly encounter an important lover who was born in a country other than one's own.

When the ruler of the Fifth is in the Tenth, there is a strong indication that one's creative drive will be incorporated into the focus of one's career. This is not always the case in life. Many people have careers that do not give them pleasure or have the quality of joy that is embodied in one's other Fifth House pursuits. Hobbies, pastimes, and leisure activities are not often one's career, sadly. But when the ruler of the Fifth is well aspected in the Tenth, the profession is usually a joy. Let us say that Sagittarius is on the cusp of the Fifth and Jupiter is in the Tenth trine Mercury. This would be a clear indication that the individual loves to write and travel and not only is well suited to work as a travel agent or travel writer, but also would be happy and successful in such endeavors. The astrologer should then examine the nature of the sign on the cusp of the Tenth and its planetary ruler to substantiate this conclusion. If the reader can look again at Madame Blavatsky's chart (see page 215), he or she will see that the co-ruler of the Fifth is Pluto in the Tenth. H. P.

Blavatsky left her family and relatively high social position in order to pursue a life and career of her own making. Pluto is in Aries (total regeneration of oneself) in opposition to the Moon in Libra in the Fourth (family roots). In order to leave her family home, Blavatsky arranged to get married at a rather young age to a much older man, and then within a very short interval, left her husband (Pluto in opposition to a Venus/Moon conjunction in Libra). This was to be Blavatsky's only marriage. H. P. Blavatsky was the *force majeure* in transforming the nature of occidental mysticism and occultism. Through her intense creative drive (Scorpio on the Fifth), she opened the door (Aries) to an intense inflow of occult spiritual teachings that change the esoteric orientation of tens of thousands of people in the Western world. In addition to the points mentioned above, because the Tenth is the Sixth from the Fifth, we also may find indications in this planetary combination concerning our children's jobs or their state of health.

When the ruler of the Fifth is in the Eleventh, our creative self-expression is strongly connected to the social groups to which we may belong. Here individual creativity is intimately linked with the larger and more collective social circumstances that surround us. The challenge issued to the person with this position (if the ruler were afflicted), would consist in an ability to individualize his or her participation within the framework of collective pursuits. This would especially be the case if the Sun was the ruler of the Fifth and Leo on the cusp of the Fifth with the Sun in Aquarius in the Eleventh. The same thing also could take place if the ruler of the First House were also the co-ruler of this domicile as well. This would occur, for instance, if Scorpio was rising and Aries was on the cusp of the Fifth with Mars in Libra in the Eleventh. It also would happen if Taurus were on the First House cusp and Libra on the Fifth with Venus in Aries in the Eleventh House. In the first example, a Scorpio/Aries, First/Fifth house emphasis indicates a person who is highly individualistic and self-motivated when it comes to his or her creative and libidinous drives. Mars in Libra in the Eleventh indicates that the individual may often encounter discordant social relationships in his or her urge to fulfill such urgings. In the second example, a person with a Taurus/Libra, First/Fifth house emphasis, when confronted by the need to be creatively self-expressive, is very partnership oriented. Venus in Aries in the Eleventh, however, indicates that this person consistently has to take a personal and somewhat confrontational stand and assert him or herself within a group context. This is something that goes against the Taurus/Libra nature, bringing challenges to the partnership urge.

We may also look at the Fifth House ruler in the Eleventh as the indication of our sons- or daughters-in-law. This is because the Eleventh is the Seventh from the Fifth and, as a result, is indicative of our children's marriage partners.

When the ruler of the Fifth is in the Twelfth, the individual is prone to having clandestine love affairs or secret pleasures. This may not always be the case, of course, but it has shown itself to be true enough in a number of horoscopes read by this astrologer. Just look at the keywords: clandestine (Twelfth House) lovers and other pleasures (Fifth House). Astrologers know that just having Venus in the Twelfth alone is an indication of secret amorous adventures. Should Venus be the ruler of the Fifth and in the Twelfth, this conclusion is even further emphasized. This combination can also point to an individual who expresses his or her creative talents best when in a secluded location: the artist in his remote studio, the writer in his wooded cabin, the poet on his island, and so on. The Twelfth House placement of the Fifth House ruler is also an indication of the nature of the death of our children, as it is the Eighth house from the Fifth.

The Nature of the Sixth House

The Sixth can be called the "house of our well-being," as it is traditionally associated with health. Yet physical wholeness is not its only concern. In a much broader yet profound sense, this is the area of the horoscope that reveals the use of those tools, techniques, processes, and methodologies by which we come to perfect ourselves. It is therefore quite correct to call the Sixth the "house of self-improvement." This is the last portion of the chart found in the northern hemisphere, the subjective half of the horoscope. The first six houses are involved with the more personal and self-developmental side of our nature: who we are (First), what we have (Second), how we think (Third), where we came from (Fourth), and the expression of our creative drive (Fifth). Once we cross the threshold into the upper, objective hemisphere of the horoscope, we reach the realm of the Seventh House of relationships first, and then move steadily onward and upward into increasingly uncharted, impersonal, and universal territory. The Sixth House serves to prepare us for this journey.

It does so by teaching us lessons of discrimination and synthesis. It shows us how to put our life together so that it may run more efficiently. It is a practical house and highlights our weaknesses—physically or otherwise—as well as highlighting our special skills and the path that leads to the refinement of our personality. It is through the training we encounter in the Sixth House that we finally emerge as a socialized unit, ready to meet others and encounter the adventures of life outside our instinctual, subjective nature. In traditional exoteric astrology, the Sixth is also the domicile of pets, jobs, and employees.

When the ruler of the Sixth is in the First, health often will be an important issue in one's life. If the ruling planet of the Sixth House is in the First House and is poorly aspected, the physical constitution may be impaired indeed. Look to the planet therein to describe the part of the body that may be affected. The Sun indicates the heart, but may also involve the vitality in general. If it is the Moon, a weakness in the lymphatic system may occur, or in the horoscope of women, difficulties arising in the menstrual cycle and with the breasts. If the signs Capricorn or Cancer are involved, then it is highly likely that such bodily illnesses may be hereditary. Water retention also is likely when the Moon is in the First, especially if in a watery sign or in difficult aspect to a planet in a fixed sign.

Mercury afflictions relate to the nervous system. Should the sign Gemini also be involved, the lungs, arms, and hands may contain certain weaknesses. Venus points to the kidneys and the urinary tract, while Mars has a lot to do with the sexual organs, the eyes, and blood in general (the red blood cells in particular). If Aries is involved, the head should be taken into consideration; while if Scorpio is the sign on the cusp of the Sixth or the First, look to the reproductive system for any problems. Jupiter afflictions in this combination tell the astrologer that the liver is weak, while Saturn indicates bones, teeth, knees, joints, and in certain charts, may indicate calcium or other mineral crystallizations or deficiencies in the body. Uranus is the significator of the circulatory system and the skin. If Mars is square, opposed, or conjoined Uranus when as ruler of the Sixth, and it is posited in the First, skin rashes are likely. If the sign Aries is involved, then it is face rashes; if Cancer, the skin on the chest or stomach is likely to be quite sensitive; if Pisces, then the feet are prone to skin irritations, etc. An afflicted Neptune as ruler of the Sixth in the First indicates psychosomatic illnesses (especially with the watery signs present) or mental imbalances (especially if Neptune is in one of the airy signs). Pluto afflicted in this position points to difficulties in cell regeneration and loss of general vitality (especially when square or opposing the Sun).

There are other areas of the Sixth House that concern primary issues of importance in an individual's life when its ruler is in the First. Relationship with pets is significant as well as work-related situations in general. If the ruler of the Sixth is well aspected in this position, the chances are that the individual will like his or her job and get along well with employees or people in inferior positions in the workplace. Should the ruler of the Sixth be found in the First and also in good aspect to the ruler of the Tenth (career), look for likely success in the individual's chosen professional field.

When the ruler of the Sixth is in the Second, the individual will be repeatedly called upon to use his or her personal talents and resources in terms of his work. If one's self-worth is low, then it will be difficult to succeed at the job. An afflicted Sixth House ruler located in the Second will lessen any sense of personal value because often the person is given tasks to perform which the individual either does not have the skills to accomplish or else is different from his or her natural life orientation. On the other hand, a well-aspected Sixth House ruler in this position will indicate an easy relationship between the individual's capabilities and their application in the workplace. Troubles with employees over money can occur when the ruler of the Sixth is afflicted in the Second. Pets also may prove to be costly to maintain if this combination of influences is afflicted in the natal chart.

When the ruler of the Sixth is in the Third, the nature of one's job will require the use of the individual's communication skills. Writing, speaking, and the implementation of one's ideas and opinions will be important facets of the person's job description. If the airy signs are featured and/or if Mercury, Virgo, or Gemini are involved, the work is primarily intellectual in nature. If the water signs and/or the Moon are the significators, the communication of feelings and emotions characterize the natural work orientation of the person in question. The earth signs in these positions point to the use of common sense and a pragmatic approach to the tasks one encounters on the job. The fire signs add creative impulse and drive, although afflictions in the fiery signs or with Mars and the Sun as significators, can point to difficulties with coworkers and employees because the need for personal recognition is strong.

Let us say, for example, that Leo is on the cusp of the Sixth House and the Sun is in Taurus in the Third opposing Jupiter in Scorpio. Leo indicates that this is a person who takes her job very personally. The need for individual recognition is always predominant in the area of life ruled by the Lion. The tendency in this chart is for this person to state her opinions and values assertively. And, the way she communicates her creative impulses affirms her personal identity through her job. The opposition from Jupiter in Scorpio would exaggerate this tendency as well as indicate a resistance to modifying her views in order to be more cooperative with coworkers or employees.

When the ruler of the Sixth is in the Fourth, a person may enjoy working in his or her own home. If this is not possible, such an individual may decorate her office with pictures of her family, or place familiar objects on her desk, walls, etc., so that the workplace feels and looks like an extension of her domestic environment. Psychologically, the use of personal skills in order to earn a living will mean a great deal to this individual. We could say that if the ruler of the Sixth is in the Fourth, the job area of life will form the foundation and base upon which everything else is structured. Success or failure at work, the choice of right livelihood, the ability to get on well with employees, all these are meaningful and affect the person's attitude to all other areas of his or her life.

This is a person who may find it difficult to be objective about his job and usually will not be able to close the office door at 5:00 PM, leaving the job behind as he sets off for the evening. Health also may be an important issue. If the ruler of the Sixth is an afflicted Saturn in Scorpio, for example (Capricorn on the Sixth House cusp), the state of one's health may be a worrisome obsession. If the ruler is an afflicted Neptune in Capricorn (Pisces on the Sixth House cusp), the individual may be more physically susceptible and personally responsive to the emotional atmosphere at work. This can give rise to psychosomatic illnesses that weaken the individual's psychological foundation, making it difficult for that person to achieve success. On the other hand, a strong and well-aspected Sixth House ruler in the Fourth will reinforce the individual's subjective attitude to health and work, giving a sense of belonging and integration.

When the ruler of the Sixth is in the Fifth and well aspected, look for the job to be a great source of fun or pleasure. The contrary would tend to be true if the ruler were afflicted. In this case, one's job could stand in the way of one's pleasures in life. In addition, this position of the Sixth House ruler indicates that animals and pets may be looked upon as one's children. At the very least, this is a person likely to have pets that are very dear to her.

The example horoscope seen on the following page is that of Robyn Smith, the first professional female jockey in the United States. The ruler of the Sixth is Venus found in Virgo in the Fifth. Virgo is the sign that usually is associated with smaller animals, but if we look at the chart carefully, we will see that Venus is in an exact conjunction with Jupiter. Anything connected with this planet enlarges and expands. In this respect, we can see Smith's contact with horses (specifically ruled by Jupiter, who is, after all, the ruler of Sagittarius, the Centaur). The Fifth House influence tells the astrologer that more than likely Smith derives great pleasure from her work. In addition, the Fifth is the house of games and gambling, and so Venus conjunct Jupiter in that domicile can indicate that animals, particularly horses, are used for that purpose. The fact that she is an "original" and a "first" in her particular job and career is easily seen in the natal map. Uranus is in the First House, indicating a rebel and someone who has to make his or her own way in life and, in addition, this planet is the ruler of the Tenth House of career and is in square aspect to Venus, which is the ruler of the Sixth. This indicates that she stands in open conflict (First House) with traditional

Example 19: The Horoscope of Robyn Smith[4]

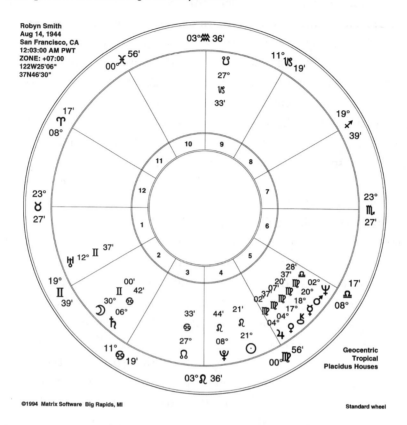

Robyn Smith
Aug 14, 1944
San Francisco, CA
12:03:00 AM PWT
ZONE: +07:00
122W25'06"
37N46'30"

03°♒ 36'

00°♓ 56'

11° ♑ 19'

27° ♑ 33'

17' ♈ 08°

19° ♐ 39'

23° ♉ 27'

23° ♏ 27'

♅ 12° ♊ 37'

28° ♎ 37'
20° ♍ 02°
02°♍37' ♍ 20° Ψ
♍ 18°
♍ 17° 08° ♎
04° ♂
♃ 17°

17' ♎ 08°

19° ♊ 39'

00' ♊ 42'
30° ♋ 06'
☽ ♄

33' ♋ 27' ♋

44' ♌ 08' ♌

21' ♌ 21' ♌

☊

56' ♍ 00'

11° ♋ 19'

Ω ♍

☉ ♌

Geocentric
Tropical
Placidus Houses

03° ♌ 36'

10 9

11   8

12   7

1   6

2   5

3   4

©1994 Matrix Software Big Rapids, MI

Standard wheel

social behavior relative to her career choices (Uranus square Venus and their associated house rulerships).

When the ruler of the Sixth is in the Seventh, you could easily conclude that the individual is married to his work. The question for us to consider is: Is this a happy or miserable union? A lot depends on the condition of the ruler. If the ruler of the Sixth House is Venus in the Seventh, for example, and Venus is trine the Moon, then the individual is likely to derive a great deal of self-nourishment from his work. Such a person would extend his sense of well-being out into his other relationships as well. It also would indicate that if he were in an executive position, he would receive support from his employees. If Venus were trine or sextile Jupiter, then the job would tend to bring regular financial and social increases into his life. But if Saturn were square to Venus in this position, the "marriage" would be a definite burden. The individual would more than likely experience his job as a great weight, one which would also cause him unwanted responsibilities.

If Taurus were the sign on the cusp of the Sixth and Venus were in the Seventh square or opposed Saturn, for example, worries would come about through not being able to make enough money in one's particular job. If the ruling sign were Libra, problems would come about either through a lack of cooperation from employees or even more likely, from one's superiors, because the area of concern is in job-related relationships.

When the ruler of the Sixth is in the Eighth and the ruler is well aspected (especially from the ruler of the Eighth or from Pluto), the job would afford the individual many opportunities for the refinement and regeneration of skills. If the earthy signs are the significators, the area of work also provides the means to improve one's income. Should the astrological indications be negative, then the job would not allow for any form of regenerative experience and the person would find him or herself stagnating in terms of one's work. This would be especially the case if such difficult aspects involved the fixed signs or Saturn.

Health could be a problem if the ruler of the Sixth is afflicted in the Eighth. Leo on the cusp of the Sixth with the Sun in the Eighth in difficult aspect to Pluto, Saturn, or Neptune could give degenerative, chronic, or psychological difficulties respectively. On the other hand, Leo on the cusp of the Sixth with the Sun in the Eighth well aspected by Pluto, Saturn, or Neptune respectively would tend to regenerate vitality, strengthen the general constitution, and increase sensitivity to others.

When the ruler of the Sixth is in the Ninth, look for a person whose job involves traveling, teaching, publishing, and the pursuit of knowledge. If well aspected, especially by Jupiter or the Sun, the individual will make every effort to increase and enlarge upon the scope of his or her skills, methods, and techniques in any job he or she undertakes to perform. If poorly aspected, the person may feel that he or she is overqualified for the job or that the work area does not meet with his or her expectations.

The Sun, Mars, or Jupiter as ruler of the Sixth in the Ninth when afflicted can point to a person who tries to move beyond the capacity or promise that the job may offer. If any of these planets are well aspected as significators of the Sixth, then advancement comes about through work at regular intervals. Those individuals whose horoscopes indicate an orientation toward healing will find that a well-aspected Sixth House ruler in the Ninth adds to one's education in these matters and stimulates all learning activities which lead to self-improvement.

When the ruler of the Sixth is in the Tenth and well aspected, there is an ability to synthesize one's various skills into one's chosen vocation. Life has a highly practical tone and the individual is eager to succeed and advance his or her social position accordingly. If Saturn is the Sixth House ruler, and well aspected in the Tenth House, for example, then the climb to the top will be slow and steady with the likelihood of eventual success. Mars in this position indicates a person who tends to push his or her way up the ladder. Venus will do the networking through one's social connections, and Venus always adds a certain charm to the personality. What gives special meaning to the Sixth House ruler in this position is that the individual may have come from a lower social class or work-related position, and has used his or her special skills to create advancements in life.

If the earth signs are involved, the individual has the tendency to be rather materialistic in his or her approach to success. If the water or fire signs are present, then there is a possibility that one is working not just for the attainment of beautiful things and economic power, but also to fulfill some ideal. The air signs will show that human relationships and communication skills are profoundly important facets of one's work orientation. Planets well aspected in the air signs as the significators of the relationship between the Sixth and the Tenth, reveal that the individual is possessed of highly developed communicative tools and techniques.

When the ruler of the Sixth is in the Eleventh, the work area involves groups and organizations. If the airy signs are the significators (or Mercury or Uranus are the qualifying rulers), communication networking is a feature of the job orientation. This is an individual who learns by being with others. When well aspected, this person can feel quite at home in a large corporation. This also is an individual who may enjoy participating in corporate activities or on a committee that represents the interests of his or her coworkers. If Virgo is on the Sixth House cusp and Aquarius is on the Eleventh, for example, and Mercury is in Aquarius in that house, the indications are that such a person would make a wonderful customer service representative for the telephone company! In terms of health, the presence of the Sixth House ruler in the Eleventh presents some interesting possibilities. We should remember that the Eleventh is a social house. House rulers in this position involve the activities of the house that they rule in the larger life experience. If Leo is on the cusp of the Sixth and the Sun is in the Eleventh in Aquarius in a square to Neptune in Scorpio, for example, this is a person who is prone to catching colds and flus that are pandemic. Such illnesses are usually caught because he works with many other people or has to commute on public transportation. In other words, the individual is open to "communicable diseases."

When the ruler of the Sixth is in the Twelfth, one may prefer a job that is secluded or deals with things of a more secretive nature. This is a person who prefers to work alone in peaceful solitude. The Twelfth House position of the Sixth House ruler is excellent for laboratory and research work. It is very good for being privy to clandestine information, hidden files, and obscure facts. Library research work also belongs in this category. This is also a combination that is often found in horoscopes of people who work in the medical professions or who deal with people who reside in institutions. If the Sixth House ruler is afflicted in this position, especially by Neptune or Saturn, it may be difficult for the individual to find a job and once found, to hold on to it.

The tendency with Neptune afflictions to the Sixth House ruler is toward being in a constant state of uncertainty about what one is doing; having the feeling that "something is missing in my job, but I don't know exactly what that something is." With Saturn either afflicted as the ruler of the Sixth in the Twelfth or afflicting the ruler, the sense is one of burden and a feeling of being imprisoned by one's work. In terms of health, a poorly placed ruler of the Sixth in the Twelfth (especially if it is the Sun or the Moon or if the ruler is afflicted by the luminaries), can indicate chronic health issues that inhibit one's job performance.

The Nature of the Seventh House

When speaking of the First House and most specifically, of the Ascendant, we refer to "you," i.e., to one's sense of self coming from the immediate, moment-to-moment contact with one's environment. As we have seen, the First House tells us much about the nature, character, and traits of the specific individual in question. The Seventh House and certainly the sign on its cusp, the Descendant, tells the astrologer about the "not you," or what most attracts you to other people. Furthermore, the Descendant describes what the individual is seeking in another person that he or she cannot find too easily in him or herself. In essence, the Seventh is the house of the personality's complement or partner. Traditionally known as the house of marriage, the current World Age requires that we broaden this definition from one's husband or wife to one's "significant other." Thus, this house tells us a lot about the kind of people with whom we seek to bond, the nature of that commitment, and the circumstances surrounding the searching and finding of that special someone.

We also may look to the Seventh for our business partners and generally to our sense of integration with others. Curiously, the Seventh also is the house of "open enemies," or people with whom we find ourselves in frequent conflict or competition. Human nature is such that very often it is with our most intimate partners that we find ourselves in our most serious interpersonal difficulties. Through attempts at resolving the differences and friction that can arise through serious relationships, we most often come in contact with the shadow side of our own nature. Our task, then, is to shine the light of the soul onto the realm of the shadow and for personal duality to cease by seeing this reflection of self in others. It is through one's intimate relationships that most men confront their own *anima* and the majority of women their *animus*. The fusion of the male and female energy within each of us allows us to achieve a state of personal integration and wholeness, a conscious androgyny that leads us to increased spiritual development and the refinement of our creative potential.

When the ruler of the Seventh is in the First, the focus on personal relationships achieves a high degree of importance and prominence in life—often to the detriment of the individual in question. If what I am and what I do to assert myself as "me in the world" (the Ascendant) is constantly related to relationships, I may easily compromise myself. In some cases, the individual is blind to the influence that other people have over him or her. This is certainly what happens if Neptune is the ruler of the Seventh and placed in the First (Pisces on the Seventh House cusp and Neptune in either Virgo or Libra in the First), especially when in hard aspect to the ruler of the First. If Venus is the Seventh House ruler in this position, the individual is charming and "made for love," but a partnership of some sort is always a requirement for individual activities and decisions. Should the ruler of the Seventh House be conjoined to the Sun in the First, then any relationship a person may be in is not so much a fusion of the two people into a third entity—the relationship—but a fusion of the other person into oneself. In other words, the sense of personal identity is so connected with that individual's reality (or one's *projected concept* of that reality) that the individual with Venus conjunct the Sun in the First is constantly defining any intimate relationship in terms of his or her subjective needs. The partner (signified by the ruler of the Seventh) doesn't stand a chance of being seen objectively and independently. Although the ruler of the Seventh in the First indicates that the individual will never be alone for too long, sometimes in life, on occasion, it is very good to have one's own space clearly defined. This is not easily accomplished when the ruler of partnerships is in the house of self.

When the ruler of the Seventh is in the Second, a partnership is very important to the definition and use of one's talents and abilities. If the ruler of the Seventh is well aspected in the Second, such an arrangement in partnership could be extremely beneficial for both parties concerned. Let us say that Saturn in Virgo is the ruler of the Seventh and is in the Second trine the Moon in Taurus. This would indicate that one is naturally attracted to older, or at the very least, emotionally mature people. Such "senior" partners would be helpful in guiding the individual along in ways that structure and define one's sense of self-worth, especially towards the success of practical goals. What if the Seventh House ruling sign were Taurus, for example, and Venus were in Sagittarius in the Second sextile the Sun in Libra? Such a person would have an easy time creating helpful and friendly relationships in general. In this case, it would be safe to assume that the individual attracts partners who can educate him or her on how best to expand his or her talents and resources.

On the other hand, let us take this same example but also have Venus square to Neptune in Virgo. Here the idealism and impracticality of the Libra/Sagittarius combination would probably predominate and throw the relationship off balance. After all, in this example, Venus is the ruler of the Seventh House as well as the dispositor of the Sun, and thus occupies the central position of this combination of influences. Here the individual whose chart we are examining should be cautioned about receiving questionable financial advice from others. This advice could result in deception and disappointment. I would be prone to saying in this instance, "My friend, do not invest financially with people with whom you share a bed!"

When the ruler of the Seventh is in the Third and the planet is well aspected, partners can be our very closest of friends. Communication with these special loved ones will be easy and effective. In fact, a person who has the ruler of the Seventh House in the Third often is attracted to people who are mentally stimulating. The urge is to see a partner who tends to have a positive effect on that individual's mind and ways of relating his or her thoughts. Please remember that the Seventh House ruler (the other person) is in the native's Third House (the way an individual expresses his or her opinions and ideas). In some cases, this position points to a brother or sister as a business partner, or may indicate that a sibling could act as a consultant to the individual in question (consultants and counselors also fall under the domain of the Seventh).

Because the Third House indicates our neighborhood, when the Seventh House ruler is in this domicile, our life partner may have come from the same ethnic, social, or geographical background as ourselves. Should the Seventh House ruler be afflicted in this house, there is a tendency for the partner to dominate one's thoughts and ideas. Let us say that Scorpio is on the Seventh and Pluto is in the Third in Cancer square the individual's Mercury. This can be an indication of mental manipulation and abuse in their marriage or partnership.

When the ruler of the Seventh is in the Fourth, there is a distinct desire to share one's home with a partner. The combination of Venus and the Moon (natural rulers of these two houses) is particularly domestic and "homey" by nature. Whenever there is a close combination of the houses that these two planets rule, the domestic nature and the urge for intimacy is an important component of one's life. The question is: "What is the *quality* of that intimacy and how *nurturing* will that partnership be for the individual?" When we have the ruler of the Seventh in our Fourth House, we allow people to enter into our most subjective space. We take them into ourselves and as a result are quite psychologically vulnerable to the men and women with whom we are intimate. If the question is, "Your place or mine?", you can be sure that the person with the ruler of the Seventh in the Fourth will always answer "Mine." Yet how safe and secure is "your place"? If there is a developed degree of emotional maturity, then this relationship will only serve to support and embellish the individual's psychological and physical home. Should there be afflictions to the ruler of the Seventh (especially with the ruler of the Fourth), the road to intimacy will definitely have its price, and in accord with the nature of the challenging planetary positions.

When the ruler of the Seventh is in the Fifth, the pull toward romance is strong. Here we have the ruler of the marriage partner in the house of lovers. Although this is an ideal situation, it does not always work out that way. Yet for all intents and purposes, the individual with this combination will want the honeymoon to go on forever. If there are afflictions between the planetary rulers of these houses, especially if in the mutable signs, there may be a tendency toward promiscuity. In this respect, the urge for partnership never loses its desire for the intense immediacy of passion. When the Seventh House ruler is Neptune or if another planet (especially Venus or the Moon) is afflicted by Neptune, look for the tendency for relationship addiction. This manifests in the life of someone who is never happy without a partner, one who must share intimacy and romance even if the quality of the relationship does nothing to support, aid, or comfort him or her. The need for relationship for relationship sake is the result. Granted, this is extreme, but highly possible, when the planetary rulers combine as described above. More often, the combination of the Seventh House ruler in the Fifth bodes well for fun and pleasure in relationship, as this is the natural objective for a person with this interchange of rulerships. If the Seventh House ruler is well aspected in the Fifth, the partner may be an extremely good parent to one's own children (whether natural or stepchildren). If there are stepchildren, look for the influence of Saturn or Uranus in connection with the Fifth House.

When the ruler of the Seventh is in the Sixth and well aspected (especially if the earthy signs are prominent), then the partner may be a good influence on the more pragmatic facets of life. Indeed, this is a positive position for business partners, especially if the other person is to be the junior partner of the team. In terms of marriage and romantic partnership, this influence tends to produce what we could call a "helpmate," a person who is there with all of his skills, tools, and techniques to be of assistance when needed or called upon. If the ruler of the Seventh is afflicted in the Sixth (or afflicts the Sixth House ruler of the person's chart), the partnership may have an adverse effect upon the individual's health. The expression, "You make me sick!", could be appropriately said in this instance. But what is it in the other that unbalances and destabilizes the individual? What is the specific quality of the partner's personality that annoys or harms? And most importantly, what does this difficulty or irritation from the partner *represent* in terms of the psychology or "karma" of the individual?

Why should something in *you* create a malaise in *me*? After all, the person whose chart is in question is *attracted* to such circumstances and therefore invites them (and the partners who embody such situations) into his or her life. What is the quality of the shadow self that needs to be healed here? The answer will be found from the nature of the Seventh House planetary ruler and the sign in which it is placed. If it is an afflicted Moon in Cancer, for example, perhaps there is too much suppressed or misplaced self-nurturing. The partner may then be too obviously needy or emotionally smothering, a condition that makes the person moody and psychologically ill. The planets will always tell the story; we just have to know how to read them correctly. Of course, what we do not want to happen when the ruler of the Seventh is in the Sixth is for our partner to become our pet!

When the ruler of the Seventh is in the Seventh, partnership is paramount. The nature of the ruler of the Seventh House in this instance will be a specific indicator of exactly the kind of person who attracts us the most. If afflicted, it also will reveal what type of relationships create the most problematic situations for us. In terms of the first situation, let us say that Taurus is on the Seventh House cusp and Venus is in Taurus and trine the Moon in Capricorn. In this case, Scorpio has to be rising in this chart and therefore the individual will often seek financial support and stability from his or her relationships (Scorpio is, of course, the sign of other people's resources). Well, look no further! The position of Venus in this example tells us that the Scorpio-ruled individual would tend to find in others exactly what he or she is looking for. In this case, not only would the partner tend to be attractive and materially secure, but also may come from a wealthy family. In terms of the second situation, let us say that Aries is on the Seventh House cusp and Mars is in Aries as well and square Uranus. We know that Libra has to be rising in this horoscope and that we have before us an individual for whom partnership is the key element to life. Also, this is a person who tends to create a peaceful and harmonious form of self-presentation. But look at what is always looming ahead and confronting our Libran—the chaos of Mars square Uranus as the significator of partnerships! Not a pretty sight; exciting, perhaps, with some unusual sexual encounters tossed into the picture, but certainly not at all complementary to the aspiration for serene unity that so much characterizes the life of the Scales. We know that with confrontational Mars in Aries as ruler of the Seventh House in a conflicting relationship with erratic Uranus, our Libra-rising friend is in for a number of unpleasant surprises as he or she seeks out the perfect partner.

When the ruler of the Seventh is in the Eighth, money and mutual resources will play a very important role in our relationships. If the ruler is well aspected, especially in and/or from other planets in the earthy signs, then the individual is likely to have success in shared investments or marry a person who is good with money. Should the ruler be afflicted, problems with finances may plague the relationship. Let us say that Capricorn is on the Seventh House cusp and Saturn is in Aquarius in the Eighth in opposition to the individual's Leo Sun in the Second. This would be a clear indication that the Leo person would seek a partnership in which the other person was extremely controlling (an afflicted Saturn in a fixed sign). This Lion has some deep father issues that he or she will be objectifying (the opposition aspect) in terms of his or her relationships (difficulties with the Seventh House ruler), and the nature of such problems will take the form of financial struggles (planetary opposition between the Second and Eighth houses).

Remember, planets are also people and they will describe themselves in the chart. This planet/house combination concerns two other areas of relationship influence in the chart: sex and transformation. It is quite natural that our sexuality is expressed with our partners. This facet of relationship will be extremely important to a person with the Seventh House ruler in the Eighth. Let us say that Sagittarius is on the Descendant. This tells us that we seek to expand ourselves through our relationships and as this position gives Gemini rising in the chart, we also like to travel and have a good time with our partners. If Jupiter, the Seventh House ruler in this example, were to be found in the Eighth in Capricorn, such expansive, fun-oriented relationships would tend to be limited in some fashion. The individual would tend to get "less than he bargained for" out of his partnerships. He might still gain, mind you, because Sagittarius is a fortuitous sign; however, the partner may be tightfisted or repressed (Capricorn). The Eighth House influence of the Seventh House ruler indicates also that relationships will play a critical role in bringing about those crises of transformation that lead to personal regeneration (or degeneration, as the case may be!).

When the ruler of the Seventh is in the Ninth, partnership is a learning experience. The general orientation is to seek out a partner with whom there are many shared (1) intellectual, (2) philosophical, or (3) spiritual interests. In (1), look in the horoscope for connections between the Seventh and the Ninth in which Mercury, Saturn, or Uranus are the significators and/or the airy signs predominate; for (2), Jupiter, the fire and water signs; and for (3), Neptune and the water signs. In all cases, the individual will want to travel with his or her partner as the urge for adventure plays a significant role in the urge for relationship. Should Mars or Jupiter and the signs Aries or Sagittarius be involved, the partner will definitely have to be a brave seeker of new horizons.

When the ruler of the Seventh is in the Tenth, the urge is to have a partner that increases one's social standing. If debilitated by sign, aspect, or any other astrological indication, the partner can be a source of difficulty in achieving these goals. Let us say that Gemini is on the Seventh House cusp and Mercury in Virgo is placed in the Tenth square to Neptune is Sagittarius. The natural inclination is to look for a partner whose intellectual advice in practical affairs would be a major focus for the relationship. The above example, however, could also point to finding a person whose counsel could be misleading, overly idealistic, or at the very least, confusing. Taurus on the Seventh with Venus conjunct a well-aspected Sun in Leo in the Tenth indicates, as with the Tenth House Leo, that the partner would wish for public recognition and could be quite helpful in stimulating success for both people concerned.

Another interpretation for this position could be that the partner is very successful in his or her own right and that such success would extend into the individual's life. As in all cases involving an individual house/planet combination, one must look at the entire chart to support one's suppositions.

When the ruler of the Seventh is in the Eleventh, the tendency is to seek out a person with whom friendship is a major facet in an intimate personal relationship. It is vital to the success of the relationship for the individual to feel that there are a number of shared common interests. The Eleventh House placement of the significator for partnership reveals that the "significant other" must be much like oneself in many ways, and it is especially important to be able to have the same circle of friends and similar social views.

Let us examine the horoscope of Prince Charles as a fine example of the ruler of the Seventh in the Eleventh House of the natal chart. Many of the problems that Prince Charles had in his marriage to Princess Diana, as well as the rapport he has in his relationship with Camilla

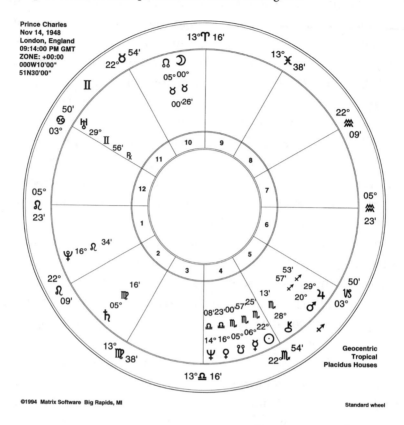

Parker-Bowles, can be seen from an examination of the Seventh, Eleventh, and Fifth houses of the prince's horoscope.

Charles has Uranus as the ruler of the Seventh in the Eleventh in exact opposition to Jupiter in Sagittarius. This placement reveals deep philosophical and sociological differences that he would have with any potential wife. It also would reveal great differences in social perspectives between his own social circle of friends and those of his spouse.

Although Lady Diana Spencer came from the perfect social background, she was thirteen years his junior, thus from a completely different astrological generation; that is, none of the outer planets were in the same signs. They had completely different friends and life experiences. As heir to the throne, Charles was educated in a highly monitored, regimented, traditional, and structured environment. This can be seen from the fact that the ruler of his Third House (Mercury) is in the Fourth closely sextile Saturn in Virgo. His life is not only totally dominated by his mother, Queen Elizabeth, but also the position he is meant to occupy as King if and when he inherits the throne. This situation is also clearly marked in his natal chart by the placement of the Moon in Taurus in the Tenth (exactly conjoined the position of Queen Elizabeth's Sun!) trine to Saturn.

The Sun, Moon, and Ascendant (plus the ruler of the Ascendant) are all in the fixed signs, indicating a life that tends to be rather immobile and set. The great passion in his life comes from sports, especially polo (Mars conjoined to Jupiter in Sagittarius in the Fifth House of fun and pleasure). But it would also come from lovers, as the dispositors of the Sun in Scorpio (which is also the ruling planet of the Leo-rising chart), Mars and Pluto, are trine to one another. When the significators of the house of lovers (the Fifth) are compared to those of the Seventh (marriage partner), the reader will see that the Prince of Wales has a destiny much better linked to mistresses than to wives.

What is interesting (and so very British!) is that Camilla's great-grandmother was the longtime mistress of Charles' great-grandfather. At best, Charles is inclined towards a (turbulent) friendship with any wife, but his real love would be reserved for his paramour. Should he marry Camilla Parker-Bowles, the result of such an action would create enormous social upheaval for him because the emphasis of the relationship would then shift from the relative ease of the Fifth House to the complications evidenced by the condition of his Seventh House ruler in the Eleventh. In addition to the other factors mentioned regarding these positions, the ruler of the Tenth House (Mars) is also in opposition to the ruler of the Seventh (Uranus). The prince's social position would therefore be severely challenged by his new marital status, just as it was by his marriage and subsequent divorce from Diana.

When the ruler of the Seventh is in the Twelfth, there is a tendency for clandestine relationships. These can take several forms depending on the nature of the planetary house ruler. Very often people who work or reside in hospitals, prisons, convents, or monasteries have the ruler of the Seventh in the Twelfth. Other astrological significators of secret or obscure relationships are: the ruler of the Twelfth in aspect to the ruler of the Seventh, Neptune in aspect to the ruler of the Seventh, or Neptune in aspect to Venus (see Prince Charles' chart for an example of this position). The Seventh House ruler in the Twelfth is indicative of a person who requires and prefers a great deal of privacy about his or her personal life. A well-aspected Seventh House ruler in this position can be a tremendous source of inner strength and act as a "hidden angel or guardian spirit," quietly helping and supporting the individual through life. On the other hand, an afflicted Seventh House ruler in this position, especially if it is Neptune, Pluto, or Uranus, can bring about scandal and enormous difficulties.

The Nature of the Eighth House

In the process of atomic fission, an instrument is used called a cyclotron. The purpose of this machine is to smash atoms so that their forms are destroyed and their energetic properties are released. This allows the power expressed by such a dangerous (and amazing) process to be channeled to other sources, both destructive and constructive. In essence, the nature of the atom has been transformed and through an act of creative will, its essential vitality may be put to other uses. The Eighth House is the cyclotron of the horoscope. No wonder it and its natural sign ruler, Scorpio, have such a notorious reputation among astrologers.

The Eighth contains some of the most challenging and compulsive areas of life: death, sex, and taxes! Yet the fundamental dynamics of this astrological domicile can be summed up by one word: transformation. We can add a couple of other words to amplify this: regeneration and recirculation. Although the Eighth House does indeed describe much about the nature of one's physical death (as well as one's attitude toward death in general), the Eighth has also much to do with the nature of those crises in life that occur in order, creating psychological and spiritual growth. It is thus that we are seen to pass away and "die" to one stage of our evolution on this planet so that we may be reborn and renewed.

Sexuality is another of those areas in human existence that on the one hand, points at the door to our immortality and on the other, the complete degeneration and degradation of the self. Through our sexual nature we create our relative physical immortality through children, and in doing so also create the subsequent birthing of future generations. Also, through the reorientation of sexual energy, the more mystically inclined can reach a state of higher consciousness. Yet for many, sexuality becomes an obsessive tool of self-annihilation and destruction. What is a natural and rather beautiful part of human nature is all too often perverted and circumscribed by fear, prejudice, crime, and now, commercial advertising. What is important, although this book is certainly not a treatise on sexuality, is our way to the Spiritual Path (the Ninth House) is preceded by our journey through the Eighth.

When the ruler of the Eighth is in the First, the need for personal transcendence is highlighted in no uncertain terms. The relationship between these two houses is unquestionably linked. In the first place, they share the same natural ruler, Mars. When the Red Planet is found in Scorpio, it brings about an intensity of personal drive that stimulates the ending and subsequent transformation of certain dynamics of the personal, emotional, and desire natures. Mars in Aries opens the door to the stimulation of *new* desires, goals, and impulses that will only have to be "killed off" and transmuted into a higher state of expression at some later stage of life.

If the Eighth House ruler is strong and well aspected in the First, then the individual has a continuous font of regenerative energy at his or her disposal. If, for example, Leo were on the cusp of the Eighth and the Sun in Capricorn were in the First, the urge would be to create a life in which each and every moment is seen as a potential for the increase and regeneration of personal potency and power. This characteristic could easily manifest as a controlling personality, in an individual who wants to create a world in which he or she is the supreme dictator. In effect, this position indicates a person who takes your resources and incorporates them into the structure of his life. Such a negative tendency is energetically supported in the horoscope if Mars and/or Saturn are in any major aspect with the Sun in this position.

In addition to the indication of the aspects, the level of the person's spiritual development would certainly help determine if such a person were a benevolent or malevolent ruler over his or her domain. The

Eighth House ruler in the First also indicates that sexuality is a primary consideration of the personality in terms of dealing with the environment. If an afflicted Saturn were the planet in question, the sense of personal sexual inhibition would dominate one's self-image and affect one's relationships accordingly. If a powerful Mars or Venus were in this position, then a great deal of the life would be characterized by a strongly aggressive urge for sexual conquest in terms of Mars, or a definite magnetic and charismatic sensually expressed "urge to merge" in terms of Venus.

When the ruler of the Eighth is in the Second, the native's partner's financial resources are intimately linked with his or her own financial condition. The astrological system of houses is logical and consistent in its number sequencing. The Eighth is the Second House from the Seventh. The Second House in one's horoscope speaks about one's own resources, so the Second from the Seventh House indicates money that comes from partnerships. This is the reason why the Eighth House also is the house of alimony (resources that come from the *death* of a partnership). If Venus were the ruler of the Eighth and well aspected by a trine from Jupiter or Pluto, for example, the tendency would be for the individual to increase personal wealth as a result of marriage or business relationships. If on the other hand, Neptune in Virgo were the ruler of the Eighth (Pisces on the cusp) and square to Mercury (ruler of the Second, as Virgo would be on the cusp of this house), then the individual could easily find that his or her personal resources were somehow imperiled by some deceitful or scandalous misuse of the partner's funds.

When the ruler of the Eighth is in the Third, the subjects of sex and death will be among the prime subjects of thought, discussion, and communication. Let us take a look at the horoscope of Elisabeth Kübler-Ross, the Swiss social worker and healer who is renowned for transforming the world's attitudes towards death and the dying. In her book, *On Death and Dying*, Kübler-Ross writes, "The dying are grateful for the chance to talk, to share and explore their experience, and to be liberated from the conspiracy of silence." Kübler-Ross has Libra on the cusp of the Eighth House with Venus in Gemini in the Third. Venus is also the ruler of the Third House (Taurus on the cusp), so that the con-

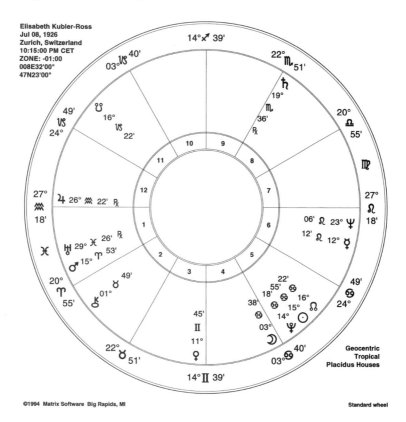

Elisabeth Kubler-Ross
Jul 08, 1926
Zurich, Switzerland
10:15:00 PM CET
ZONE: -01:00
008E32'00"
47N23'00"

Geocentric
Tropical
Placidus Houses

©1994 Matrix Software Big Rapids, MI

Standard wheel

nection between the Eighth and the Third is an intimate reality in her life. In addition, Venus is sextile Mars (natural ruler of the Eighth) in Aries in the First House, showing that she would pioneer this subject. Venus also is sextile to its own dispositor, Mercury, which is found in the Sixth House of health and healing. In esoteric astrology, Venus is the ruler of Gemini, as Venus' true nature is to harmonize polarities.

Esoteric rulerships only function from the level of the soul, when individual actions are oriented for the well-being of others and are totally non-egotistical in their goals.[7] Here Venus functions to unite the primary polarity, life and death, through *conscious communication*. The transformational dynamics of this chart and their association with death are also seen by the fact that Kübler-Ross has a tight conjunction in her natal chart of Pluto and the Sun. The placements of these planets (plus the Moon) in Cancer reveals the nurturing energy field through which she operates. Aquarius rising with Uranus in Pisces in the First House are prime indicators of the compassionate, humanitarian nature of this courageous woman's life.

When the ruler of the Eighth is in the Fourth, the individual will find that life brings a number of challenges to personal growth centering on the person's relationship with the family and place of origin. Quite often, the death of one's parents is the source of such transformational occurrences. There often is an experience of loss and subsequent release from the nature and structure of one's psychological roots, so a greater freedom to interact less from the instincts and more from objectivity is made possible. This powerful position indicates that in order to assure psychological growth, a "re-rooting" has to take place. In this respect, developmental growth occurs when one moves from a subconscious attachment to the biological karma and the process of individuation is consequently accelerated.

Let us remember that the Fourth is also known as the "house of endings." When the ruler of the house of death is in the house of endings, there is no other way to go than to create a focus for reincarnation. I do not mean this in the metaphysical sense. I am using the term here in a more euphemistic and figurative sense. When the ruler of the Eighth is in the Fourth, a step has to be made for the purpose of personal growth. We "reincarnate" in this sense by bringing the "inner child" home and merging it with the adult human being through a continuous process of psychological synthesis.

Another indication of the significance of this placement has to do with sexuality. Early sexual conditioning, as well as the possibility of there being early sexual abuse in the life, will show in the natal chart. Finding corroboration of sexual abuse is possible with the careful assessment of the Eighth House ruler when in this position.

When the ruler of the Eighth is in the Fifth, opportunities present themselves for refinement of personal creativity. Anything to do with the Eighth House, Scorpio, and Pluto, involves the "cyclotronic process." This means that the association of any other astrological significator with the Eighth House, its natal and/or natural sign and planetary rulers, points to crises of transformation. In the case of the

Fifth House, this has to do with one's creative self-expression. If I am to "turn up the volume" on my creative potential, then climbing the energetic spiral which will permit such an augmentation of my potential will also require a periodic purging of previous patterns. I cannot expect to grow in my creative output nor in the quality of its manifestation, if I stay attached to the energetic level in which I have learned to become comfortable. I can complain all I want to about not being sufficiently creative or that my potential in this respect is being squashed by someone else.

In terms of the Eighth House, this could be by the condition of my partner's resources, so that I may give myself such excuses as: "My partner needs the money," or "My spouse doesn't have enough money so I cannot make a change," and so forth. When the ruler of the Eighth is in the Fifth, the only way to grow creatively is to make a change in my creative orientation, a qualitative one, one that will definitely require a true release and detachment from my previous self-concept. Wherever the ruler of the Eighth lands, it brings its regenerative gifts or its degenerative challenges.

Let us say that Gemini is on the cusp of the Eighth with Mercury well aspected in the Fifth. The individual in question would find that his or her mind is a great tonic, a great restorer of creative vitality. The individual may also find that his or her road to personal regeneration or transformative gifts is found by working and communicating with children and young people.

If Pluto is the ruler of the Eighth and found in Leo in the Fifth and sextile the Sun in Gemini, for example, the individual is likely to notice that his or her way of communicating works magic on youth. This is a person who can stimulate the intelligent curiosity of kids as well as bring humor and versatility to the process of education. Such an individual would find that by helping the creative life force emerge from young people, he would also be regenerating his own vitality.

When the ruler of the Eighth is in the Sixth, the focus of regeneration is on health and healing. This would be the case especially if the Eighth House ruler was in Scorpio, Pisces, or Virgo and in mutual aspect with the ruler of the Sixth. Example: Pluto in Virgo in the Sixth sextile to Mercury in Scorpio in the Eighth. The impetus is to refine the tools, techniques, and methods that he or she uses to create wholeness in her own and in other people's lives. There are strong and natural connections between the functions of these two houses and their natural signs, Scorpio and Virgo. The latter is always seeking refinement and a better, more efficient way of using energy. Scorpio is the process by which energy is released from its form. Usually, although not always, Scorpio learns through tests requiring the transformation of desire and a consequent emotional loss.

If the ruler of the Eighth is well aspected in the Sixth, the horoscope reveals that the path to destruction, and consequent refinement of form, finds a "home" that supports this transformational orientation. It is revealed by providing information in symbolic form of processes and skills that bring healing to this difficult work.

In the example above, the person who has Scorpio on the cusp of the Eighth House and Pluto in Virgo in the Sixth is always in search of how to "build a better mousetrap." In other words, there is a ceaseless urge to improve upon the conditions in one's life through finding a better job, refining personal skills, and seeking in general to bring a sense of wholeness into one's life. These traits can be said to characterize the entire Pluto in Virgo generation (1957–1971), but with much more specific emphasis for a person with Pluto in Virgo in the Sixth House. The regenerative sextile to Mercury in Scorpio in the Eighth would indicate that individual tends to find the means (most probably through his or her job) to improve his or her life skills.

When the ruler of the Eighth is in the Seventh, the sexual component of relationships is most important. Here we find the natural energies of the house belonging to Mars occupying the house that is naturally ruled by Venus. The astrologer should keep in mind that *whatever* the natal sign and planetary rulers may be, this particular Mars/Venus relationship underscores the interchange between these two houses. The urge for personal regeneration, the process by which the individual creates those crises that permit psychological or spiritual growth to take place (Eighth House), will occur most naturally through relationships (Seventh House).

Let us say that Capricorn was on the Eighth House cusp, and Saturn was in the Seventh, but in Capricorn. Capricorn on the Eighth indicates that the price for having the freedom to move up the evolutionary ladder (and this is the purpose of Eighth House crises) will occur through challenges of control in his or her personal relationships. The individual with this placement will find that he would tend to structure sexual encounters so that his feelings of personal dominance in relationships would be paramount. On the other hand, Saturn in Capricorn in the Seventh ruling the Eighth might indicate that the individual would be attracted to people who tend to control the sexuality in the relationship and thus the native would feel limited in his ability to be sexually expressive. The entire chart would have to be examined to see if the individual is the activator or the receiver of such limiting and controlling circumstances.

In this instance, if Capricorn were on the Eighth House cusp, Gemini would most likely be rising. The astrologer could then come to the conclusion that *both* sides of this situation take place and that there is an alternation between being the controller and being the one controlled. One thing for sure, this combination would most definitely bring tension into the sexual component of partnership. If this were a business connection, then the energy that is limited and controlled would be financial (Eighth House). The question being asked in this instance is: "Who is in charge of the way partnership funds are being structured in my relationships?"

When the ruler of the Eighth is in the Eighth, the regenerative crises and/or sexual components of life are definitely heightened. There would be no doubt at all that if Scorpio were on the cusp of the Eighth and Mars was there as well, the individual's sexual orientation would be intense and powerful. If Mars was in a difficult aspect to Saturn from this position, enormous sexual frustration could be expected; in the extreme, the urge for sadomasochistic activity arises, especially if Uranus were involved in this particular combination in some strong aspect.

If Neptune were conjoined Mars in Scorpio here, for instance, and square the Moon in Leo, a man would tend to have emotionally deceitful and complex sexual relationships with women. The tendency would be toward sexuality dominating one's relationships to the point that real emotional nurturing would be denied. This is an individual who may tend toward promiscuity as he or she searches for an emotional content to sexuality that is obscured by pure lust. Should Taurus be on the cusp of the Eighth, for example, and Venus in her own sign in this house, trine to Jupiter in Capricorn, the urge for sensual pleasure will also be very strong. This also is an indicator for finding powerful financial alliances through marriage and intimate personal relationships. The nature of those personal regenerative crises that so characterize one's Eighth House experience will be described by the planet that rules the cusp of this house, the sign the planet is in, and the aspects it receives from the other planets. Leo on the cusp of the Eighth with the Sun in that sign and square to Pluto in Scorpio in the natal chart, for example, indicates a person who will seek power and recognition early in life. This will be a man or a woman who can be subtly manipulative so that he or she may take center stage at all times.[8] Strong identity crises will occur at regular intervals (usually signified by the transits of Pluto, Saturn, Neptune, and Uranus to the Sun) that challenge the individual's personal identification with his or her egocentricity. These crises and the necessary adjustments in the ego structure that must come about are usually resisted by the power of the personality (Sun and Pluto are square in the fixed signs) until later on in life.

When the ruler of the Eighth is in the Ninth, look for transformational crises in life to come through religion, philosophy, education, and travel. The individual is on a search for a higher aspect to his or her nature. Very often, especially if the Moon, the ruler of the Fourth House, or the sign Cancer is involved, there is a need to challenge the spiritual beliefs of one's family background. If Sagittarius were on the cusp of the Eighth and Jupiter were placed in the Ninth, the individual would be open to transformational influences coming from foreign countries, or from the amassed knowledge of human experience found in historical references. If well aspected, this can be a very fortuitous placement for the Eighth House ruler because the Ninth is the Second from the Eighth and as such, opens the mind to intellectual or spiritual resources resulting from the transformational crises. This is indicated by the Eighth House ruler.

Should the ruler of the Eighth be afflicted in the Ninth, especially in a fixed sign, difficulties may ensue in the establishment of a personal belief system. One's philosophical ideals and principles may not move with the times, leaving one dissatisfied or at the very least, backward and outmoded. If there are afflictions to the Eighth House ruler in the Ninth in the mutable signs, then too many paths to higher knowledge are attempted, leaving one dissipated and diffused, filled with inner conflict and internal crosscurrents.

Cardinal sign afflictions in this position tend to motivate people in the wrong direction. Mars in Aries square to Jupiter in Cancer as the ruler of the Eighth in the Ninth, for example, would tend to produce a self-righteous individual, one who is motivated to action by a highly personal set of ideals that are not universally applicable—as much as he or she might think that they are. As the purpose of the Ninth House is to open and widen an individual's perspective, and the nature of the Eighth is to stimulate personal growth through conflict, neither of these goals is supported by a strict adherence to a personality-centered, and therefore limited, life philosophy.

When the ruler of the Eighth is in the Tenth, ambitions and goals are high in focus. The urge is to regenerate achievements, making the most out of what has been established through one's profession. The sexual and procreative urges, the need to refine and regenerate oneself, the ability to rechannel creative energies into new directions, are all then placed in the house of career and public standing. If the condition of the ruler of the Eighth is strong and positive in this position, then support for personal achievement may come through the financial assistance of one's partners. Even if this is not the case and the individual has to go it alone, a powerfully placed Eighth House ruler in the Tenth is a great help to achievement. The individual finds the power within him or herself as long as one element is included in all the plans and goals that are particular to this planetary/house combination—detachment.

In order to make the most out of any Eighth House-related position, the individual has to realize that death will demand its due. Something, someone, or some archetype of relationship must be relinquished in order for anything better to take its place. The attitude that one develops towards the transformation of instinct and the cultivation of the intuitive nature allows one to see the true relationship between essence and form. This is a most important transition to make if one is to profit from a strong Eighth House ruler in the Tenth. Should the Eighth House ruler be afflicted, personal reticence to one's necessary transformations will inhibit success in terms of career goals. If Venus is the ruling planet, these inhibitions stem from an inability to regenerate one's personal values or the nature of one's relationships. If it is Saturn, the need to be in personal control obscures the possibility of real achievement. If it is Mars, one's sexual desires or urge to dominate in career environments or situations stand in the way.

When the ruler of the Eighth is in the Eleventh, a direct link is created between transformational crises that release personal attachments, and the possibilities of a wider social application and acceptance of the individual's talents, resources, and general creativity. It is important here to understand the relationship of the succedent houses (Two, Five, Eight, and Eleven).

Briefly, the Second House is the bank in which our potential assets are stored. The Fifth allows those raw and unformed potentials to be invested in terms of the nature of the individual ego — the effects and projections of these personal talents and abilities are still rather personal. In the Eighth House, challenge to this personalization of life takes place. This is the "cyclotronic process" to which I made earlier reference. In other words, one's creative abilities have to be stripped from their acute personalization (after all, the Fifth House natural ruler is Leo) so that they may be used for more evolved, social, and humanitarian purposes. In this respect, it should be reiterated that a major goal of human evolution is to bring the individual into the understanding of the One.

This is done through a process of socialization symbolized by Aquarius and the collective activities of the Eleventh House. When the ruler of the Eighth is in the Eleventh and afflicted, there is a resistance on the part of the individual to this process of depersonalization and socialization of resources. One feels rejected or opposed by society and one refutes collective opinions or creative group direction. Should the ruler of the Eighth find a comfortable dwelling place in the Eleventh, then the natural human evolutionary process is allowed to continue unimpeded. One's talents, resources, and abilities (as signified by the actual planetary ruler) are accepted by the collective of which he or she is a part. The individual is therefore allowed to transform and regenerate his social group, organization, or association in such a way that rewards (social and financial) also may come to that person. As a result, his or her own life force is sustained, nurtured, and increased.

When the ruler of the Eighth is in the Twelfth, two directions are possible and both are rather subtle in nature. In the first case, the individual is open to a more mystical transformation of any leftover personality refuse. This means that a final meltdown of any resistance to growth (as symbolized by the actual planetary ruler) is indicated. If the ruler of the Eighth is well aspected, there is absolutely no need to personalize the planetary energy in question. Life will take care of any and all situations involving that planet. If this planet is Venus, as ruler of the Eighth in the Twelfth in a trine to the Moon in the earthy signs, for example, the individual does not have to be concerned about monetary issues in personal relationships. This area will just seem to flow of its own accord. The more mystical astrologer would say, "She has earned good financial relationship karma in a past life so that in this life, all she has to do is smile and open her purse and life will provide the necessary substance." Whatever one's views on the subject of reincarnation may be, the point is that there is no need for this individual to have to objectify lessons that involve the right use of finances in human relationships. The job is done and done well.

In the second case, if the Eighth House ruler is afflicted in this position, the resistance to learning the lessons of the planet in question will likely prove quite troublesome. If this is Saturn (Capricorn on the cusp of the Eighth), then the individual finds herself uncomfortable with structure and control. Lessons concerning personal regeneration come from the need to learn about the correct restructuring of shared resources, and/or there is a sexual control issue that is incomplete and must be dealt with—or trouble lies ahead.

The Nature of the Ninth House

From the soul-centered perspective of astrology, we can say that the Ninth House represents the spiritual path. It is only after the transformative crises of the Eighth House are successfully achieved that an individual has the wisdom, life experience, and self-awareness to enter into a wider field of more universal understanding. It is here that the ego and the dynamics of the personality are used not so much as attached vehicles of personal identification, but as objective tools to greater evolutionary development. This lofty status, which only comes about through an intensely devoted period of a one-pointed focus of spiritual orientation, is simply not available to all people at the same time. The highest gifts of the Ninth House are reserved for those who have earned them, but they are there and waiting for everyone who has prepared him or herself for the long journey known as "the Path."

In traditional humanistic astrology, the Ninth House is seen as one containing many fortuitous experiences. It is first and foremost the house of stored and collective knowledge, and to the more esoterically inclined astrologer, the Ninth House is also the way to wisdom. In essence, it can be said that the Ninth is the encyclopedia of the horoscope. It is associated with archeology, history, foreign travel, higher education, and jurisprudence (man-made law). Your lawyer is found in the Seventh House, as he will take sides against your accuser or opponent and work on your behalf. His place is relative, and depending on the nature of the case and the client, he can be on either side of the scales of justice: prosecutor or defender. The judge sits in the Ninth House, objective to both sides of a case but defending the Law: the encompassing structure of codes of conduct that define the morality of a given civilization. While the Seventh is the house of relative truths and the Third is the house of personal truths, the Ninth is the house of universal truths.

When the ruler of the Ninth is in the First, we are looking at the horoscope of a person who is a seeker to broaden his or her horizons for better self-expression. The urge for the expansion of life experience links such an individual personally to the issues and affairs of the Ninth House. This is a person who will have important experiences relative to foreign travel, higher education, religion, and philosophy. Yet are such interests supported by the whole chart? Does this orientation bring conflict or rewards? As in all cases, one has to examine the conditions of the ruling planet in this position. If this is a well-aspected Jupiter as ruler of the Ninth in the First, then there is no doubt about the importance of Ninth House affairs in one's life. Call the travel agency and book the flight! Call the church and assemble the elders, our friend has a revelation to share, a commentary on an issue of great theological importance to relate! In fact, this is a person with a definite calling to the literal or figurative cloth, and wants everyone to know it. If Mars is in Aries, Aquarius, or Sagittarius, and the ruler of the Ninth in the First, then his is a *cause célèbre*, and he will need the length of his entire lifetime to assert his beliefs and spread his particular doctrine. If Mars is afflicted, then his beliefs are likely to oppose many other people's opinions, but as a spiritual warrior he will battle on. If Saturn is the ruler of the Ninth and poorly aspected in the First, the individual may find the road to higher education impeded by money (earth signs), social opposition (air signs), emotional conflicts (water signs), or an overpowering and thus limiting sense of his or her own beliefs (fire signs).

When the ruler of the Ninth is in the Second and well aspected, the tendency is for the pursuit of higher knowledge and insights into life to increase one's self-esteem and harmonize with one's innate talents and abilities. Education can do a great deal to further the individual's financial security and travel can be a source of potential for his worldly success. This would especially be the case if the ruler of the Ninth was in the Second and in positive aspect to the ruler of the Tenth (worldly status) or to a planet posited in the Tenth.

Let us say that Taurus was placed on the cusp of the Ninth House. This would indicate that the individual would seek to further his or her education in a practical field of study—for example, real estate. In this hypothetical chart, we would find that Venus, ruler of the Ninth, is in the Second in Libra sextile to Mercury as ruler of the Tenth.[9] We could interpret this chart as follows: Through the individual's higher studies in real estate (Taurus on the Ninth), she has a natural talent for creating relationships that foster her own financial wealth (Venus in Libra in the Second). This could easily take place by choosing real estate as a career (Gemini, significator of agents and agencies on the Tenth, with Mercury ruling this house as well as the Ascendant and sextile Venus).

By following the pattern of dispositorships around the chart and using the astrological keywords and phrases, separate elements move easily together, revealing the natural inclinations in any horoscope. If the Ninth House ruler were afflicted in the Second, a logical response from a person with this position would be: "No matter how much education I get, I cannot seem to find a path to greater self-esteem and increased personal wealth."

When the ruler of the Ninth is in the Third, higher education and foreign voyages enlarge the scope of personal ideas, beliefs, and opinions. As both the Third and the Ninth are travel houses, having the Ninth House ruler in the Third increases the individual's natural inclination for movement. This tendency would be especially accentuated with Gemini and Sagittarius on these house cusps or the rulers of the Ninth or Third in aspect to a planet in either of these two signs.

Let us say that Pisces is on the cusp of the Ninth with Neptune in Virgo in the Third in square to Mercury in Sagittarius. These configurations characterize a person who has a great thirst for spiritual truth but gets caught between what she would like to believe and what she actually knows and thus is confused and conflicted. In this case, a small detail from a holy scripture (Neptune in Virgo ruling the Ninth) can be exaggerated into a doctrinal and everlasting truth (square Mercury in Sagittarius). This is the kind of aspect that is symbolic of a certain fundamentalist sect of snake handlers that take a single phrase in the New Testament, then go about telling people that their beliefs will protect them against poisons and dangerous serpents, using it as the central core of their worship. This group (originating in the Appalachian Mountains) drinks strychnine and dances with venomous snakes as they seek salvation.

The drawback to having the Ninth House ruler in the Third is that it can exaggerate a person's belief that what he believes from his personal education or experience is tantamount to universal truth. The result can be an individual with a narrow mental focus thinking he has a much broader comprehension of reality than he really does. Rather like a pocket dictionary trying to impersonate the *Encyclopedia Britannica*.

When the ruler of the Ninth is in the Fourth, a person's philosophical or religious beliefs are central to his or her life. If we understand the Fourth House to be the psychological anchor of the personality, then the Ninth House ruler in this domain brings the urge for a wider worldview "home." Let us say that Libra is on the Ninth House cusp and Venus is well aspected in Taurus in the Fourth. This position would indicate to the astrologer that the individual in question is open to making relationships that widen and broaden his or her knowledge and understanding. "Higher education" in this sense may come from the people one encounters in foreign countries, or through partnership, or one's general involvements in intimate relationships. The positive condition of the Ninth House ruler in this example tells us that such relationships add to the individual's sense of self-worth or even result in some financial gains. Having the Ninth House ruler in the Fourth also indicates that the home is a place where we like to study, meditate, and contemplate some of the deeper issues of life.

If Mercury or Jupiter is the ruler of the Ninth and placed in the Fourth, then it is quite likely that a home library is important. If the sign Cancer or the Moon is involved, that person may be a book collector. In any case, the individual will express his or her urge to learn, study, and develop spiritually—all taking place in the home.

The Ninth House ruler in this astrological location may also describe a parent who acts in a true teaching role in one's life. If the ruler of the Ninth is in the Fourth but in a square, opposition, or inconjunct aspect to the Sun or the ruler of the horoscope (especially in the fixed signs), the philosophical orientation of the parent may be quite different from that of the individual, which would lead to profound interpersonal challenges. This also is particularly apt if these positions involve the fixed signs.

When the ruler of the Ninth is in the Fifth, all matters related to this domicile tend to be experienced with pleasure. Travel may be a passion and ongoing education can be a most enjoyable hobby or pastime. Should the ruler of the Ninth be Mercury in Aquarius in the Fifth, for example, the individual would delight in going to workshops, seminars, and all other events in which learning takes place in a group setting. This position of the Ninth House ruler is also indicative of a person who is a natural-born teacher, as it speaks about an individual who likes to take what he or she learns and experiences about life (Ninth House) and bring this understanding to children and young people (Fifth House).

Look for support of this supposition if the Fifth House ruler is in positive aspect to the Ninth House ruler. However, look for difficulties in transmitting what one believes across to one's children should these two rulers be inharmoniously aspected with one another. Fads, hobbies, interests, and pastimes of foreign origin can also be of great interest and constitute what a person does in the way of enjoyment. If Jupiter is the ruler of the Ninth in the natal chart and placed in the Fifth, a person could be a history buff or enjoy foreign sporting events (or both). Libra on the cusp of the Ninth with Venus well aspected in the Fifth may indicate that relationships made while traveling or in the pursuit of higher knowledge result in affectionate friends or even lovers. The horoscope is a road map. Once we know how to follow the route of the planets, signs, and houses, the path the journey takes becomes very clear.

When the ruler of the Ninth is in the Sixth, studies are geared towards improvement of practical skills that the individual may use to further his or her advancement in work. If the ruler of the Ninth is in harmonious aspect to the ruler of the Sixth when in the Sixth House, then this conclusion has strong support from the natal chart. An even greater emphasis to this supposition will come if the sign Virgo is involved and, to a somewhat lesser extent, Taurus and Capricorn. The Ninth House ruler in the Sixth may also indicate a sincere interest in animals, as well as in herbs and other forms of healing methods. Look for connections with the signs Virgo, Cancer, or Pisces to support this conclusion. Should the ruler of the Ninth be Mercury, and the latter is located in the Sixth, then the approach to higher education, philosophy, and religion tends to be rather pragmatic and rational. If Pisces or Cancer and their rulers are involved, then the urge to heal and nurture through one's chosen field of education is highlighted. Mystical healing, psychic healing, and religious associations with healing are likely if Neptune or Jupiter are connected to this combination of house influences (especially in the water or fire signs).

When the ruler of the Ninth is in the Seventh, the road to personal expansion through higher education, philosophy, or religious aspiration needs to be shared. This position often is seen in the horoscope of a person who wants to share his or her experience of the spiritual path with a partner. If the Ninth House ruler is afflicted in the Seventh (especially in the fixed signs), then such a goal is difficult to achieve. Should Venus be the afflicted Ninth House ruler in the Seventh or be in a square, opposition, or inconjunct with the ruler (again, especially in the fixed signs), then look for distinct differences in social values between oneself and one's partners. If Jupiter is the "offending" influence, there is a tendency for religious, philosophical, or moral differences between oneself and one's spouse or "special other."

Should Saturn in Sagittarius in the Seventh be the ruler of the Ninth (Aquarius on the cusp of the house), the individual has orthodox religious beliefs which can bring conflict to relationships, especially if Saturn is in difficult aspect with the ruler of the Seventh or Venus. If Uranus is the ruler of the Ninth in Sagittarius in the Seventh, the individual is usually possessed of some unusual and/or very inclusive philosophical or spiritual orientation. This could open and expand his or her relationships when well placed with the various planetary significators of the Seventh (the ruler of the house cusp or Venus) or, in turn, challenge the relationship, if in conflict with these planets. In any event, Uranus in this position certainly invites a lot of other people with interesting beliefs into partnership.

When the ruler of the Ninth is in the Eighth, a road to the transformation of one's philosophical or religious beliefs and understandings is strongly indicated. It is important to see that the Eighth is the *Twelfth from the Ninth.* As such, it points to a melting down, a total and final dissolution and release. When we add the implication of this particular placement of the Ninth House ruler to the general indications of the Eighth House itself—death, regeneration, transmutation—we can see the potential crisis that is evoked when the Ninth House ruler is so posited. Almost everyone reading this work in one way or another has made the symbolic journey that this rulership/house embodies.

It is safe to say that the vast majority of us were born into rather traditional Christian, Jewish, or Muslim homes. Very few of us had a *metaphysical* background when growing up and even fewer were fortunate to have a parent or a grandparent who was an astrologer. We had to leave behind our "natal" religion as we opened ourselves to something that not only included our biologically inherited creed but also was not limited by it. A person who has the Ninth House ruler in his or her Eighth House will have to make such a journey, but with a lot more emphasis, challenges, and potential victories than the rest of us whose Ninth House ruler is elsewhere in the chart. Look to one's personal philosophical orientation to be a source of renewal and regeneration of the spirit, but not before this kind of philosophical battle takes place.

When the ruler of the Ninth is in the Tenth, philosophical or religious doctrines take a prominent role in life. Such a position indicates a person who easily could be a public advocate for his or her religious or philosophical beliefs. This would especially be the case if the ruler was in a fire or air sign, especially Aries, Sagittarius, Gemini, or Aquarius. Education also would take on a significant role in terms of the individual's career or social image. These factors are clearly in evidence in the horoscope of one of the greatest spiritual leaders of the twentieth century, Mahatma Gandhi. The Sanskrit word *mahatma* can be translated as "great soul." The function of the soul is to bring wholeness. A soul-realized individual, a "mahatma," will embody this principle as he or she endeavors to reveal the essential unity standing behind all the apparent variations of all the forms of life.

Cancer is the ruler of Gandhi's Ninth House, indicating his spiritual background anchored in the cultural past. This sign/cusp combination speaks generally about the relationship of a person's religion and their biological karma, that is, their attachment to their family and the cultural, national, or racial background. Also, it can indicate the urge to nourish and support others through one's religion. In soul-centered astrology, the ruler of Cancer is Neptune. This indicates that in the lives of advanced human beings, the entire ocean of humanity is regarded as one's family.

In Gandhi's chart (see page 259), Neptune is trine the Moon, revealing the integration of his soul purpose with his personality in terms of his Ninth House. Gandhi received his higher education in law (ruled by Sagittarius and the Ninth House), and worked for many years in

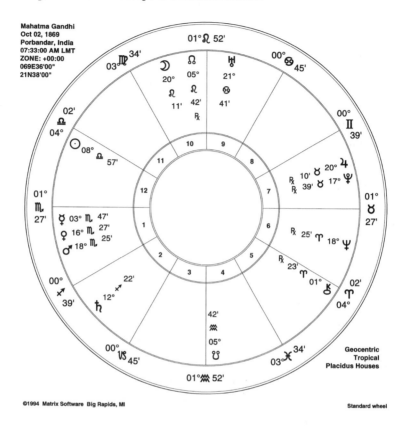

Mahatma Gandhi
Oct 02, 1869
Porbandar, India
07:33:00 AM LMT
ZONE: +00:00
069E36'00"
21N38'00"

Geocentric
Tropical
Placidus Houses

©1994 Matrix Software Big Rapids, MI

Standard wheel

South Africa to help liberate the large Indian population of that country from its policy of racial intolerance.

The Moon, ruler of the Ninth, is in Leo in the Tenth, showing the public application of his higher learning. In mundane astrology, the Moon signifies the mass of humanity. In esoteric astrology, the Moon signifies the mass consciousness. Here the Moon is in a fixed sign and the apex of a powerful T-square with Venus and Mars in Scorpio on one side with both in opposition to Jupiter and Pluto in Taurus on the other. Gandhi strove not only to unify the two great populations of the Indian subcontinent, Hindus and Muslims, but also to break down the ancient Hindu caste system, so oppressive to that vast segment of the population known as "untouchables." Gandhi renamed them *Harijans*, or "Children of God." He thus put himself under a double social *and* religious burden.

Scorpio rises in his horoscope, revealing a destiny that is based on a transformational orientation to life. Pluto, the ruler, is conjunct Jupiter in Taurus, indicating the urge to transmute social concepts and established moral values. The co-ruler of the chart is Mars in Scorpio conjunct Venus. This emphasizes a path that can be summarized as "harmony through conflict."

All four of these planets (as noted above) square the Moon, indicating the intensity of social conflict that he chose for himself. The focus on the fixed signs, culminating in the Moon in Leo, reveals his immutability and strength of will. His public work required that he transform his own powerful sexuality (Mars conjunct Venus in Scorpio) to free himself to total public devotion.

Many times Gandhi risked death through fasting, as well as public confrontation with the forces of the British Raj. His presence changed the lives of hundreds of millions of people and his influence in the world continues on long after his assassination by a Hindu religious fanatic. Another Mahatma, the late Dr. Martin Luther King, Jr., modeled his methods of civil disobedience on Gandhi's program of passive resistance.

When the ruler of the Ninth is in the Eleventh, one's religions and philosophical beliefs tend to express themselves through a group focus. This combination of influences indicates a person who likes to be part of a church congregation, specialized political group, or other secular or non-secular organizations. The individual feels very comfortable when his or her ideals are being shared by a number of like-minded people. This is a person who enjoys speaking in the common jargon and specialized vocabulary common among any such social entity. He or she feels at home with structured rites, rituals, and rallies. When the Ninth House ruler is in the Eleventh, especially in the air or fire signs, they can proselytize.

An Eleventh House influence in a horoscope indicates the distribution and diffusion of ideas, aspirations, hopes, and wishes. A person whose Ninth House ruler is in this domicile wants others to believe as he does, especially if the Ninth House significator is in strong aspect to the ruler of the Third House, Mercury, or the sign Cancer when placed in the Eleventh. Another point to be made about this position is that it reveals a person who either likes to educate the masses or who is educated by the masses, or both.

When the ruler of the Ninth is in the Twelfth, the urge to explore hidden knowledge is an important facet of one's life. If the person is so inclined, this position indicates someone who has an interest in metaphysics, mysticism, or the occult. It may also point out a person who likes to study human psychology, especially if it entails one's dream life (look to a connection to the ruler of the Eighth House to support this conclusion). This is an excellent position for someone who does laboratory or library research. At its most basic level of interpretation, when the ruler of the Ninth is in the Twelfth, we have an individual who enjoys, or who derives benefit, from studying in solitude.

If the sign Scorpio is connected to this position or there is a Mercury/Pluto contact to the Ninth/Twelfth House relationship, this is the horoscope of someone who would make a great spy! This combination points to the urge to get below the surface of things, ferret out the most profound information and the deepest secrets, as well as the ability to keep one's mouth shut about what one has discovered.

The Nature of the Tenth House

In terms of the houses, the next in importance to the natal Ascendant and the First House is the Midheaven and the Tenth House. In fact, when (and if) the integration of the personality comes about (often beginning around or within a few years after the first Saturn return at age 29), most of the energy of the Ascendant (who I am) fuels the indications of the Midheaven (what I stand for in the world). In one's early years, one is the son or daughter of one's parents. That is, their lifestyle is your lifestyle, their religion is your religion, their environment is also your environment. But when a person chooses a career, he is less apt to say: "I am the son of John Smith and my father is a doctor," and much more likely to say, "I am William Smith, the painter (or the teacher, or the CEO, etc.)." In essence, while the Ascendant and the First House reveal the potential of the personality, the Midheaven and the Tenth express the maturation and culmination of these creative seeds.

In a broader context, the Tenth represents the father archetype because it is the area of the chart of authority figures or authoritative social structures, such as the government or a corporation. A careful analysis of the Tenth House and its natal and natural rulers reveals much in the way of our attitude toward these influential figures along with the way we respond to matters of social control, rules, and regulations.

Finally, the Tenth House is representative of our career, the focus of our vocation, and the nature of our professional participation in life. The Midheaven is like the title on our business card, the logo on our stationery, the social function we embody, and the social level we achieve as we pass our adult years on this planet.

When the ruler of the Tenth is in the First, a person's career and need for worldly success holds a place of dominance in one's life. This is a most important contact in a natal horoscope because it blends one's own sense of self with the need to accomplish a concrete goal which is a direct reflection of one's personal identity. The astrologer should examine the horoscope to see if there is a contact by major aspect between the Tenth House ruler and the First House ruler. If Capricorn is on the Tenth House cusp, for example, and Saturn is in the First House in Aries, the individual in question will be highly motivated to succeed, but at the same time feel a tremendous sense of personal limitation in this respect. The key to success with Saturn in the First is always connected with the individual's ability to impose and accept a self-created schedule, a positive routine, a set of self-imposed perimeters, which would result in a personal sense of expertise and authority. In this example, if Saturn is well aspected by Mars, the drive that allows one to create the necessary self-discipline for success in life will be natural and relatively easy to bring about. But should Saturn be square to Mars, the individual will have the sensation of driving a car with the brakes on — frustration and personal setbacks will tend to accompany the intense urge for personal accomplishment.

When the ruler of the Tenth is in the Second, success in one's career requires the right use of personal resources, talents, and abilities. This can be a very good combination of influences, especially if the Tenth House ruler is well configured in this position. The horoscope of Gloria Swanson is a perfect example of these astrological conditions. Many

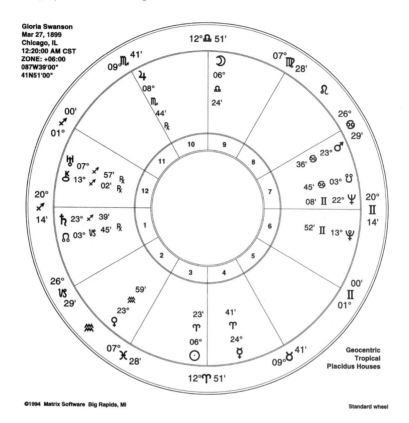

Gloria Swanson
Mar 27, 1899
Chicago, IL
12:20:00 AM CST
ZONE: +06:00
087W39'00"
41N51'00"

Geocentric
Tropical
Placidus Houses

©1994 Matrix Software Big Rapids, MI

Standard wheel

years ago, the author was called upon by Miss Swanson to visit her in her rather luxurious Fifth Avenue, New York apartment to read her horoscope. Her question to me was delightful and surprising. Miss Swanson was in her 70s at the time and she wanted to know: "Why have I had such a wonderful life?"

The answer to this rare question was clear to me. Libra is on the cusp of the Tenth with Venus in Aquarius in the Second House and quite well aspected. The international success and wealth that she acquired can be seen by the fact that Venus is sextile to Saturn, which is both the natural ruler of the Tenth as well as one of the dispositors of Venus. Uranus, the other dispositor, is sextile her Moon in Libra, which is disposited by Venus. This particular triple mutual reception certainly is helpful in linking a person to large numbers of others through the use of personal talents (Venus in the Second) in the pursuit of one's career (Venus as ruler of the Tenth). In addition, Venus also is closely sextile to Mercury, the natal Seventh House ruler of the chart. This is a powerful sextile in terms of the Seventh because it links harmoniously both the natal and the natural rulers of that domicile and, through Venus, connects the Seventh to the Tenth.

Miss Swanson had some very prosperous husbands and lovers who were very supportive of her career. These included Cecil B. DeMille and Joseph Kennedy, Sr. I'd like to mention one more factor that illustrates why Gloria Swanson had such "a wonderful life": Pluto is in Gemini in the Sixth House of work trine the MC. This position reveals the ability for renewal and regeneration in terms of career. Gloria Swanson was one of the most famous of silent film stars; however, in the 1940s her career lagged quite a bit. But she rose again in 1950 and starred in the classic film *Sunset Boulevard*, a work that has stamped her memory into the minds and hearts of cinemaphiles ever since.

When the ruler of the Tenth is in the Third, career dynamics will have a great deal to do with the individual's ability to communicate. There is a strong need to capitalize upon one's ideas, thoughts, and opinions, using the mind to further one's goals. For example, if Gemini or Virgo are on the Tenth House cusp and Mercury is in Aquarius in the Third, look for writing and the use of computers and other communicative tools as a prominent feature of one's life. Another example of this same combination that brings out the more limiting qualities of this position would be if Capricorn was on the Tenth House cusp and Saturn in early Gemini in the Third square the Moon in late Leo. This placement of the Tenth House ruler in this case can point to a person whose mindset was anchored by early parental influences and environmental conditioning. The psychological dynamics of such an individual, as reflected by the natal planetary placements, make it quite difficult for him or her to expand the mental outlook or adapt the thinking process to new circumstances that are bound to come up in the pursuit of one's career. Communication is thus limited to safely established forms, and does not easily allow for the renewal of career opportunities.

When the ruler of the Tenth is in the Fourth, career activities are likely to take place in the home. This combination often appears in people's charts who are either self-employed (especially if the signs Aries, Leo, or Capricorn are involved) or who have their office in their residence (especially if Cancer or Virgo are present). These two houses are intimately related in human psychology. The Fourth House is where we find our psychological roots, while the Tenth reveals how these roots condition our worldly success. Therefore we could call the Tenth House the realm of fruition.

If the roots are stunted or harmed because the Fourth House ruler is badly afflicted in the natal chart, then it makes it difficult for the fruits of our labors to ripen. When the Tenth House ruler is in the Fourth, the astrologer should pay careful attention to the relationship that the two rulers of these houses have to one another. This observation should be supplemented by an examination of the relationship of Saturn and the Moon—the natural rulers of these houses.

Let us say that Leo is on the cusp of the Tenth and the Sun is in Aquarius in the Fourth trine Saturn in Gemini. This is a good, strong interchange because the co-dispositor of the Sun is trine to the solar position. In addition, Saturn is the natural ruler of the Tenth House. The indications are that the individual would use her home as a base of operations (Fourth House) to create structures of communication (Saturn in Gemini) so that her professional, creative ideas and impulses (Sun as ruler of the Leo Tenth House cusp) may be used to network with large numbers of people (Sun in Aquarius).

When the ruler of the Tenth is in the Fifth, the career orientation is geared to the use of the individual's highly personalized creative abilities. The Fifth House placement advances the indications of the Second House, and the Tenth fully matures them. If the Second House is where one's personal gold mine is located, the Fifth House is the piece of jewelry that is shaped from that ore by the individual's creative self-expression. The Tenth House is a jewelry shop or gallery that he or she may own or administer in which these creations are shown and made available to the public. A well-placed Tenth House ruler in the Fifth is therefore an excellent position to support a career based directly upon one's creative urges. As the house of pleasures, it is quite possible that the Fifth House influence upon the Tenth House ruler adds a lot of fun and enjoyment to an individual's career orientation. In addition, as the

Fifth is the house of young people, this combination can point to a career that is involved with children or youth. This indication is augmented by the presence of the sign Leo and/or a major aspect, or other primary contact—such as mutual reception—between the Sun and the ruling planet of the Tenth House.

Let us use an example for this combination: Virgo on the Tenth House cusp with Mercury in Aries in the Fifth House. The nature of the career is therefore likely to be very service-oriented (Virgo on the MC). The individual with this configuration has highly developed writing and communicative skills as well as an innovative and original turn of mind (Mercury in Aries in the Fifth). He would use his mental talents within the larger field of service that constitutes his career. Let us further state that Mercury in this position is trine Jupiter in Leo in the Ninth. This would make it clear to the astrologer that this person also does a great deal of professional traveling and, more likely than not, he is published and his work is available in foreign editions (all Ninth House/Jupiter influences).

When the ruler of the Tenth is in the Sixth, a person with this combination may find that the career orientation consists of numerous and various jobs. There is a natural and positive affinity between these two houses, as they are both related to the earth signs. In addition, the two natural rulers of these domiciles, Mercury (Sixth) and Saturn (Tenth), also "enjoy each other's company." Mercury represents the communicative and rational dynamics of mind, while Saturn rules the entire mental structure of human consciousness. Saturn is very happy when it can put all of the little Mercurial pieces of information into larger and cohesive structures and patterns, and this is done well when these two planets are in sextile or trine to each other in the natal chart.

We can state the positive relationship in terms of our general assessment of the placements of house rulerships as follows: If the Sixth House and Tenth House rulers find themselves in a harmonious aspect, then the many little skills that I have (Mercury and the Sixth) fit very nicely into the larger, overall picture of my profession (Saturn and the Tenth). If the ruler of the Tenth is in one of the mutable signs and located in the Sixth and there also is a mutable sign on the cusp of this house, there is a distinct tendency to move from job to job or to shift the focus of one's larger goals. In a positive sense, this can add a lot of versatility to one's career. The potential success of this position requires a person to be able to synthesize his or her various tools and techniques into a one-pointed professional focus. If there is a good aspect between the ruler of the Tenth and the ruler of the Sixth, such an achievement is likely. When well placed in the Sixth House, the Tenth House ruler will stimulate the use of one's skills towards inclusive professional goals. Should there be a square, opposition, or inconjunct between these two significators, the individual will face many challenges. An afflicted Tenth House ruler in the Sixth also may indicate that health issues can impede career objectives. Health in general is connected to one's career and the individual with this placement may find that his or her interests involve one of the healing professions.

When the ruler of the Tenth is in the Seventh, partnership will figure prominently in the success or failure of career objectives. In effect, we are seeing the placement of the planet that signifies career objectives and social standing in the house of marriage as well as open enemies. A natural and positive affinity exists between these two houses from the perspective of planetary powers because Saturn, the natural ruler of the Tenth, is exalted in Libra, the natural sign ruling the Seventh. In order to bring out the best of this combination of planetary influences, it is necessary to create harmonious structures of partnership equality. If the planetary indications are contrary to creating harmony in partnership, then trouble from one's business or personal relationships will interfere with worldly success.

Let us say that Aries is on the MC and Mars is in Capricorn in the Seventh square to Saturn in Aries in the Tenth House. This position will cause a great deal of frustration. The individual has a tremendous amount of ambition, as is indicated by the placement of Saturn and Mars in their respective locations. These very same planetary positions can also point to the individual's need to have a partner who is in authoritarian and executive positions, which then would further his own career ambitions. Yet this is a person who will find himself in competition with the very same executives he needs to cultivate as allies. This is seen by Capricorn on the Seventh (partnerships with older and/or established people) with Mars in the Seventh (open hostilities with partners or the urge to dominate in relationships) square to Saturn in the Tenth (problems with people in senior positions).

When the ruler of the Tenth is in the Eighth, a powerful position presents itself as the regenerative possibilities in the horoscope come to the region of career and public standing. If the rulership factors connecting these two houses are well placed, especially if the signs Capricorn, Scorpio, Virgo, or Aries are involved and the rulers of these signs are well situated in relationship to each other, then there is great support for worldly success. As we have seen, when the Eighth House influences in a horoscope are positive, the possibility for regeneration and added vitality are present.

A successful man or woman is a person who can pick him or herself up after a fall, wisely use the experience of that failure, and continue on to make an even greater success in life. A strong and well-aspected Tenth House ruler in the Eighth permits a person to do just that. Naturally, this indication is highlighted if there is a trine or sextile between the Tenth House ruler in the Eighth, and the natal or natural ruler of that house.

Thus, Gemini on the cusp of the Tenth with Mercury in Aries in the Eighth both in a sextile to the Midheaven and Mars in Aquarius in the Sixth is quite the blessing to any career. This is a person who has the ability to renew and revitalize his mind. She is an idea woman who knows how to find the core issue in any career-related situation and is precise and exact, quick and alert in her attitude. This position also indicates that the individual will have continuous support from her employees or coworkers, who will collectively defend and support her.

When the ruler of the Tenth is in the Ninth, help in one's career advancement can come from an understanding of history—either the specific history of the company or field in which one is employed (the Ninth rules archives and records) or history in general. This position also indicates a person whose profession may involve teaching, publishing, long-distance travel, and other Ninth House affairs. A person with the Tenth House ruler well aspected especially by the natural or natal ruler of the Ninth will find that his higher education and philosophical beliefs are harmoniously linked to his occupation. Should Jupiter be this planet, then his knowledge will be a sure vehicle for his advancement up the ladder of his professional goals. However, if Jupiter is poorly placed in relation to the Tenth House ruler in the Ninth, especially if in hard aspect to the Sun or Saturn, he may have ambitions far beyond the scope of his abilities.

When the ruler of the Tenth is in the Tenth, the planet/sign combination will clearly indicate the profession. Should this be Mercury in Gemini, then the career involves active communication through writing, speaking, and travel. If it is Mars in Aries, then the individual will be a pioneer in his or her career and most likely will be self-employed or, at least a highly specialized consultant. A well-placed Jupiter in Sagittarius in this position indicates that the individual is a natural-born teacher, a man or woman with definite world views and the urge to imprint his or her beliefs through the chosen career field. This is relatively an easy rulership position to delineate because the astrological keywords and phrases will apply with great accuracy.

What is important to keep in mind is the position of Saturn relative to the Tenth House ruler when in the Tenth. If it is Saturn in Capricorn itself, and Saturn is well aspected, professional success should come about but not until after the forty-second or even the fifty-sixth year of age. Even if the person has achieved a modicum of acclaim in his or her field before this time, the individual will not *feel* successful until later on in life. If Saturn is in any other position in the horoscope and is in good aspect to the ruler of the Tenth in the Tenth, success is likely but gradual in coming. Ambition is very strong should such an aspect fall in the cardinal signs, but there is also great impatience.

If the fixed signs are well featured, success may come at an even later date, but the person has the willpower and the stamina to see things through to their positive conclusions. The mutable signs usually give more ups and downs in terms of the career, but if Saturn is well aspected to the ruler of the Tenth in the Tenth, even if the mutable signs are featured, success is the eventual outcome. Should Saturn afflict the Tenth House ruler in the Tenth, impediments, restrictions, discouragement, and many delays are indicated, but if the lessons of Saturn are well learned, even this individual may eventually reach his or her goals. No matter where Saturn is placed in a chart, it is a ladder: You have to respect its hierarchical structure and climb it carefully and patiently.

When the ruler of the Tenth is in the Eleventh, the career will be connected to group dynamics and collective interests. This is a typical combination for a politician because to achieve public office, the individual needs the support of his political party as well as his constituents. You cannot make it to any elected office without such positive interactive group participation. Even a dictator needs a power machine behind him or her, as well as the tacit support of the governed.

A well-aspected Mercury as the ruler of the Tenth in the Eleventh is an asset to communicating one's plans and ideas with others, and even more so when in an air sign. An afflicted Mercury in this position—especially by the natal ruler of the Eleventh—indicates that one's opinions will not be easily accepted by the group. Should Uranus, the natural ruler of this house, be the afflicting planet, then a person has too many ideas and too many, often conflicting, group alliances. This would be especially the case if the mutable signs were involved.

Like the Ninth, the Eleventh is a house of ideals. After all, it is the domicile of hopes, wishes, and aspirations. Should Jupiter be afflicted in the Eleventh or afflict the ruler of the Tenth in the Eleventh, one's aspirations can be completely out of sync with more practical realities of life. Because the Eleventh is the *Second from the Tenth*, it indicates money or other (usually social) resources coming to the individual as a direct result of his or her professional efforts or worldly position.

If Neptune, for example, is afflicting the ruler of the Tenth in the Eleventh, especially if the earth signs are featured, look for difficulties in company or group finances. The Eleventh also is the house of peers, associates, and friends of the same social level as oneself. A well-aspected Tenth House ruler in this location, especially if the aspecting planet is Venus or the Moon, indicates much support of a person's professional objectives from one's social equals.

When the ruler of the Tenth is in the Twelfth, a person will feel most comfortable with a career that is not highly visible. This makes an excellent position for an executive that likes to wield control from behind the scenes. A typical example of the latter would be Saturn as ruler of the Tenth in Aries, Capricorn, or Leo in the Twelfth trine to Mars. This is also a natural placement for a person engaged in research, corrections, psychology, hospital work, or in any of the healing professions.

An afflicted Tenth House ruler in the Twelfth, especially by Neptune, Pluto, or the rulers of the Eighth or Twelfth houses, may do a great deal of harm in terms of scandals adversely affecting one's public standing. Neptunian afflictions with the ruler of the Tenth in the Twelfth may make it difficult to define a career choice. On the other hand, should Neptune be trine or sextile the ruler of the Tenth in this house, especially if the water signs are involved, look for a successful career in anything to do with marine biology, and professions involving water, oil, cosmetics, or the arts. This is also a position that indicates a career as a psychic, mystic, or other form of occult worker.

The Nature of the Eleventh House

As we enter into a study of the rulership dynamics of the last two houses of the horoscope, we are far removed from the personal sphere of expression of the Ascendant. The Eleventh is directly related to the consciousness and collective activities of the human race. Planets and positions connected with this astrological domain take the individual into the larger society and thus beyond the scope of the status quo of one's life. This is the reason why we associate the Eleventh with the study of sociology, computer networking (especially the Internet), public relations, advertising, and astrology. This is the house where we branch out into the world in terms of our social contacts. The Eleventh, therefore, is particularly concerned with groups, organizations, committees, and the general social contacts that constitute our wider circle of friends, acquaintances, and professional colleagues. The Eleventh House is also known traditionally as the house of "hopes, wishes, and aspirations," as its purpose is to stimulate the individual to experiment with creative impulses that enlarge his or her potential. This leads to his ability to affect and integrate with the greater society, rather than with the small circle of one's immediate surroundings. Like the Third and the Seventh, this is a house connected to the element of air. As such, it relates to the faculty of communication. While the Third House speaks about our personal communication skills in general and the Seventh about our most intimate and important social relationships, the Eleventh takes us beyond the mundane and into higher realms of communication. The

Eleventh, its natural sign, and especially its planetary ruler Uranus, signify the amplification of consciousness beyond the five physical senses. In this respect, the significators of this house are associated with the sixth sense, intuition, and by extension, mental telepathy and ESP.

When the ruler of the Eleventh is in the First, the individual is going to be strongly affected by the groups of people with whom she associates and the social conditions of the times in which she lives. I can remember my parents telling me as I set off for university: "Choose your friends wisely, as you will be judged by the company you keep." This counsel would apply quite aptly to a person who has the Eleventh House ruler in the First. In addition, the *kinds* of associates one has are described by the planet and sign combination of the Eleventh House ruler in this position. If Mars was the ruler of the Eleventh and placed in the First in square to Uranus, for example, the individual would be attracted to social rebels and/or to people with alternative sexual orientations (and would most likely embody these characteristics himself).

Let's compare the difference in influence of (1) the Fifth House ruler in the First with a chart that (2) has the ruler of the Eleventh in the First:

(1) This is the horoscope of someone who will most likely project his or her highly personalized likes and dislikes into the environment and seek acknowledgment for his or her special talents and individuality. Depending on the astrological conditions of the planetary rulers, the surrounding environment would either support or challenge that individual's need for personal recognition.

(2) When the Eleventh House ruler is in the First, the emphasis in the life is totally different. We now have an individual who is *personally* affected by the larger social circumstances or political events of the society in which he or she lives. In terms of the effects of this position on one's life, the statement could be made: "I am consciously aware of the larger social issues of my times and these totally affect the nature of the projection of my ego into the environment."

Let us say, for example, that Libra is on the cusp of the Eleventh and Venus is in Sagittarius in the First House. This is a person who would tend to embody her ideals and higher aspirations for social peace and justice. Such an individual would use her Venusian magnetism and charm not so much to attract people to her for the purposes of personal pleasure and recognition (as she would if Venus were the ruler of the Fifth and placed in the First), but to proselytize and advance her causes and beliefs. Her hopes, wishes, and aspirations would therefore be connected with the urge for social equality and freedom (and on a personal level, she would seek out a partner who feels the same). In addition, this position can simply indicate the liking for making friends from foreign countries.

When the ruler of the Eleventh is in the Second, the nature of one's friendships would greatly affect the way one uses one's personal talents and resources. On the most practical level, this position, especially if the earthy signs were involved, indicates a relationship between friendship and money. If the Eleventh House ruler is afflicted in the Second, then one should take care that the way one uses one's finances is not dictated by the wrong influences coming from friends or associates. If Mars is the ruler of the Eleventh and is afflicted in the Second, friendships will be a cause of financial discord. If it is an afflicted Saturn, friends or the larger social environment in which one lives tend to inhibit a person's use of their individual resources, talents, and abilities. This is a person who may feel very shy or personally unworthy in comparison to the group of people with whom he or she normally associates.

There is a natural connection between the Eleventh and the Second. While the latter is the house of one's intrinsic sense of self-worth and the depository of one's money, the Eleventh is the house in which the financial, and especially the social, rewards coming from our career are found. If I have an harmonious aspect between the ruler of the Eleventh and the ruler of the Second, then what I have to offer life in terms of my nascent talents and abilities and what I receive from society as a result of harnessing and actualizing those talents will pay off very well in my career. Naturally, this supposition should be supported by an examination of the ruler of the Tenth House in relation to these other two.

When the ruler of the Eleventh is in the Third, social trends and attitudes affect the individual's ideas, opinions, and the way he or she tends to communicate. If I am closed off from the "outside world," if my way of thinking is totally conditioned by my biological karma, or limited by my social contacts, or motivated solely by personal desires, then one could rightly say that I was a close-minded, egocentric individual.

But if the Eleventh House ruler is in the Third, I hear the news around me and I tend to be eager to watch CNN and surf the Net for information that expands my way of thinking. On a personal and socially immature level, this position of the Eleventh House ruler can mean nothing more than a person who is always aware of the gossip around town about his or her friends and group of associates. But in the life of an individual objectively seeking a path of personal evolution, then the ruler of the Eleventh being in the Third can be most helpful.

One of the primary indications of an individual who is growing spiritually is his or her awareness of life apart from the domain of the ego. This allows one to be in a position of service to people who may either be totally unknown or else with whom one has only an impersonal relationship. Another clear indication of this rulership combination is the effect that friends have on the way we think. Should Neptune be the ruler of the Eleventh and either posited in the Third or afflicting any other Eleventh House ruler in this position, one can be easily deceived or lied to by one's friends. When Neptune is so configured in the natal chart, it is also easy to blind oneself to larger social issues in life or to misinterpret them.

When the ruler of the Eleventh is in the Fourth, we tend to take our friends home. Should Libra be on the cusp of the Eleventh, for example, and Venus in the Fourth, look for a person who loves to socialize and who feels most comfortable when the party is taking place at his or her house. If an afflicted Mars is the ruler, friends, and associates may bring dissension to our home or be the cause of some very deep personal agony. This social dynamic relative to the relationship between the ruler of the Eleventh and the Fourth House, although true, does not speak of the deeper meaning to this planetary interchange. Also, we can say this position means that we take our friends as well as the issues of our society, deeply within ourselves. Friendships mean a great deal. The causes in which we believe, the sense of social injustice or oppression that we experience in the wars and conflicts between people and nations are very real to us, and there is a profound subjective response to such conditions. Remember that the Eleventh House is the house of "social equality," and truly is a democratic domicile (The

Fifth is a monarchy or a principality, the First can easily be a dictatorship, and the Tenth may be interpreted as an empire).

When the ruler of the Eleventh is in the Fifth, our creative self-expression is conditioned by our perception of social needs or demands. Let us say that Virgo is on the cusp of the Eleventh and Mercury is in the Fifth in Pisces trine to Pluto in Scorpio (a position easily found in horoscopes of individuals born between late 1983 and late 1995).

In a spiritually mature individual, this is a position that reveals the urge to be of service to society. The mind is sensitive to other people's requirements for a better life and the individual would find no difficulty in reshaping his or her creative talents to meet these social exigencies (mutable signs on the cusps of the Fifth and Eleventh). He or she would have the kind of intelligence that can profoundly affect many other people by transforming their opinions (Pluto in Scorpio trine Mercury) and opening them to greater social compassion (ruler of the Eleventh in Pisces) through his or her own writing, speaking, and all forms of communication (Mercury).

In some cases, the focus of one's creative contribution to society would take place in the realm of children (Fifth House). But let us say that Mercury in Pisces in the Fifth were square the Moon in the Second House in Sagittarius in the horoscope of an egocentric person. The emotional needs of this individual (Moon) would tend to be connected to his or her personal financial state (Second House) and the use of personal talents and resources to anchor and secure him or herself in life. These highly personal considerations and the level of consciousness of the individual in question do not support a more altruistic interpretation of Mercury as the Eleventh House ruler in the Fifth. A likely interpretation for this combination of planetary influences would be that the person uses his persuasive mind (Mercury trine Pluto) and perception of social situations in order to further his or her urge for personal security (Moon square Mercury from the Second House to the Fifth).

When the ruler of the Eleventh is in the Sixth, the influence of the larger demands of society would tend to shape one's skills, tools, and job orientation. If the mutable signs are strong and positively connected within this planetary interchange, it can lead to a person who does whatever is required based on arising opportunity. "If they need a plumber, I'm the plumber. If they need a gardener, I'm the gardener. If they need a painter, I'm a painter, etc.," can be the attitude of such an individual. In addition, our friends and associates can be the vehicle through which we find job opportunities.

A person who has Sagittarius on the Eleventh and Jupiter in Gemini well aspected in the Sixth should not be surprised if many fine job openings come about through his or her circle of acquaintances and friends. On the other hand, afflictions of the Eleventh House ruler in the Sixth can thwart or inhibit an individual from finding ways of self-improvement through his or her social connections.

Capricorn on the Eleventh with Saturn in Cancer in the Sixth square the Sun in Libra, for example, can give rise to experiences in life that make a person say: "No matter what I do, I can't seem to find the right job. All the social connections I make do nothing to support me in my urge to use my working skills and techniques." The ruler of the Eleventh in the Sixth also can be influential in terms of increasing a person's awareness of public health issues. There are many people born in the middle to late 60s, with Aquarius on the Eleventh House cusp and Uranus conjunct Pluto in Virgo in the Sixth House, who are very aware of the need to bring improvement, change, and transformation into the areas of public health and social welfare and are doing something about it.[12]

When the ruler of the Eleventh is in the Seventh, we may easily find ourselves married to a friend or in a primary partnership with friends. Often people find that the person with whom they are sharing their life and their bed is *not* their friend. Therefore, they look outside of their marriage for the delights of platonic, heart-centered contacts. There is nothing wrong with this at all, but those people who have a well-aspected Eleventh House ruler in the Seventh may easily discover that not only are they married to their lover but to their best friend as well. In the Aquarian Age, all partnerships that produce regenerative, life-promoting, healthy energy have to be founded upon friendship. In esoteric, soul-centered astrology, the ruler of Libra is Uranus, the natural ruler of the Eleventh. This means that for personal relationships to be a vehicle for soul growth, they must be based on a firm foundation of impersonal service. In other words, "I am there for you not just for the pleasure of your body or to make our families happy. I am there for you as your brother or sister on the Path of human evolution. In this respect, I am very definitely your best friend and together we can do something that makes our relationship a vehicle of service to others." This is the true nature of soulmates in the current and future world age. If the ruler of the Eleventh House is afflicted in the Seventh, especially by the ruler of the Seventh, Venus, or Uranus, friendships outside of marriage may be a source of great challenge to primary partnerships. Social opposition to the choice of partners or to the nature of the partnership also may be indicated by this position.

When the ruler of the Eleventh is in the Eighth, we are looking at a horoscope in which there are factors in the relationship with friends and/or with society in general that need to be transformed. There is a very strong natural planetary affinity between these two houses. The natural ruler of the Eleventh, Uranus, is exalted in the natural sign ruler of this house, Scorpio. Although this affinity is positive, it is not necessarily easy. Uranus is the revolutionary planet that is constantly working against some aspect of the status quo in order to bring life to some new and innovative dynamic, thus furthering the person's sense of his or her own individuality.

Uranus is very helpful in this respect in terms of evolutionary progress, but the means and manner he uses to effectuate these changes are not always so gentle. Thus, when the ruler of the Eleventh House is in the Eighth, an aspect of the relationship to society has to change, often manifesting itself through friendships. Let us say that Libra is on the cusp of the Eleventh and Venus is in Cancer in the Eighth House of the natal chart. This can be indicative of a person who can be too possessive of his or her friends. It may also mean that there is some confusion about making personal contact with others. In other words, the individual tends to be too personal (Cancer) in contacts that are more impersonal in nature (Eleventh House ruler). The lesson here is clear: The person needs to achieve balance in terms of friendships (Libra on the Eleventh) in which personal needs are met (Venus in Cancer) but are not killed off (Eighth House) by being too needy and demanding. One great problem that can arise from the Eighth House placement of Venus as the ruler of the Eleventh (especially if square Neptune in Libra), is an inability to see and respect the difference between a sexual and a platonic relationship.

When the ruler of the Eleventh is in the Ninth, the individual may be very idealistic about life. These two houses have a natural positive affinity with one another. When their natural rulers, Uranus and Jupiter, are harmoniously configured in a horoscope, the individual is open to many adventures and experiences that serve to develop and expand one's beliefs. The sextile, trine, or even the conjunction of these two planets is an indication of a person who seeks a wider horizon of understanding through his or her education, travel experiences, and general social contacts. In this combination, the ruler of the Eleventh House of social movements, politics, and sociology (along with one's hopes, wishes, and aspirations) is in the Ninth House of one's religious and philosophical beliefs. We can therefore conclude that the need to belong to religious and/or political groups and organizations of like-minded individuals will be an important facet of this person's life orientation. Should the ruler of the Eleventh be afflicted in the Ninth, there is a good chance that one's religious or social views will be in conflict with the beliefs of one's friends or with the general social environment in which one was raised or in which one lives.

Let us say that Aquarius is on the cusp of the Eleventh and Uranus is in Sagittarius in the Ninth square to Mars in Virgo. This position would produce a person who is actively critical of the social standards and beliefs of his or her environment. Conforming to the prevailing social trends would definitely be anathema to such a personality.

When the ruler of the Eleventh is in the Tenth, an individual seeks to personally embody or represent the society in which he or she lives. This is the perfect position for a political leader, for example, or a man or woman who is aware of social demographics in terms of his or her chosen career. A Mars and Uranus significator of this position—Aries on the cusp of the Eleventh with Mars in Aries in the Tenth opposing Uranus in Libra, for example—would indicate a social combatant. This is a person who has a definite social agenda of his own and who doesn't care how many people he offends or how many people will oppose him (and there will be many) as he rallies around his own flag.

At the least, the ruler of the Eleventh in the Tenth indicates a person who is socially minded and whose career is highly affected by social opinion. Let us say that Gemini is on the cusp of the Eleventh with Mercury in Gemini in the Tenth trine to Uranus in Aquarius. This is a perfect combination for a pollster. A person with Uranus in Aquarius (active in people's charts who were born on the cusp of the millennium, between 1996 and 2003) will have a natural inclination to codify data. This also is an individual whose path of individuation will be intimately connected with society at large and the groups and organizations to which he or she belongs. This orientation is a "generational stamp" and will affect in a like manner the lives of all people born in this seven-year period. The placement of Mercury in Gemini in the Tenth as the ruler of the Eleventh accentuates the communicative urge of Aquarius and the Eleventh House and also helps the individual to travel and move around in his or her search for information about the public and for the public.

When the ruler of the Eleventh is in the Eleventh, one's hopes, wishes, and aspirations will be intimately connected with large social issues, groups, and organizations. The sign on the cusp of the Eleventh and the nature and condition of its dispositor will describe the nature of such social contacts and the circumstances surrounding one's involvement with them. The horoscope of Madalyn Murray O'Hair is a perfect example of the effects of this combination. O'Hair is probably the world's most famous atheist. In particular, her battle was to make sure that prayer in public schools was outlawed in keeping with the separation of church and state, a proposition fundamental to the American political, social, and public educational system. This stance, of course, brought her into a great deal of conflict because the United States of America is also "One nation under God indivisible…" as well as having a provision in its Constitution that guarantees freedom of religion (and by extension, the freedom of "nonreligion"). O'Hair, a lawyer by profession, brought her case all the way to the U.S. Supreme Court and emerged victorious. Mars in Aries in the Eleventh certainly ruled in this instance.

O'Hair's horoscope is a perfect example of the Eleventh House ruler in its own house. In this case, the ruler is Mars conjunct the Sun in

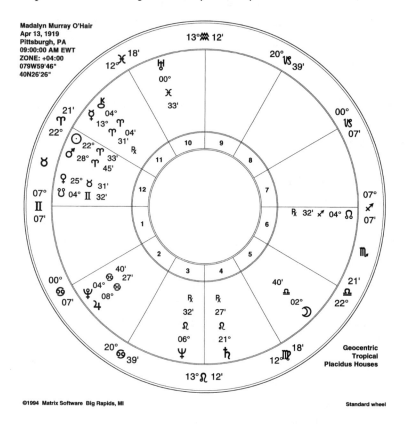

Madalyn Murray O'Hair
Apr 13, 1919
Pittsburgh, PA
09:00:00 AM EWT
ZONE: +04:00
079W59'46"
40N26'26"

Geocentric
Tropical
Placidus Houses

©1994 Matrix Software Big Rapids, MI

Standard wheel

Aries. The fact that her "religious" and philosophical beliefs were so important to her is shown by the fact that Uranus is the ruler of the Ninth House in this chart and is prominently positioned in the Tenth House. Her career is an embodiment of what she believes. O'Hair's chart reveals her tendency to stand strong no matter what the social opposition to her philosophy might be. This is not only indicated by fiery Mars conjunct the Sun in Aries in the Eleventh as the natal ruler of this house, but also the natural ruler of the Eleventh, Uranus, is trine Pluto, the co-ruler of Aries in her First House, the natural domicile of this sign. In addition, Pluto is conjunct Jupiter and trine Uranus. This contact is a potent astrological influence because it unites both the natal and the natural rulers of the Ninth House, along with Pluto therein.

The transformation of public opinion, or at the very least, an incredible effect on that opinion, is seen by the Pluto/Jupiter/Uranus combination and its effects through the First and Tenth houses of her chart.

When the ruler of the Eleventh is in the Twelfth, the individual primarily is prone to having many private friends and acquaintances. This is a person who may have several circles of social contacts, but one or more is bound to be clandestine in nature. The Eleventh House ruler in this position also points to associations with secret groups and organizations and may even indicate a person's participation in an esoteric brotherhood, lodge, or other type of occult group. In extreme cases, especially if Pluto or Neptune is involved, there can be contacts to gangsters, the sexual underworld, spy networks, and hidden intelligence organizations such as the CIA or the FBI. Mars in Scorpio as ruler of the Eleventh conjunct to Neptune in that sign in the Twelfth and sextile to Uranus in Virgo easily could be the significator of a computer hacker, a person who likes to infiltrate (Mars/Neptune combinations in water) into complex computer networks (Uranus in Virgo/Eleventh House contacts) and implant viruses (Neptune/Twelfth House influences). The position of the Eleventh House ruler in the Twelfth also may be explained more simply with a much less sinister intent: The individual may not be sure or distinct about his political and social views and prefers to keep his opinions (or lack of same) to himself.

The Nature of the Twelfth House

One of the most beautiful results of spiritual growth is the more evolved our consciousness, the more we tend to see ourselves as individualized "units" intimately connected within the functioning of a totally inclusive Whole. What was once a frightened and/or overly self-involved ego, separated by the exclusive dynamics of the personal desire and mental natures, has now become a vehicle for the activities of the soul. Thus, the focus of self-awareness of personal identification as seen through the lens of the Ascendant gradually gives way to the mystical awareness of union with the universe.

The Twelfth House and its natural ruling planet, Neptune, are the "keepers of the seal" surrounding this evolutionary process. Many astrologers call the Twelfth the "House of Karma," as well as the "House of Self-Undoing." But this is not exactly true, as *all* the houses of the horoscope contain the karma of one's life and how it is associated specifically with the nature of that particular house. Much of karma consists also of rewards and riches, not only difficulties and punishments.

The special "karma" of the Twelfth House has to do with the collective. The Twelfth synthesizes what has been stored from previous turns of the astrological wheel, that is, other life cycles. Thus, it is the storehouse of our secret treasures as well as the strength we have gained from experience. The last house of the horoscope contains our oceanic reserves of power and potency from all the good we have done and all the positive services we have performed. In effect, it is also the repository of our "good karma."

One of the central characteristics of being human is duality of nature, until we reach an advanced state of spiritual initiation. There is, therefore, a bipolar aspect to oneself, to one's general karma. This human characteristic is the magnetic shadow that is self-destructive and harmful. Locked away within our treasury of hidden potencies are also our (not so) hidden weaknesses and addictive vulnerabilities. We could say that right next door to our protective guardian angels live our worst enemies, and all of these entities comprise parts of ourselves.

The Twelfth is the house of convents and monasteries, esoteric schools and lodges, but it is also the domicile of insane asylums and torture chambers. The Twelfth is where hope for healing may be found in hospitals and medical clinics and, too, where the dying are comforted by kind souls working in hospices. Yet, we also know that the Twelfth is the location where slave quarters, jails, and concentration camps may be found. The great healing wonders of the plant kingdom are ruled by Neptune, the natural Twelfth House ruler, but so are heroin, crack cocaine, alcohol, and all other life-destroying addictive substances.

We may not believe in reincarnation and therefore the Twelfth House may not interest us as "the house that teaches us what we need to overcome from past lives," as it is often called. The fact is, however, that the Twelfth House tells us what we have to overcome in *this* life and that alone is quite the job in itself. The Twelfth also reveals some of our greatest tools with which we may accomplish such a task. As we leave the realm of the Twelfth, we come once again to the Ascendant. If we have managed to purify our nature and therefore externalize much more of our latent consciousness, love, and light, we may then be reborn *in this lifetime,* and be able to say, "I and the Universe are One."

When the ruler of the Twelfth is in the First, the person with this position can bring the hidden elements, talents, and weaknesses of his or her nature to the forefront of life. This position makes it much easier to tap into one's concealed or secret potentials. It certainly does not allow us to escape from ourselves too easily. A person with Mercury as the ruler of the Twelfth in the First square to Neptune is likely to be told by his or her experiences in life: "God loves you so much that whenever you lie, you always get caught!" The message from Neptune in the Seventh opposing Mercury in this position is likely to be: "What you lie about to yourself about yourself is reflected in the deceit coming to you from your relationships."

Many astrologers, including the author, use a system of house division called Placidus to interpret the horoscope. In a number of cases in horoscopes calculated in this way, the same sign appears on the Twelfth House cusp as on the Ascendant. The more mystically inclined astrologers say that when this occurs, the individual "has not completed his or her karma from a previous life and must do so in the present incarnation." With all due respects, to me this is very simplistic "New Age speak." What is certain when the sign on the Twelfth House is also on the Ascendant is that the influence of that sign is very profound. One could say that when the same sign is on the Twelfth House cusp as is on the Ascendant, that one's karma rises up very quickly from the collective in terms of one's personal confrontations and moment-to-moment contacts with life. In other words, if we agree that the Law of Karma is the same as the Law of Cause and Effect (which in many ways it is), then when the Twelfth House sign is on the First House cusp, what you get is definitely what you deserve (and you could deserve something wonderful!) in terms of the nature of how these Laws affect your life. Therefore, should the Twelfth House ruler be the same planet as the ruler of the horoscope and located in the First, watch for immediate karmic returns.

Let us say that Taurus is on the cusps of the First and Twelfth houses and Venus is located in Gemini in the First and well aspected by a trine to the Moon in Aquarius. This position indicates a person who would easily circulate his or her resources, both material as well as mental. As a result, the Law of Circulation would be in positive effect in this person's life and he or she would be the recipient of many social invitations, good deeds, wise counsel, emotional support, and other "karmic goodies" from friends, groups, and organizations.

When the ruler of the Twelfth is in the Second, and poorly aspected (especially by Venus or the ruler of the Second), care must be taken with our personal resources. There is a tendency to waste money (especially if Jupiter is square or opposed to this planet) or to invest it poorly (especially if the ruler of the Eighth afflicts this position). Such difficulties in finances could definitely lead to our own "self-undoing." Conversely, if the ruler of the Twelfth is well aspected in the Second, we can profit from an inner knowing about how to best use our money or talents. If the Twelfth House ruler is well aspected in this position (especially by Venus, Jupiter, or Pluto), look for added and often surprising or unknown and surprising help to come to us in financial matters (earth signs), ideas and general relationships (air signs), creative vitality (fire signs), or in our general resourcefulness (water signs).

When the ruler of the Twelfth is in the Third and well aspected, look for an "inner guidance system" to be part of one's personal radar. Many indications of the presence of the ruler of the Twelfth House and its influence upon our life are not always clearly in evidence, nor are they logical. If Aquarius is on the cusp of the Twelfth and Uranus is well aspected in the Third, the individual in question is bound to be profoundly intuitive and display the ability to see things as they will probably manifest before all the facts are in or the events played out.

Uranus afflicting Mercury (or the Third House ruler) from this position can mean that our intuition is wrong, that we jump to false conclusions, making statements that are highly illogical and do not sustain with the passage of time and unfolding events. In effect, the idea that one is highly intuitive is misleading and can be a contributor to our own "self-undoing."

The presence of the Twelfth House ruler in the Third may also indicate a special bond, a deep "karmic connection" linking us to a brother or sister. The nature of this connection can be determined through a careful assessment of the particular planet and signs involved in this combination.

When the ruler of the Twelfth is in the Fourth and well aspected, in the chart of one who is spiritually mature, it can indicate that the person has an understanding of life that is far beyond his or her years and/or personal experience. If in the water signs, this position shows that the person has enormous compassion for others and a deep empathy with life's events. If poorly aspected, especially by Neptune or Pluto, there can be deep fear of being exposed in some way, and thus one may be apprehensive about people and life in general. If Saturn is the afflicting planet, a state of chronic depression or an inferiority complex can easily be present. The results of all of these positions are emphasized if the Moon and/or the sign Cancer is involved. What we are seeing in this combination of astrological influences is the interplay of what is most inclusive within us (the Twelfth) being brought into our personal, psychological roots (the Fourth). In effect, our instinctual nature is being touched by a universal element of understanding. In the examples given above, this can lead to an exaggeration of our deepest fears or an expansion of our natural goodness.

When the ruler of the Twelfth is in the Fifth, there can be a universal element connected to our creative self-expression. This can result in an artist being able to paint using common symbolism that is understood by all people regardless of religion, race, or nationality (look to Venus or Neptune as significators). It may indicate a writer whose words link all people in a common bond of experience (Mercury, Jupiter, or Uranus as significators). It can point to a sculptor who can depict universal emotion (the earthy signs and the Moon or Neptune as significators).

On the other hand, a poorly aspected Twelfth House ruler in this position, or even a well-aspected one in the horoscope of an emotionally immature person, can overly stimulate the search for romance and sensual pleasures and thus become a source of personal self-undoing. Addictions to alcohol or other drugs may impede or harm one's creativity should the Twelfth House ruler be Neptune in the Fifth or the latter is afflicting another planet as Twelfth House ruler in this house. If the Twelfth House ruler is in the Fifth and in difficult aspect with the ruler of the person's Eighth, there can be an unnatural sexual attraction to children, including one's own. This would especially be the case if the Moon were also afflicted in the natal chart (most likely by Saturn, Neptune, or Pluto) and the Eighth House ruler were afflicted in Pisces or by Neptune. The latter would indicate an unclear understanding of correct sexual boundaries.

When the ruler of the Twelfth is in the Sixth, it indicates difficulties in health, especially when the significators are afflicted. Should Neptune be the ruler of the Twelfth and inharmoniously placed in the Sixth (square or opposed the ruler of the Sixth, for example) or if Neptune as Twelfth House ruler is afflicting a planet in the Sixth, look for drug addiction or serious medical issues requiring overmedication. If Capricorn, Pisces, or Scorpio are the sign indicators and their ruling planets are also connected, addictions or illnesses are chronic in nature and not easy to cure.

Yet if the connections are positive between the ruler of the Twelfth and its placement in the Sixth, look for a person whose skills, tools, and urge to be of service draws them to people in prisons, hospitals, asylums, and other institutions. This position can bring out a deep urge to be of help to people in distress and to be available to those in need. Because the Sixth is the house of self-improvement, when it is linked to the ruler of the Twelfth, a universal element is added, thus enlarging one's knowledge. He or she can turn five loaves into enough bread to feed the multitudes.

When the ruler of the Twelfth is in the Seventh, one's choice of partners and the general orientation to intimate relationships stimulates spiritual advancement. Or, conversely, relationships can be a vehicle for tremendous pain and suffering. As always, so much depends on the other astrological conditions surrounding the ruler when it is found in this house. Very often when the ruler of the Twelfth is in the Seventh, we meet people with whom we feel we have a very strong karmic tie. "I know we have met before." "It's like we have been together for all of our lives even though we have only recently met." "There is a great mystery surrounding our relationship that will take us a long time to uncover." "I am sure that we are soulmates."

These are typical responses and feelings when the ruler of the house of universal experience is found in the house of partnership. Well, all of the above can be true. But I would caution an individual who has this placement (and/or the ruler of the Seventh in close aspect to Neptune) to stop and contemplate the reality of such a thing if it happens repeatedly in his or her life. Just how many people do you meet that are soulmates? How many partners or potential partners are leftover lovers from past lives? The author is a firm, convinced, and proselytizing "minister" for the reality of life everlasting and the immortality of the soul, but he is all too familiar with the ridiculous hype of the New Age spiritual supermarket. Caution must be used in this astrological combination not to overamplify the astral glamour that is a natural feature of human relationships. One reason why it is easy to feel, see, and know that "we have met before," when the Seventh House ruler is in the Twelfth (or Neptune is in close contact to Venus or the ruler of the Seventh), is that it is easy to see the universal in the personal. This is especially true when the personal emotional nature is being stimulated by hormones.

When the ruler of the Twelfth is in the Eighth, the sexual dynamics of one's life are usually linked to the nature of one's progression or retrogression along the evolutionary path. Should there be afflictions to the Twelfth House ruler in this position (especially from Mars, Pluto, Neptune, and/or the ruler of the Eighth), incorrect or addictive sexual behavior can lead to a person's self-undoing. In extreme cases, mishandling sexual energy can eventuate in financial ruin, prison, or even death.

When these significators are in positive contact with one another and the ruler of the Seventh is involved, the individual may be a sex counselor, helping regenerate the lives of people who have misdirected their sexuality in this respect. This counseling capacity especially is the case if the Moon or the sign Cancer is well placed in the chart and in close connection with the ruler of the Twelfth in the Sixth. Sexual healing (or misconduct) and the regeneration (or degeneration) of sexual energy (one's own or other people's) is strongly indicated by the condition of the ruler of the Twelfth in the Eighth.

If the ruler of the Twelfth House is well placed in this house, look for the ability to regenerate previous life experiences or one's contact to what is known in metaphysical literature as the akashic records. In practical terms, this means that the individual can dip into the collective experiences of humanity and draw out the energy and wisdom of the ages and transform this potency on behalf of one's own resources. Naturally, the more advanced one is on the spiritual path, the more available such collective human experiences are to us. This is like a person saying, "I have never been to your country but I can immediately relate to your experience and it gives me strength. That strength comes through my ability to accept you for who you are and use that universal acceptance as a source of my own regenerative potency." In essence, this is unconditional love at work.

When the ruler of the Twelfth is in the Ninth, there often is an attraction to deep metaphysical or occult knowledge. The author has Scorpio on the Twelfth House cusp and Pluto in the Ninth in Leo trine the Sun. Since I was a very small boy, I have always been attracted to learning about religious or spiritual subjects. Astrology and the Ancient Wisdom Teachings, as found in theosophical literature and especially in the Alice Bailey books, provide a never-ending source that allows me to probe the depths of the Twelfth House ruler in the Ninth.

When the ruler of the Twelfth is well aspected in this domicile, especially by Jupiter or the planetary ruler of this house, foreign travel is another major source for unlocking the "secrets of the ages." Should there be afflictions to the Twelfth House ruler in the Ninth, one may feel that he or she is a "victim of the Inquisition." In other words, one's particular philosophical or religious beliefs are not accepted, or one may even get into a great deal of trouble as a result of one's way of looking at the world or worshiping Divinity. Should the affliction of the Twelfth House ruler in the Ninth come from the Moon or the ruler of the Fourth House, then such profound opposition comes from one's parents and family background. Should this difficulty involve the ruler of the Eleventh House, then one's friends and general social environment believe things that are different from one's own beliefs, and this can result in ostracism which causes great pain.

When the ruler of the Twelfth is in the Tenth and well placed, the individual may have a special gift for professional strategy. This is a person who is familiar with the patterns of business or world events and who knows how to bring that understanding into his or her own career interests. Such a person may be privy to secret information about one's competitors. This would especially be the case if the ruler of the Twelfth in the Tenth were in a major aspect to the ruler of the Seventh House. This position is excellent for being able to "draw a rabbit out of a hat," because it provides an access to hidden resources that can be used to one's own career advantage. "I don't know how I know what I do, but boy am I glad that I know it and also how to use it in a practical context. I usually do not have all the money or help that I need for my projects right at hand, but all I have to do is fish around a bit and call upon my spiritual guide and I always have what I need." These sentences do much to describe the way the Twelfth House ruler acts in the Tenth when well aspected. On the other hand, subterfuge and deceit, the influence of unsavory and dishonest people, can ruin one's career should the Twelfth House ruler be afflicted in the Tenth, especially by the ruler of the Seventh and/or Neptune or Pluto.

When the ruler of the Twelfth is in the Eleventh, either it can give a tremendous understanding of human behavior or one can lose oneself too easily in the activities of social groups or organizations. If the Twelfth House ruler is well aspected in the Eleventh, there is a close connection between one's inner understanding of human nature and the objectification of that awareness of society. In the intellectually sophisticated, it allows for some amazing political and sociological insights and offers a sense of where society is going and why it is going there.

In the lives of those less formally educated, this position can bestow a good dose of common sense about people. The individual with this aspect in their chart seems to be saying: "I know people and their habits and customs. Nothing anyone or any group of people may do surprises me."

Should the Twelfth House ruler be afflicted in the Eleventh, there is a tendency to join groups and organizations that are not supportive or

Example 25: The Horoscope of Margaret Mead[13]

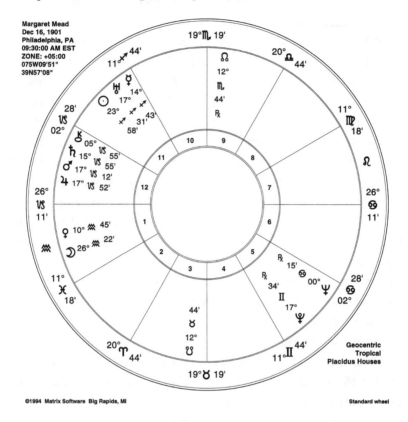

Margaret Mead
Dec 16, 1901
Philadelphia, PA
09:30:00 AM EST
ZONE: +05:00
075W09'51"
39N57'08"

©1994 Matrix Software Big Rapids, MI

Geocentric
Tropical
Placidus Houses

Standard wheel

helpful to one's growth. If the ruler of the Ascendant and the ruler of the Twelfth are the same planet, and are located in the Eleventh House, this indicates a tendency toward cults or sects that impersonate themselves as being the elect, thereby losing one's own personal will (which was initially weak) in the process. This road has been a common path to self-undoing during much of the twentieth century and will continue to play an active role in addictions to political or spiritual glamour well into the twenty-first century.

When the ruler of the Twelfth is in the Twelfth, look for the person to require seclusion and a deep-seated need to probe the depth of his or her special interests. The ruling planet and its sign and aspects will guide the astrologer to what that special interest may be. Should, for example, the ruler of the Twelfth in the Twelfth be in difficult aspect to the Moon and/or the ruler of the Fourth, then such a profound interest will center on a person's own navel! This is a man or a woman who can be totally absorbed in his or her own emotional problems to the exclusion of everything else. It is the type of individual who tends to see him or herself in everything and what they are seeing is not particularly uplifting. On the other hand, should the ruler of the Twelfth be in harmonious aspect to the ruler of the Fourth or the Moon (even if afflicted) in the horoscope of a person inclined to be of help and service to others, then this ability to see everyone in oneself and oneself in everyone only adds to a sense of universal love and compassion.

Margaret Mead is probably the world's most famous anthropologist. She spent many years of her life in isolated locations, especially on remote islands (ruled by the Twelfth House) in the South Pacific living with and studying local cultures. The author of numerous books, the most well-known of which is *Coming of Age in Samoa*, Mead contributed much to changing the view of many millions that so-called "primitive societies" are quite socially evolved. At the early age of twenty-five, Mead became the director of ethnology at the American Museum of Natural History in New York and won numerous honors throughout her life.

It is important to note that this is a chart with a strong Eleventh House emphasis. Sagittarius is on the cusp with the Sun, Mercury. and the natural ruler of this house, Uranus, posited therein. These positions tell us that this is a woman with a deep sociological interest, one that would take her traveling to many cultures far removed in location and orientation from her native Philadelphia.

The ruler of the Eleventh House, Jupiter, is in the Twelfth, indicating long periods in relative isolation studying the cultures and social ramifications of the groups of people that were of interest to her. The ruler of the Twelfth is Saturn (which is also the ruler of the Ascendant and hence of the chart), which is placed in its own ruling sign of Capricorn. The importance of this position and the fact that Saturn is conjunct Jupiter tells the astrologer about Mead's particular interest concerning the structures of the societies that she studied. It reveals an interest in the sociological development of these cultures and how she could find the roots of all common human activity in these specific ethnic groups.

The ruler of her Tenth House of career is Mars, also conjoined Jupiter and Saturn. This adds a sense of adventure and much courage to her character as well as bringing the affairs of the Tenth into isolated settings. The co-ruler of the Tenth, Pluto, is in Gemini in the Fifth House. A great deal of Mead's work concentrated on the sexual customs of the people she studied (Scorpio on the Tenth), especially as it related to courtship among young people (Pluto in the Fifth House of romance and youth). In essence we have a conjunction of the rulers of the First, Tenth, Eleventh, and Twelfth in the Twelfth. It is no wonder that Mead was a "professional exile," specializing in the study of the evolution and structure of societies and cultures of profound interest to her. Yet in recent years, a lot of her work, especially her data regarding sexuality and mores in Samoa, was determined to be unfounded and spurious. Although she devoted a great deal of her life and positive creative energy to the field of anthropology, some of the more negative Twelfth House influences of self-undoing led to the discrediting of portions of her major academic contributions.

1. Data source: *Profiles of Women*, op. cit., p. 257.
2. Data source: Jones, Marc Edmund, *The Sabian Symbols*, Great Eastern Book Company.
3. Data source: *Profiles of Women*, op. cit., p. 149.
4. Data source: Rodden, Lois, op. cit.,, p. 145.
5. Data source: Reliable contacts known to the author in the U.K.
6. Data source: March, M., and McEvers, J., *The Only Way to Learn Astrology*, Vol. III, ACS Publications, p. 66.
7. Please consult the author's previous work, *Soul-Centered Astrology* (The Crossing Press, 1996), for a detailed description of the esoteric rulers of the horoscope and their implications.
8. A First, Fifth, and Tenth house placement of the Sun is far more obvious in its expression. The Fourth, Eighth, and Twelfth houses obscure the solar light and dim the effects of the more apparent solar dynamics.
9. It might be helpful here for the reader to draw a horoscope wheel placing Taurus on the Ninth and the other signs in their natural order around the wheel. This would give Virgo rising, Gemini on the Tenth, and Libra on the Second House cusp.
10. Data source: Jones, M. E., op. cit., p. 351.
11. Data source: Personally given to me by G. S. to the author.
12. In order for this position to occur, Leo would be on the Sixth House cusp and Virgo on the Seventh. The placement of Uranus and Pluto would also have to be in an earlier degree of Virgo than is found on the Descendant, a situation that is not uncommon.
13. Data source: Rodden, Lois, M. op. cit., p. 261.

Recommended Reading List

Arroyo, S. *Astrology, Psychology and the Four Elements*. Reno, NV: CRCS Publications, 1975.

Guttman, A. and Johnson, K. *Mythic Astrology*. St. Paul, MN: Llewellyn Publications, 1993.

Heindel, M. *The Message of the Stars*. Oceanside, CA: Rosicrucian Fellowship, 1940.

Jones, M. E. *Essentials of Astrological Analysis*. New York, NY: Fabian Publishing Society, 1960.

Leo, A. *The Art of Synthesis*. Edinburgh, Scotland: International Publishing Co., 1961.

March, M. and McEvers, J. *The Only Way to Learn Astrology*. San Diego, CA.: ACS Pubs., 1990.

Oken, A. *Alan Oken's Complete Astrology*. New York, NY: Bantam Books, 1988.

_____. *Soul-Centered Astrology*. Freedom, CA: The Crossing Press, 1996.

_____. *Houses of the Horoscope*. Freedom, CA: The Crossing Press, 1999.

Rudhyar, D. *The Astrology of Personality*. New York, NY: Lucis Publishing Co., 1936.

Sasportas, H. *The Twelve Houses*. London: Thorsons Publications, 1985.

Sullivan, E. *Retrograde Planets: Traversing The Inner Landscape*. London: Arkana CAS, 1992.

Wickenburg, J. *A Journey Through the Birth Chart*. Reno, NV: CRCS Publications, 1985.

Index

To receive a current catalog from The Crossing Press
please call toll-free, 800-777-1048.
Visit our Web site: **www.crossingpress.com**